WINDOWS ON THAT WORLD

Essays on British Art Presented to Brian Allen

WINDOWS ON THAT WORLD

Essays on British Art Presented to Brian Allen

'It is a landscape and a life that is fast disappearing, and these beautiful
windows on that world may in future years be the only reminders of a world gone by.'

PAUL MELLON
at the opening of the Yale Center for British Art
1977

The Paul Mellon Centre for Studies in British Art
2012

Contents

ACKNOWLEDGEMENTS

This volume is a gift to Brian Allen, on the occasion of his retirement in 2012 as Director of Studies of the Paul Mellon Centre for Studies in British Art, from all his colleagues at the Paul Mellon Centre (including the present writer).

Brian's considerable achievements since taking the helm at the Paul Mellon Centre sixteen years ago are well recognized, here and elsewhere – and quite rightly so. Behind the scenes, however, he has been ably supported by a devoted staff who have contributed in no small way to these many achievements. A great big thank-you should be extended to them all for what they have done in the past and what they will do in the future.

Particular thanks should go to Guilland Sutherland who has tirelessly worked 'undercover', with co-conspirators Gillian Malpass and Sally Salvesen at Yale University Press and all the contributors, to produce this handsome publication. Guilland's abundant good humour, which has seen her deal over the past twenty years with a very mixed bag of authors, never misses a beat. A huge thank-you should also go to Emma Lauze who in her quiet and modest way has done so much for the Centre, both as Photo Archivist and one-time assistant to Brian. Her undoubted intelligence, gentle nature and personal courage are a lesson for us all. Along with Guilland, Emma Lauze is part of the 'old guard' from 20 Bloomsbury Square and together have witnessed the many changes to the Centre over the years.

Thanks also to our much-loved Viv Redhead, who has co-ordinated the Yale-in-London programme for the past sixteen years and who has dispensed advice throughout her tenure on every 'not-to-be-missed' activity in London, Europe – and indeed the rest of the world! Her energy and enthusiasm for a wide range of subjects, particularly travel, puts us all to shame. Another colleague who has consistently kept us all on our toes is Emma Floyd. With enormous diligence and determination, Emma has heroically carried the Centre's Library into the 21st century, and over the years we have all relied upon her quick mind and forthright, no-nonsense ability to get right to the heart of the matter. Many thanks too to Mary Peskett Smith, who started life at the Centre assisting Christopher Wright in producing *British and Irish Paintings in Public Collections*, a task requiring both patience and accuracy in large measure. Mary then moved seamlessly into administering our Grants and Fellowships programme, transforming this complicated system into an easy-to-follow, utterly clear part of our operations and arguably is second only to the Director of Studies in both knowledge and experience in this significant area of the Paul Mellon Centre's activities.

A huge thank-you should be extended to Maisoon Rehani who, more than any of us, has been involved in every aspect of the Paul Mellon Centre's activities, from on-line publishing and picture research to assisting Brian in how to open an attachment in Word! Maisoon has always maintained the sweetest disposition, despite being sorely tried on a weekly basis: we are all enormously dependent on her expertise and willingness to help.

Thanks too to Harry Smith, arguably the best-dressed member of staff, who for the past seven years has kept a weather eye on the Centre, not only during evening functions but on a daily basis. We can depend upon Harry to let us know precisely what is happening in our area and rest assured that we are well protected – a single glance from Harry is usually all it takes.

Many thanks also to Martin Postle, who took on the role of Assistant Director for Academic Activities a mere five years ago. Since then he has put us firmly on the map with his superb exhibition, *Johan Zoffany RA: Society Observed,* shown both at the Yale Center for British Art and Royal Academy of Arts. The Centre has relished basking in the reflected glory of Martin's scholarly achievement, the first of many.

It certainly seems more than four years ago that Ella Fleming started work at the Centre as a young graduate. Sitting on the front line she has unfailingly managed to make everyone feel welcomed at the Centre. Juggling the many demands that her role requires, Ella has most ably demonstrated how to handle any situation with quiet restraint – and perhaps a little irony too?

Last of all, but certainly not least, we have been extremely lucky to add Charlotte Brunskill, our Archivist and Records Manager to our ranks. First coming to the Centre on secondment from the National Portrait Gallery in 2008, Charlotte acquired an overview of the workings of the Centre (which had taken most of us years to acquire). When she returned to the NPG we realized we could not do without her and negotiated her permanent return. We have not looked back.

There is one person, however, whom we should thank above all others and that is Brian's wife of thirty-five years, Katina. Without Katina's unfailing support in every aspect of Brian's life, from bringing up their two wonderful sons Andrew and Nick, to attending countless private views, and sitting through an endless number of official dinners, it is certain that Brian would not have had the time or opportunity to achieve so much.

When encouraged to produce this volume we faced the impossible task of whom to ask. There are literally hundreds of scholars, colleagues and friends of Brian's, over the past four decades of his working life in British art, who would have enthusiastically agreed to contribute. We decided that there was only one solution and that was to limit this tribute to his immediate colleagues: to people who have worked with Brian. This book comes with affectionate appreciation from colleagues at the Yale Center for British Art and the Paul Mellon Centre (Amy Meyers, Jules Prown, Christopher White, Duncan Robinson, Patrick McCaughey, Steven Parissien, Frank Salmon, Martin Postle); from research fellows appointed over the years by Brian (John Ingamells, Elizabeth Einberg, Alex Kidson, Hugh Belsey, Paul Spencer-Longhurst, Eric Shanes); and from all the staff at the Paul Mellon Centre in London, including

Kasha Jenkinson

Foreword

In contemplating Brian Allen's retirement as Director of Studies of the Paul Mellon Centre for Studies in British Art (PMC), members of the Centre's staff desired to honor their esteemed colleague with a volume of essays both assessing the excellence of his thirty-six years of service to the field and addressing subjects of scholarly inquiry that have received support through the Centre's Senior Research Programme under his aegis. Intended as an expression of admiration and affection from those who have worked most closely with Brian at the Centre itself, invitations to contribute were extended to past Directors of the Yale Center for British Art (YCBA), who have served as the Paul Mellon Centre's Trustees and ex-officio Chief Executives (Jules Prown, 1970–76; Duncan Robinson, 1981–95; and Patrick McCaughey, 1996–2001); the Director of Studies of the PMC under whom Brian first worked as Assistant Director and Librarian (Christopher White, 1973–85); the past and present Assistant Directors of Academic Activities (Steven Parissien, 1995–2001; Frank Salmon, 2001–6; and Martin Postle, 2007–present); and Senior Research Fellows (John Ingamells, 1992–2010; Elizabeth Einberg, 1998–present; Hugh Belsey, 2006–present; Eric Shanes, 2008–present; Alex Kidson, 2009–present; and Paul Spencer-Longhurst, 2009–present). The excellence of the resulting contributions serves as a testament to the time and effort that Brian's closest colleagues were prepared to commit to crafting essays that would do their revered friend justice. And, of course, there could be no one more deserving of such tributes. As Christopher White and Jules Prown have indicated in their eloquent discussions of Brian's leadership of the PMC, few people have stood at the helm of a research center with such steadfast dedication over so many years. He has shaped its programs with extraordinary attention to the needs of the field, and his emphasis on parity has allowed scholars from many walks of life, reflecting the most varied points of view, to enrich the conversation. In point of fact, Brian's insistence on pluralism as the key to the Centre's success has been a hallmark of his stewardship of the institution, enabling the PMC to serve as a platform for the healthiest exchange of ideas on the broadest range of topics in the most civilized of ways.

Brian's interest in promoting scholarship on British art well beyond the bounds of the British Isles has led him to serve as an important cultural diplomat. He has developed collegial friendships with scholars across Europe and the United States, placing the Centre at the heart of an international community of individuals and institutions that has expanded the very definition of the field, and immeasurably nuanced and enriched its study. His curiosity about the ways in which British art is studied abroad, coupled with his personal love of travel, has drawn him across the Atlantic, to Yale University, well over one hundred times, enabling him to forge an extraordinarily productive working relationship between the PMC and its sister institution, the Yale Center for British Art, which has benefited both organizations immensely over time. Imbued with the beneficent spirit of the American philanthropist and collector, Paul Mellon (Yale, Class of 1929), who founded these linked research centers, Brian has fostered this special collaboration in a multitude of ways, including the support he has offered Yale undergraduates through the PMC's Yale-in-London program of study, and the warm welcome he has extended to Yale faculty teaching in the program; his mentorship of Yale graduate students traveling to London for their dissertation research; his readiness to cooperate on the organization of workshops, study days, and symposia on topics of mutual institutional interest; his support of the two centers' joint publication, *Studies in British Art*; his nurturing of international collaborations that have allowed the Yale Center to pursue important exhibition and publication projects with British and European institutions; and, most recently, his assistance in the promotion of a free and open-access policy for the YCBA's electronic collection catalog. In the ten years of my directorship of the Yale Center, I could have asked for no more congenial and steadfast collegial friend, and this sentiment is shared by all of my colleagues here and across the University. We shall miss Brian immensely in the role he has played at the PMC, but we know that he is leaving our sister institution in the best of health, to flourish most happily under its able new director, Mark Hallett. Indeed, we shall look forward to working with Brian in new and exciting ways as he takes on the non-executive Chairmanship of Hazlitt, Gooden & Fox, and we extend our congratulations and our best wishes to him as he embarks on this stimulating new chapter of his professional life.

Amy Meyers
Director, Yale Center for British Art

BRIAN ALLEN: A PERSONAL MEMOIR

Christopher White

For thirty-five years Brian has been an essential part of the Paul Mellon Centre for Studies in British Art, so that his departure in September 2012 will leave a significant hole in its fabric. After taking his degree at the University of East Anglia, then postgraduate study at the Courtauld Institute of Art, followed by a brief spell working in the Witt Library, Brian was appointed to the newly created post of Assistant Director and Librarian at the Mellon Centre in 1976. In 1987 he was promoted to Deputy-Director of Studies and finally in 1993 he succeeded Michael Kitson as Director of Studies. Perhaps unusual for the *mouvementé* world in which we now live, his whole career has been devoted [*sic*] to one institution, undoubtedly to its benefit.

On his arrival Brian was put to work in a pokey dark office at the back of the building on the ground floor. It also served as the principal entrance to the conference room in the front of the building so that willy-nilly he became a silent witness to much of what took place at 20 Bloomsbury Square. If he writes his memoirs, he will undoubtedly recall numerous incidents which took place before his eyes. Perhaps none more piquant than the arrival of his thesis supervisor for an Advisory Council meeting, characteristically late and suffering from guilt that Brian's manuscript had been sitting unread in his in-tray for months on end. Unable to face up to making any eye contact with Brian, Professor Michael Kitson, for it was he, made his way through Brian's office, with his face resolutely to the wall, in a strange crab-like movement towards the central door, around which he folded his body as he entered the conference room, like one of those seemingly weightless underwater archaeologists wrapping themselves around a sunken wreck. And hey presto, the door closed and Michael was safely inside, ne'er having cast a glance at his expectant graduate student. And of memories, perhaps none more diverting than, on the occasion of an Advisory Council lunch, coming face to face with Professor Michael Jaffé, who, like a latter-day Don Giovanni, was consuming, with magisterial satisfaction, his second cold grouse, held daintily between his fingers. The amused look on Brian's face betokened the only possible response: '*che barbaro appetito*'.

Building on what had been achieved by that master librarian, Frank Simpson, Brian served the library well, expanding its collections of books and photographs with an archive of the working papers and library collections of art historians associated with the Centre. In its new home the Paul Mellon Centre has become a most valuable resource for visiting scholars in British art.

When Brian arrived in 1977 the Centre was embarking on a new important branch of activity. Until that time its operations had, apart from its publications programme channelled through the Yale University Press, very largely been devoted to serving people and institutions in the United Kingdom. Members of Yale University could be forgiven for their ignorance of what went on in that mysterious foreign out-station, umbilically attached to the Yale Center for British Art. To contribute something more eye-catching to the basic purpose of the University, it was decided to set up an annual Summer Term Programme for about fourteen students at the London Centre, which would offer stimulating opportunities for visiting museum collections and buildings around the country, even on one occasion venturing as far as Rome. This has grown over the course of time into a programme now offering three self-contained sessions, one in the spring and two in the summer.

In playing a major role in the Yale-in-London programme, Brian's duties varied from the academic to the domestic to the emotional. A number of students found themselves ill-at-ease in a large foreign metropolis, and needed hand-holding and occasional handkerchief-work. With his friendly and relaxed personality, Brian was ideal for the job, quickly gaining the confidence and friendship of the students, at the same time maintaining a sharp eye on any less desirable activities. On one of our travels outside London, when I was driving the mini-bus, I noticed in the rear-mirror, several students seated in the back row passing a bottle from hand to hand. Enquiring what they were drinking, I was told it was cold tea and I was welcome to have some. I declined the easily resistible invitation, and in any case was not totally convinced that the account of the contents would meet the trade descriptions act. It was only when we arrived at our destination that Brian, who was of course *au fait*, whispered in my ear, 'single-malt'.

On assuming the directorship, Brian took the decision that he would give his primary energies to the institution, and allow his own research and teaching to take second place, although it must be added that his contributions in those two areas were by no means negligible. What this has meant to the Centre has become abundantly clear in the well-presented volume celebrating the Centre's fortieth anniversary, *The Paul Mellon Centre for Studies in British Art. A History 1970–2010*, a piece of writing by Brian, which, it should be said, humanises a mass of dry documentation in a masterly way. With its punctilious acknowledgement of the achievement of his three predecessors, the book is in no sense an 'ego-trip', but the facts clearly speak for themselves. There is no hiding the fact that the Centre's activities have been enormously increased and developed during Brian's directorship. As he states, 'he has been most fortunate to be in post at a time when the Centre's funds have grown significantly as a result of Yale University's careful investment of Paul Mellon's endowment', but the important thing is that he knew what to do with this increased income to the Centre's best advantage. One can say he has moved it from the fringe to the centre of the capital's cultural institutions.

One excellent decision was to move the Centre from its cosy, agreeable but cramped home in Bloomsbury Square to much larger and, as it turned out, much grander premises in Bedford Square, which can incorporate all the activities which now take place. In the early days in the new home, when some of the Yale Center's British eighteenth-century pictures hung very decoratively on the walls, to visit Brian seated behind a magnificent desk in the grand room on the *piano nobile* of an eighteenth-century house imposed an attitude of respect on the part of the visitor. But any seeming affectations of grandeur were quickly dispelled by Brian's innate modesty and relaxed charm. And even with mezzotints replacing the pictures, sadly returned to New Haven, he cannot be accused of slumming it. As he looks out at those elegant private gardens in Bedford Square, he must feel satisfaction at his progress from what was essentially a coalhole at the back of Bloomsbury Square to what is one of the most stately offices inhabited by anyone in the art world in London.

With its increased space and stylish ambience it provided an opportunity to play host to conferences on aspects of British art and culture, an idea introduced by Michael Kitson when the Centre was still in Bloomsbury Square. But, as a glance at the record shows, it has really taken off in Brian's day. A conspectus of the varied subjects under discussion at the conferences, as well as the regularly held research seminars, give a clear *aperçu* of the concerns of British art history today, so very different from those of a few generations ago. Although brought up in a different tradition of art history, Brian has shown himself commendably open to new areas of investigation.

Limited by the funds available, grants were in the past decided upon by the Advisory Council under one simple heading. Now, with more money to dispense under Brian, they have been expanded into numerous discrete categories, covering curatorial research, publication grants for both author and publisher, educational programmes and individual research. The Centre now plays a major role in funding all the various activities connected with British art. And from 1997 a substantial number of individual scholars has greatly benefited from the programme of senior, Rome, postdoctoral, junior and conservation fellowships, some of whom have taken up office in Bedford Square, greatly adding to the life of the Centre.

Publications have from the beginning been a major contribution of the Centre to the study of British art, and one can claim that not many books on the subject of real significance were not published in this way. It represented an activity which had been started by the old Paul Mellon Foundation, and was indeed the principal role

Fig. 1 *Yale in London Summer 1977,* The Paul Mellon Centre for Studies in British Art Archive

for its existence, but once again with more money available, the number of new publications as well as their scope has greatly expanded during Brian's years as Director of Studies. In earlier days monographs or *catalogues raisonnés* of artists were the principal titles, but now the titles of the publications, running to on an average of twelve a year, have greatly broadened to include architecture, as well as reflecting current interests in art history.

Following the example of the Andrew W. Mellon Lectures held at the National Gallery of Art in Washington, Brian, in 1994, set up a biennial series of lectures named after Paul Mellon, which have been delivered by distinguished scholars in the field of British art in the National Gallery in London, with one exception, and subsequently at the Yale Center for British Art in New Haven.

One particularly agreeable activity introduced by Brian has been the study days, when a group of invited scholars make a day visit to such houses as Arundel Castle, Welbeck Abbey and Castle Howard. It provides a mixture of formal investigation into a house, its history and collections, and at the same time an opportunity for informal discussion. Whether or not it has been the skill with which Brian chose the participants, the occasions have been notable for the bonhomie which has suffused the assembled company.

It is a tribute to both the enhanced status of the Centre in this country and to Brian's own qualities that cultural institutions looking for trustees or governors should turn so regularly to the former's Director of Studies. The list of bodies on which he serves or has served is very impressive, not to say overwhelming, and it comes as no surprise that in a number of instances he has been appointed chairman, such as in the case of the National Art Collections Fund, as it then was, and the Walpole Society, as well as serving as Vice-President of the Foundling Hospital. He built up particularly close relations with museums in Moscow and St Petersburg, from which emerged his part in *British Art Treasures from Russian Imperial Collections in the Hermitage* (1996), and at a different level his award of Honourable Life Membership of the Museum Friends, State Kremlin Museums, Moscow.

Fig. 2 *Brian Allen in his office,* The Paul Mellon Centre for Studies in British Art Archive

Apart from the indication, as old photographs show, that along the way he met a Delilah, Brian, to the delight of his friends and colleagues, has remained essentially the same person, unchanged by success and the course of time. It is a commonplace to say, when someone of distinction retires after a long career, that it represents the end of an era but in Brian's case, as the longest serving member and a greatly influential director in the history of the Centre, it is literally true. He has left his successor with a wonderful legacy, but also a challenge.

Brian Allen: A Personal Memoir

Jules David Prown

I first met Brian Allen about thirty-five years ago when he came to the Paul Mellon Centre while still a graduate student at the Courtauld Institute to work in the library with Frank Simpson. Frank was an amiable and knowledgeable librarian who had been helpful to me years earlier when I was in England doing dissertation research on John Singleton Copley. I had recently stepped down as Director of the Yale Center for British Art in New Haven to return to full time teaching, but continued to travel to England, initially to teach at the Centre and subsequently to pursue research. Sharing an interest in finding and acquiring books on British art, he for the Centre and I to build up a personal library, Brian and I exchanged information about books and visited booksellers together. And we liked pub lunches, beer, and sports. He was a delightful companion.

As Brian assumed greater responsibilities at the Centre, he increasingly visited New Haven. Once when he and Katina came over for a term, my wife, Sam, and I took them to see a Yale–Princeton football game. Brian dressed in good British fashion for a November outing, as if he were going to watch his beloved Arsenal. He wore a light raincoat. The temperature held at a windy seventeen degrees Fahrenheit (eight degrees Centigrade). Sam and Katina had the good sense to leave at halftime but Brian and I, aided by a flask, remained to the bitter end.

In terms of scholarship, Brian and I shared a particular interest in the eighteenth century. I admired his knowledge of Francis Hayman, Vauxhall Gardens, the Society of Artists, the Foundling Hospital, and myriad aspects of the British art world of the middle years of the century, especially those leading up to and including the founding of the Royal Academy. But Brian's scholarly interests have not been parochial. One of the traits that has marked his productive career has been his willingness to foster worthwhile projects regardless of field, date, medium, or geography. When we were collecting books on British art four decades ago, the literature was thin and uneven. In the broad perspective of the history of art, British art was regarded as inferior. If the arts, like the course of empire, moved westward, as Bishop Berkeley would have it, from classical antiquity in Greece and Rome to Renaissance and Baroque Italy, to France from Poussin and Claude to the Impressionists, they had yet to reach Britain. But during the last forty years there has been a transformation in the understanding and appreciation of British art and its history, in which the Mellon Centre has been instrumental through its support of scholarly research, writing, and exhibitions and the dissemination of scholarship through a vigorous program of publication, especially in concert with Yale University Press.

Brian, as head of the Centre, has played a key role in bringing about this efflorescence. His influence has been international, spreading awareness of the importance and quality of British art to Europe and beyond. He is admired and trusted by colleagues not only in London and New Haven but in St Petersburg and Madrid, in Italy, Germany, and throughout the Continent. In part this has been a direct result of his personal qualities as well as professional ability. What is it about Brian that inspires the affection, confidence, and high regard of so many friends and colleagues? I think it is 'authenticity'. With Brian, what you see is what you get; what he promises, he delivers.

Although modest and unassuming, he holds firm convictions. An able administrator, he knows how to make things happen, to achieve his and his institution's goals, befriending rather than offending those with whom he works. Perhaps springing from his Irish roots, Brian has, and refuses to set aside, a common touch and basic values. He could have settled into elegant digs in London, but he and Katina have always preferred to live modestly in Windsor. A low-profile style also characterized his predecessors at the Centre – Ellis Waterhouse, Christopher White, and Michael Kitson – but Brian has gone still further in deploying these virtues to good effect. His achievements rest on a core of personal integrity wedded to a devotion to scholarship. They are a gift he has given to his friends and colleagues, a legacy to the Mellon Centre, and a major contribution to the ongoing growth of interest in and understanding of British art.

TRAVELLERS IN AN UNSEEN LAND

John Ingamells

A man who has not been in Italy, is always conscious of an inferiority, from his not having seen what it is expected a man should see. The grand object of travelling is to see the shores of the Mediterranean.

Samuel Johnson, 11 April 1776

Fig. 3 Joshua Reynolds, *Parody of Raphael's 'School of Athens'*, 1751, oil on canvas, 97 x 135 cm, National Gallery of Ireland, Dublin

TRAVELLERS IN AN UNSEEN LAND

John Ingamells

There was a standard image of the eighteenth-century Grand Tourist: privileged, young, educated, and anxious for souvenirs. Young men like THOMAS PORTER (1788–89), fresh from Christ Church, Oxford, embarked on the Grand Tour 'merely with a view of Amusement & in the hope of passing agreeably the period between College & Matrimony'. His gap year had to be filled, for the relief of parents and, in theory, for further education. But in the course of the century there were increasing numbers of travellers (in Florence in 1776 the painter THOMAS JONES could scarcely help but 'fancy myself in England'), who form a wonderful miscellany, covering the whole range of the human condition, each pursuing a particular scheme which, apart from discovery, could also involve escape or duty. A glimpse at some of the less conventional travellers (fig. 3) might usefully flavour the overall concept.

Sir Brinsley Ford had become increasingly aware of this variety as, for some thirty years, he accumulated contemporary evidence from letters and archives documenting British and Irish travellers in Italy from 1701 to 1800. While he had always been a serious student of eighteenth-century art, he had also remained alert to, and appreciative of, the oddities of human behaviour. He had urged me, as I began to write up his notes (which were written in a large, distinctive, backward-sloping hand on thin, foolscap paper), never to omit 'the racy bits'. At that stage I had no idea what he implied, still believing that the disciplines of art history and connected studies were, perforce, very short of spiciness. Yet the young, fastidious HORACE WALPOLE (1739–41) had observed of travellers that 'there are no people so obviously mad as the English' – and perhaps he was right.

Walpole may have heard of GEORGE HUTCHINSON (1742), the Presbyterian weaver from Ireland, who was preaching 'mightily' in Rome 'against statues, pictures, umbrellas, bag-wigs and hoop-petticoats' (then an identikit for a traveller). And much later THOMAS HACKMAN (1779–94), seen in Rome and Naples, thought to be the father of the murderer James Hackman, had turned 'almost mad, travelling always on foot', as he 'walked on and took no notice of anything', looking like a beggar. These melancholy eccentrics were extreme examples of ungentlemanly conduct, neither prepared to acknowledge his peculiar location.

Yet travel in the eighteenth century was enhanced by an element of surprise, as well as recognition. In the absence of illustrated guides, the dedicated traveller was intrigued above all by history and literature, although the privileged HESTER THRALE (1784–86, fig.4) suggested that the paintings she saw in Venice 'were all known in England', but quickly added 'but nothing can give one a just Idea except the Sight'. To see what Horace saw or Vergil imagined mattered initially more than Titian or Tintoretto. The English thronged to Rome, where the histories of Livy and Caesar had been enacted, to stand and stare and rememember. The 2ND EARL OF MORNINGTON (later Marquess of Wellington) confessed in 1791 that, in Italy, 'all the old ideas of Eton and Oxford' employed his mind; and without them, he thought, 'the journey through Italy would lose the greatest part of its amusement'. When he visited Cicero's Villa in Rome the 5TH EARL OF CARLISLE (1768) wrote excitedly that it was 'where the Tusculan questions [*Tusculanae Disputationes*] were wrote [and] you may easily fancy with what reverence I beheld this scene'. Without such education Italy could be more arduous. As Mornington pondered in Rome, so MRS SUSAN COUTTS, wife of the celebrated banker, was reflecting that the Colosseum would be 'a very pretty building' once it was finished and whitewashed. Her apathy did not prevent her husband commissioning in Rome portraits of their three daughters from Angelica Kauffman, 'all dressed in white, attired like the muses or the graces'. Similarly LADY MALMESBURY (1791–92) had thought it very clever to lure her husband, the accomplished diplomat James, 1st Baron Malmesbury, 'to a country which furnished nothing but the things he detests – antiquities, cameos and intaglios'.

Mrs Coutts was just one of the many disinterested, perhaps reluctant, travellers dutifully following the fashionable, Johnsonian trail. The 4TH EARL OF ABINGDON (1763–65) was overtaken by boredom as he roamed to escape from his home, accompanied by three hounds, some punch and his mistress, having been taught,

Fig. 4 Unknown Italian artist, *Hester Lynch Piozzi (née Salusbury; Mrs Thrale)*, 1785–86, oil on canvas; 75.6 x 62.9 cm, National Portrait Gallery, London

Fig. 5 Pompeo Batoni, *Alexander Gordon, 4th Duke of Gordon*, 1763–64, oil on canvas, 292 x 192 cm, Scottish National Gallery, Edinburgh

it was alleged, nothing but hunting and music. Such apathy was splendidly (if unintentionally?) illustrated by Batoni in his portrait of the handsome 4TH DUKE OF GORDON (1762–63, fig.5). The Duke had previously shown 'scarcely a trace of animation as he sat in his carriage, while [the erudite] Winckelmann described to him, with the choicest expressions and grandest illustrations, the beauties of the ancient works of art', and when Batoni painted him in Rome he showed the Duke standing by his fine bay horse surrounded by dead game and hunting dogs, as if he had never left the Scottish Borders. The comparatively erudite 5th Earl of

Carlisle 'had amused himself with the thought that his dog Rover should be painted by Batoni', although nothing more is heard of this commission. ADAM WALKER (1787, fig.6), an energetic inventor, having visited twenty churches in a morning in Venice, found that by the time he reached Rome he had 'began to grow sick of palaces, pictures and statues', while the Scot, CAPTAIN JOHN CLERK (1769–70), became jaded after seeing the *Apollo Belvedere* and decided that most of the other statues 'seem to have been Carvd by Sandy Thompson or some such Artist'.

Fig. 6   after Samuel Drummond, *Adam Walker*, 1792, stipple engraving, 19.3 x 13.2 cm, National Portrait Gallery, London

The disillusionment of such older visitors was contrasted by JOSEPH ATWELL (1729–30) with the conduct of those 'Boys just escaped from the lash of a severe master, & the tedious confinement to Books and Studies[,] to visiting a foreign Country where they first give a full swing to their Passions, & lead such lives as they are sensible would be attended with shame at Home'. Here we are not concerned with their inevitable sexual adventures – the 5th Earl of Carlisle had noted that 'sins during the Carnival are so very numerous that I believe the monks are forced to absolve them by the lump' – but with demonstrations of cultural apathy. The DAMER BROTHERS, the Hon. George and John (1764), in the long gallery at Florence, 'submitted quietly to be shewn a few of the pictures. But seeing the gallery so immensely long, their impatience burst forth, and they tried for a bett who should hop first to the end of it'. The young PETER BECKFORD (1766) tried to appreciate the guidance of James Byres in Rome: 'no schoolboy ever toiled harder or at times more unwillingly; hurrying over pleasing objects to visit stones and rubbish of very little importance, for *what* – to say I had visited all the antiquities of Rome'. The despairing CHARLES BALDWYN (1711–12) wrote, 'I believe the whole present Rome has not so many People in it as the ancients had Statues' (doubtless recalling Addison's slightly earlier remark that 'there are more statues in Rome than there are men in several other [cities]').

Yet an even greater difficulty for many travellers was their xenophobia. The same Joseph Atwell, who was in any case suspicious of the educational value of the Grand Tour, recognised the 'advantage the English have over Forreigners in the Goodness of our Climate and the happiness of our Civil Constitution', a sentiment richly exaggerated by THOMAS, later 2ND EARL, PELHAM (1778) when he wrote (not, one hopes, without some irony), 'Italy would be a most delightful Country if there were not so many Italians'. But one might trust the sincerity of the elderly LORD GARDENSTONE (1788) who found the atmosphere in Rome depressing: 'how can men of free thoughts, humanity and British spirit expect to be happy, or even altogether at their ease in Rome, the seat of slavery and priestcraft, erected on the monumental ruins of very ancient liberty, grandeur and empire. The fine arts are wholly subservient to the vile arts of superstition and tyranny.' Even Mgr. Alban Butler (1746), accompanying James and Thomas Talbot, both to become Catholic priests, considered the 'softness and grace of life' of the *Medici Venus* 'too dangerous for any one to look upon…' (thus subscribing to the concept of the fine arts as subservient to superstition and tyranny?).

Lady Malmesbury (1791–92) had observed, 'I think my journey to Italy has given me a very perfect idea of the excess to which dirt, disease and deformity may reach, without causing death, or even disgust, to some millions of human creatures'. The common people of Rome, according to the merchant Robert Harvey (1773), were 'a compound of Pride, roguery, laziness & poverty', while the nobility were 'all for vanity, much ceremonial, but no cordiality'; he concluded triumphantly, 'Thanks to ye Gods, I was not born a Roman'. Hester Thrale found Rome a mixture of squalor and splendour, like Rembrandt's pictures 'composed of the strongest lights and the darkest shadows possible' (it would appear then a paradox that in such a repellent city eight thousand artists from different nations, were constantly employed, according to Lady Phillipa Knight in 1778). Elsewhere Lady Holland (1766) found the common people of Naples the most lazy in the world, while the great people were made up of 'ignorance, pride, debauchery and show'. To the Marquess of Kildare (1768) Venice seemed 'the most disagreeable place I ever was in'.

There was a small band of fugitives, anxious to leave a reputation behind them. The glamorous Georgiana, Duchess of Devonshire (1792–93) was compelled to go abroad to conceal her illicit pregnancy by Charles Grey, the future prime minister, and her daughter Eliza Courtney was duly born in Aix in 1792; as the Duchess later progressed through Italy she took a deep interest in a foundling hospital at Pisa. Sir Erasmus Philipps, 5th Bt. (1738–41) was one of many who went abroad (in vain) for his health, dragging about 'a miserable life of Pain and Anguish for some time'. But there were inevitably less pitiable exiles. An adventurer named Black (1731–34) had been a protestant minister in London but was forced to fly following unspecified crimes. He came to Florence, where the British chargé d'affaires described him as 'a composition of infidelity, Religion, Vice, rattle, literature, poverty and affectation of riches'. Black went on to Rome (where he was known as 'Lewis Smith') and later styled himself a Bishop in England. He was last heard of as a victim of the Spanish Inquisition. Where Black failed, one HENRY FISHER (1730–86) apparently succeeded. He had lived in Florence as Howard, and in Leghorn as John Warner. With the protection of the Catholic Church, according to Thomas Jones, and further helped by a little robbery, he set up as a merchant and succeeded in becoming the eccentric 4th Earl of Bristol's banker in Rome in the 1770s and 1780s. The young painter THOMAS JONES met him in May 1778; his blood had shivered in his veins as he beheld this 'old, shrivel'd assisin' and Jones 'could not help conceiving a Dagger lay concealed in every wrinkle'. A Londoner called MORIN (1765) had arrived shabbily dressed in Naples, where he bought himself 'the compleat dress of an Abbé', got blind drunk, and was found next day expiring in a chair with no papers upon him but, sewn into the lining of his waistcoat, 'two Purses containing 470 Guineas'. The adventuress ELIZABETH GALLOWAY had come to Rome in 1725 disguised as a man, to consort with Jacobites.

There were also, inevitably, some physical oddities. CORNELIUS MAGRATH (*c*.1755), an Irish giant, was persuaded to exhibit himself in Italy. In complete contrast TABITHA MENDES (1760–61, fig.7) was 'a young Lady about 4 feet & a half high', as Nathaniel Dance observed, 'and in every respect, with regards to person, one of the ugliest figures I ever saw, but the qualifications of her mind are as amiable as her person is disagreeable'. Finally CLOTWORTHY-SKEFFINGTON, 2ND EARL OF MASSEREENE (1762–63) had a passion for dancing but, it was said, 'he does not carry his ballast in the right place' and his figure was 'the worst calculated for such an exercise'. Poor man.

This brief glimpse shows some of the motley assembled round more dedicated travellers, like the young EDWARD COKE (c.1738–40), whom the rather pretentious Lady Pomfret assessed as 'one of the few I have met with who *ought* to have been sent abroad'. There were earnest students who absorbed what they saw and unmistakeably modified British taste. Those we have been remembering here, who seemed only to stress the imperfections of the Grand Tourist, may also serve to emphasise the achievements and discretion of their more attentive fellow travellers.

Fig. 7 Thomas Patch, *The Golden Asses* (detail showing Tabitha Mendes), 1761, oil on canvas, 142.2 x 229.7 cm, The Lewis Walpole Library, Yale University

Fig. 8   Sir Brinsley Ford and the author of this essay share 'a racy bit',
The Paul Mellon Centre for Studies in British Art Archive

Note

This essay is based entirely on John Ingamells, *A Dictionary of British and Irish Travellers in Italy 1701–1800 Compiled from the Brinsley Ford Archive*, Paul Mellon Centre for Studies in British Art, 1997.

Travellers' names are cited in small caps to permit identification in the *Dictionary*. The dates in parentheses that immediately follow their names indicate when the traveller was in Italy.

'SUBJECTS *I* CONSIDER'D AS *WRITERS DO*'
Hogarth and Swift

Duncan Robinson

Fig. 9 William Hogarth,
The Painter and his Pug,
1745, oil on canvas, 90 x
69.9 cm, Tate, London

'Subjects I Consider'd as Writers Do'
Hogarth and Swift

Duncan Robinson

Among the many references to literature in Hogarth's paintings, those to Shakespeare, Swift and Milton in the portrait of *The Painter and his Pug* of 1745 (fig.9) are perhaps the best known. It has often been pointed out that the inclusion of leather-bound volumes by these authors (fig.10), beside his palette and beneath his image of himself, illustrates not only Hogarth's dependence upon literary sources but also his insistence on the literal nature of his own work; 'subjects I consider'd as writers do.'[1] Significantly, the paint on the palette takes the form of words, spelling out 'the line of beauty', the precept Hogarth was to expand upon eight years later when he published *The Analysis of Beauty.*[2] There, on the title page, the line of beauty is defined quite literally as 'serpentine' by means of a quotation from Milton's account of Eve's temptation in the Garden of Eden. This helps to explain why the bottom of the three books which support Hogarth himself in *The Painter and his Pug* is *Paradise Lost*, the epic poem which in the eighteenth century earned for Milton the epithet of the English Homer, once he had been rehabilitated from his republican past and enshrined along with Shakespeare in the Temple of British Worthies.[3] Shakespeare is also represented, somewhat cryptically, on the title page of *The Analysis*. The single word 'VARIETY', inscribed on the base above which the serpent(ine line) is encased, refers to none other than 'Shakespear, who had the deepest penetration into nature, [and who] has sum'd up all the charms of beauty in two words, INFINITE VARIETY.'[4] To turn once more to the self-portrait, on the top of the pile of three books, Shakespeare lies closest, as it were, to Hogarth's heart, while Swift's *Works* are

Fig. 10 *The Painter and his Pug* (detail)

sandwiched in the middle, resting upon *Paradise Lost*, with its reference to the Fall and, as a consequence, to human nature as it was understood by both Hogarth and Swift. Hogarth's promotion of Swift to keep company with Shakespeare and Milton may seem surprising at first, but it did enable him to represent the three different literary genres of drama, poetry and prose. It was also a typically Hogarthian tribute to a disillusioned author who died in the year that the picture was painted. Above all, however, the inclusion of Swift, the master of ironic commentary with whom Hogarth undoubtedly identified, must have involved a measure of wish-fulfilment for an artist who was beginning to realise that his own fame was likely to rest in future on his reputation as a satirist.

Jonathan Swift (1667–1745) was thirty years older than Hogarth. He was at the height of his influence as a Tory journalist when Hogarth was a child, during the final years of Queen Anne's reign. With Pope, Arbuthnot and Gay he established the Scriblerus Club, a literary society formed with the explicit aim of opposing pedantry. It was Swift who wrote to Pope in August 1716 that 'I believe further the Pastoral ridicule is not exhausted, and that a porter, foot-man or chair-man's pastoral might do well. Or what think you of a Newgate pastoral, among the whores and thieves there?'[5] His comment was occasioned by the success of Gay's sextet of mock heroic pastorals, published as *The Shepherd's Week* in 1714, and it was Gay, of course, who took up Swift's challenge when he wrote his 'Newgate pastoral', *The Beggar's Opera*, which was first performed at the Theatre Royal in Lincoln's Inn Fields in 1728 under the direction of its proprietor John Rich. Seen for what it was, a highly entertaining satire upon the Walpole ministry and its self-interests, it was an instant success, making Gay rich and Rich gay in the cry of the hour. Its appeal to Hogarth was a foregone conclusion. Questions of attribution aside, no fewer than six versions exist of his painting of the denouement (fig.11), when the shackled anti-hero Macheath shrugs off his dilemma as to which of his two brides to favour by posing centre-stage like a frustrated Hercules and singing 'How happy could I be with either / Were t'other dear charmer away.'

Throughout *The Beggar's Opera* values are reversed. The Beggar has the choric voice: 'Through the whole piece you may observe such a similitude of Manners in high and low life, that it is difficult to determine whether ... the fine Gentlemen imitate the Gentlemen of the Road or the Gentlemen of the Road the fine Gentlemen.' The theme is one which runs like a *leitmotif* throughout Hogarth's

Fig. 11 William Hogarth,
The Beggars Opera, 1729,
oil on canvas, 59.1 x 76.2 cm,
Yale Center for British Art,
Paul Mellon Collection

graphic satires, beginning with his print of *Masquerades and Operas* or *The Bad Taste of the Town* of 1724 (fig.12), in which 'the English Stage [is] Debauch'd by fool'ries,' while the works of Shakespeare, Dryden, Congreve and Otway are wheeled away by a hawker, crying 'waste paper for Shops.' In the background a foppish 'connoisseur' points out to his two companions the statue of William Kent, which tops the pediment above the 'Academy of Art', with those of Michelangelo

Fig. 12 William Hogarth,
Masquerades & Operas, 1724,
engraving, 12.7 x 17.1 cm,
The British Museum

and Raphael looking up admiringly from below. The irony is Scriblerian,
reminiscent of Swift's Preface to *A Tale of a Tub*, published twenty years earlier, in
which 'it is intended that a large Academy be erected, capable of containing nine
thousand seven hundred forty and three Persons; which by modest Computation
is reckoned to be pretty near the current number of Wits in this Island.' Hogarth's
visual diatribe also anticipated by four years Pope's *Dunciad*, in which the ageing
and increasingly bitter poet attempted to settle by similar means his scores with a
raft of literary and political opponents.

   In 1726 Hogarth seized a further opportunity to demonstrate his sympathies with
the Scriblerians, who regrouped that year to mount a scathing attack in the pages
of the *Craftsman* on Walpole and his administration. Swift's *Gulliver's Travels* was
published in October and two months later Hogarth issued his print of *The
Punishment inflicted on Lemuel Gulliver* (fig.13). It was an invention on his part, as
opposed to an illustration of the text, in which he responded to Swift's narrative

Fig. 13 William Hogarth, *The Punishment inflicted on Lemuel Gulliver*, 1726, engraving, 20.7 x 31.4 cm, The British Museum

by rendering its implied criticism of the government in his own, equally feculent, visual terms. In the book, Gulliver was condemned to lose his sight after he put out the fire which was threatening the royal palace of Lilliput by urinating on the flames. Alerted to his sentence, he escaped before it could be carried out. In Hogarth's variant, the gull(ible victim) allows himself to be subjected to a gigantic enema, administered 'by applying a Lilypucian fire Engine to his Posteriors.' He is surrounded in the print by all the usual butts of Hogarth's satirical rage. Among them, a priest looks down approvingly from the elevated chamber pot which serves as his pulpit while a large rat savages a naked infant among the ruins of the city. In other words, church and state are implicated in this humiliation of the body politic just as, twenty-five years later, Hogarth held the same agencies responsible for the social evils he represented in his engraving of *Gin Lane*.[6]

In 1736 Swift repaid the compliment in the scathing attack on the Irish Parliament he mounted in his poem *The Legion Club*; addressing 'Humorous Hogarth', he

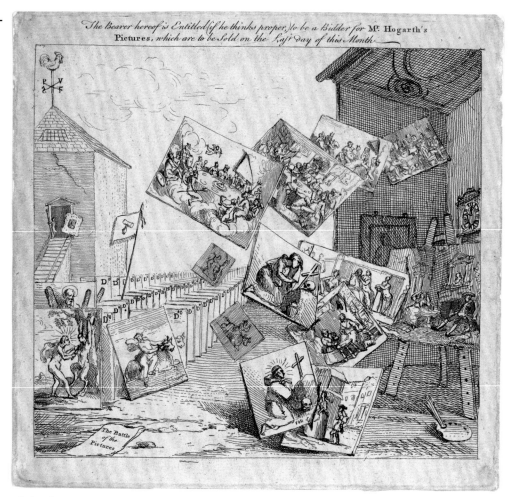

Fig. 14 William Hogarth, *The Battle of Pictures*, 1745, engraving, 20.1 x 21.3 cm, The British Museum

advised:

> You should try your graving Tools
> On this odious Group of Fools.

Perhaps as a result of this, in 1740 Hogarth sent Swift one of the first folios of his prints. It was acknowledged by Swift's publisher, George Faulkner, who wrote: 'I have often the Favour of drinking your Health with Dr Swift, who is a great Admirer of yours … and desired me to thank you for your kind Present.'[7] By then Swift's mental and physical health were in decline; in 1742 guardians were appointed to manage his affairs and he spent the last three years of his life in a twilight of dementia. On the other hand, as the inclusion of Swift's collected works in *The Painter and his Pug* demonstrates, Hogarth maintained his share in the mutual admiration pact and indeed made a significant contribution to his fellow satirist's enduring reputation as a literary giant. In the same year, 1745, he added a further, albeit indirect, compliment when he illustrated the ticket he designed to advertise the auction of his paintings with *The Battle of the Pictures* (fig.14). The image is a self-interested one, in which an army of dubious old master paintings attacks authentic contemporary art in the form of Hogarth's works; with deliberate irony, a penitent Magdalen slices through the canvas of scene three of *The Harlot's Progress* for instance.[8] But as Hogarth's contemporaries would have recognised at once, his iconography is derived from Swift's *Battle of the Books*, a polemic he wrote in 1697–98 to defend his patron Sir William Temple, whose *Essay on Ancient and Modern Learning*, published in 1790, had been attacked by the Revd. William Wotton in his *Reflections* of 1694, and even more roundly by Richard Bentley in his *Dissertation on the Epistles of Philaris* which appeared as an appendix to a second edition of Wotton's *Reflections* in 1697. What followed was all-out literary warfare between the 'Ancients' and the 'Moderns', in which Swift's *Full and True Account of the Battel fought last Friday between the Antient and the Modern Books in St James's Library* may be seen as a significant but indecisive skirmish. It was not published until 1704, when it appeared together with *A Tale of a Tub*, but the controversy rumbled on to reappear in the fourth book of Pope's *Dunciad*, which was dedicated to Swift. In it Bentley, by then Master of Trinity College Cambridge, was invoked:

> Where Bentley late tempestuous wont to sport
> In troubled waters, now sleeps in port.
>
> . . .
>
>   is Aristarchus yet unknown?
> Thy mighty scholiast, whose unwearied pains
> Made Horace dull, and humbled Milton's strains.
> Turn what they will to verse, their toil is vain,
> Critics like me shall make it prose again.

For Hogarth, the parallel was irresistible. Swift had written in his Preface to the *Battel*: 'SATYR is a sort of Glass, wherein Beholders do generally discover every

Fig. 15 George Bickham the
Elder, *The Whig's Medly / The
Three False Brethren*, 1711,
engraving, 38.7 x 28 cm,
The British Museum

body's Face but their Own; which is the chief Reason for that kind of Reception it
meets in the World, and that so very few are offended by it.' The same figure of speech
was used by Hogarth in his later versions of *The Beggar's Opera*, in which 'veluti in
speculum' ('just as in a mirror') is inscribed in a cartouche above the scene in which
the action encompasses members of the audience as well as the cast of the play.

Hogarth's contemporaries would have recognised his visual sources for *The
Battle of the Pictures* as readily as his literary reference to Swift. Composite images
such as George Bickham's *The Whig's Medly* were commonplace in the print
culture of the early eighteenth century (fig.15). As Mark Hallett has pointed out,
that particular image served to attack the writer Daniel Defoe who, like Swift, was
fully engaged in party political controversy.[9] It was a form of visual satire which

Fig 16   Nathaniel Hone I,
The Conjuror, 1775,
oil on canvas, 145 x 173 cm,
National Gallery of Ireland

retained its currency throughout the century, as Nathaniel Hone's painting of *The Pictorial Conjuror, displaying the Whole Art of Optical Deception* shows (fig.16). Exhibited at the Royal Academy in 1775, it was recognised at once as a satire aimed at the theory and practice of the Academy's first President, Sir Joshua Reynolds.[10] Once again, the underlying theme is the relationship between the ancients (old masters) and the moderns (contemporary artists).

One of Hogarth's last words on the subject was his etching of *Time smoking a Picture*, published in 1761, and in many ways a prelude to his final engraving, made shortly before his death in 1764. *Bathos* is also a kind of medley print, a despondent 'tailpiece' to what was for him 'the world's end', his palette cracked, and the exhausted figure of Time, derived from Salvator Rosa's *L'Umana Fragilità*, uttering

Fig. 17 Luke Sullivan after William Hogarth, *Satire on False Perspective*, 1754, engraving, 22.2 x 17.6 cm, The British Museum

one word, FINIS. While there is truth in Horace Walpole's assessment of Hogarth, 'that in so many scenes of satire or ridicule, it is obvious that ill-nature did not guide his pencil,' and that 'his views were more generous and extensive,'[11] his final pessimism recalls that of Swift who, we must remember also wrote of himself (in the third person):

> His Satyr points at no Defect
> But what all Mortals may correct.[12]

There is, perhaps, one image which sums up that combination of humour and seriousness, the essence of irony, which was common to both Hogarth and Swift. In his *Satire on False Perspective* of 1754 (fig.17) Hogarth depicts a topsy-turvy world which offers a visual counterpart to that described by the author of *Gulliver's Travels*. In each of them the norms of size and scale are distorted to undermine all sense of physical and psychological equilibrium. Just as the conventions of proportion and pictorial space which governed representation in the visual arts are subverted in Hogarth's imaginary landscape, so the factual and scientific nature of contemporary travel literature is parodied in Swift's absurdly fictional geographies.

1   Autobiographical Notes, BM Addl. MS 27,991, f.10, repr. Joseph Burke, *William Hogarth. The Analysis of Beauty*, Oxford 1955, pp.201–31. For a recent discussion of the painting, see Mark Hallett and Christine Riding, *Hogarth*, London 2006, pp.42–44.

2   William Hogarth, *The Analysis of Beauty*, 1753, ed. Ronald Paulson, New Haven & London 1997.

3   At Stowe, for example, where they joined William III, Elizabeth I, Hampden, Locke, Bacon and Newton to personify the principles upheld by the 'Glorious Revolution' of 1688. Jacob Tonson published the first complete edition of Milton's *Works* in 1695.

4   *Analysis of Beauty*, ed. Paulson, p.10.

5   Swift to Pope, 30 August 1716, in *The Correspondence of Jonathan Swift*, ed. Harold Williams, vol.2, Oxford 1962, p.215.

6   Published in 1751 to coincide with the passing of the Gin Act, which was designed to curb consumption by regulating the distillation of spirits.

7   Quoted by Ronald Paulson, *Hogarth, vol.II, High Art and Low, 1732–1750*, New Brunswick 1992, p.47.

8   For a detailed analysis, see Paulson, *Hogarth, vol.II, High Art and Low*, pp.231–35.

9   Mark Hallett, *The Spectacle of Difference: Graphic Satire in the Age of Hogarth*, New Haven & London 1999, pp.46–55.

10 For a detailed analysis, see John Newman, 'Reynolds and Hone: "The Conjuror" Unmasked,' in *Reynolds*, Royal Academy of Arts, London 1986, pp.344–54.

11 Horace Walpole, *Anecdotes of Painting in England*, London 1879, pp.358 and 360.

12 *Verses on the Death of Dr Swift*, 1731.

A Cure for the Captain
A Sober Look at Hogarth's *Captain Lord George Graham in his Cabin*

Elizabeth Einberg

An affectionate testimonial to Brian Allen who also has an 'invincible fund of good humour'.

Fig. 18   William Hogarth, *Captain Lord George Graham in his Cabin, c.*1745, oil on canvas, 68.5 x 88.9 cm, National Maritime Museum, London

𝒜 Cure for the Captain
A Sober Look at Hogarth's *Captain Lord George Graham in his Cabin*

Elizabeth Einberg

The conversation piece of 'Captain Lord George Graham in his cabin'[1] (fig.18) is usually interpreted as a roistering celebration of the young Captain's participation in a successful naval action off Ostende in 1745, for which he was rewarded with the command of the 60-gun *Nottingham*.[2] Yet to an eighteenth-century viewer this picture might have appeared too informal, too private, and altogether too odd to represent an event that would have been more usually marked with a formal portrait in full dress, with ships firing broadsides in the background. Intimate and personal the picture certainly was: bequeathed by the Captain in his short will[3] to his brother, the 2nd Duke of Montrose, it remained in the family, never engraved or recorded, until the end of the nineteenth century.[4]

Firstly, to Hogarth's contemporaries a gathering of five men 'in their own hair', with only a dog wearing a formal wig, would have signalled a huge joke of the 'world turned upside down' kind. Since this is not a group of children at play but of seriously professional adults, none of them drunk, this would suggest more than a throwaway pleasantry.

The other oddity is the total absence of alcohol in what should be a convivial male gathering for which the main reason would normally be to raise and to down one toast after another. Although food is being served to at least two of those present (only two places are laid), there are no wine glasses on the table and the punch-bowl has been placed on the floor in the left foreground. This could be in order to show that it is filled with pure water through which the Chinese pattern at the bottom is clearly visible (fig.19). It is placed at the feet of the Captain's table-

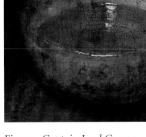

Fig. 19 *Captain Lord George Graham in his Cabin* (detail)

companion, whose collared spaniel joins, as sensitive dogs often do (fig.20), in the musical performance that visibly fills the room. Dog-lovers usually interpret this kind of canine involvement as an expression of extreme sympathy or empathy. The only glass, big enough to serve as a water glass, has been kidnapped to serve as a lectern for another, more highly placed, dog. This is a pug, majestically enthroned on a chair in the right foreground, wearing a large campaign wig (almost certainly the Captain's) and holding a rolled paper as a master of ceremonies would hold his white staff of office (fig.21).

The focus of attention is the Captain himself, thoughtfully puffing at a pipe of unusual length. Placed in his 'natural' environment of a captain's cabin,[5] he is presented in richly elegant undress that in no way marks him out as a sailor: wrapped in a fur-lined coat, he is wearing red slippers, a tasselled satin or velvet cap, and an old-fashioned twisted Steinkirk cravat still sometimes favoured by the military. He is surrounded by companions of lower rank than himself: a cook, a hired singer (no place is laid for him at table), a black musician, who might also be his servant, and the aforementioned soberly dressed table-companion who, while often reasonably described as a parson, doctor, secretary or some other non-aristocratic professional, nevertheless exudes an air of relaxed and easy authority. To these one can add the unusually anthropomorphic pug.

None of these elements make for a triumphalist picture and many details are genuinely puzzling. For all its casual air, this is a large (for Hogarth), elaborately conceived and expensive picture, such as one would paint to mark a life-changing event, albeit perhaps a private rather than a public one. Many of its enigmatic details, however, fall into place when one considers Captain Lord George Graham's career and life in greater detail.

Lord George Graham (1715–1747) was the youngest son of the 1st Duke of Montrose (d.1742). He was a midshipman in the Navy by 1730, aged 15, and became a dedicated career sailor. Helped no doubt by his family's superior connections, he rose rapidly and was made lieutenant on 13 April 1734, seeing service in the Mediterranean. On 15 March 1740 he was promoted to post-captain and was reported to have been given various commands in quick succession, including that of the *Adventure*, ostensibly for a tour of duty to protect English fishing off Newfoundland, a seasonal assignment that carried with it the title of Governor of Newfoundland. These reported appointments, however, seem to have been either

Fig. 20 *Captain Lord George Graham in his Cabin* (detail)

Fig. 21 *Captain Lord George Graham in his Cabin* (detail)

based on rumour or purely nominal, for the *Adventure* remained laid up at Deptford in poor condition and was broken up the following year. On 3 June 1740 Graham and the crew of the *Adventure* were reassigned to the 40-gun man-of-war, the *Lark*, as part of a naval squadron that, under the overall command of Captain Philip Vincent in the *St Albans*, was to escort a convoy of well over thirty merchant ships of the Turkey Trade on a round trip to Smyrna (now Izmir) and Tenedos (now Bozcaada). They were ready to leave Spithead on 22 June 1740 (though held back by contrary winds for over two months) and returned almost exactly twelve months later, anchoring in the Downs off Deal on 25 June 1741. The ship's logs[6] record a relatively uneventful voyage, with victualling stops at Lisbon, Gibraltar, Minorca and elsewhere, in reasonable weather conditions for most of the time, the daily routine punctuated by regular readings of the Articles of War to the crew and the usual steady stream of burials at sea due to sickness and accidents.

The Captain has come down in history as a popular figure, a successful and brave officer and, above all, one who cared deeply for his crew. The late eighteenth-century naval biographer Charnock writes about him:

> From a multitude of concurrent testimonies he appears to have been an officer who attained a great share of popularity, and was indeed, very deservedly, the idol of all seamen who knew him, as well as on account of the high opinion entertained of his gallantry, as an invincible fund of good humour, which latter quality conciliated the affections of men in the same degree that the first related excited their admiration and esteem.[7]

The Captain's letters to the Admiralty Board[8] on his return home in 1741, however, strike a far from happy note. After receiving a clean bill of health on arrival ('there is in her no Distemper but the Scurvy', and that in 'none of ships from the Levant is there any Disease but what is incident to Seamen who have lived near Twelve Months upon Salt provisions') he was immediately instructed to fit out other ships before attending to his own leaky vessel, the *Lark*. Reporting on her condition on 25 June 1741, he writes that 'she is Exeeding Foule and Very leaky … although I had her Caulked all Round at Smyrna', and that, among many other defects, her decks were so rotten that the men below were 'mostly wett in their Hamacoes when it Rains'. There must have been problematic circumstances that brought him into conflict with Admiralty orders (only the Captain's letters have been located so far) but the upshot was that Graham got into arguments with at least one other captain and that he was reprimanded for disobedience in a manner that stung him to the core. His letter of 30th July 1741 sets out his situation:

> Sir,
> This moment Mr. Helby delivered to me your letter of the 29th July, and as I humbly conceive it my duty to clear up this point, I shall answer it by an express. … Monday, the 26th, came Lord Montagu Bertie in the Lime [*Lyme*]. His Lordship honoured me with a visit on board my ship and communicated his orders to me. I must acquaint you, Sir, that Captain Reddish told me that as he was a transient man here … he would take no cognaizance of the trade, but said I must do it in pursuance to their Lordships' repeated commands. I have fitted out two Privateers with proper officers and seamen on board of them. I have had the honour to be twice seven years in the Navy, and never in that time or in my life read a letter that went so near my heart as did yours of the 29th. … Permit me to say, Sir, in regard to the Privateers I have acted like a seaman. I hope I shall never be susceptible to vanity, but this I will venture to say: I know my trade. …
> In all this affair Captain West has been warm, I have been cool, as can be witnessed by gentlemen of undoubted veracity.…

Assuring their Lordships of his desire to serve them with utmost obedience and diligence, he appeals to them to check with his former commanding officer Lord Vere Beauclerk if, even as a boy, he had ever neglected his duty or disobeyed a command, also with his commodore on the Turkey voyage, Captain Vincent, and with the captains of the Levant Company as to whether he had the interest of trade at heart. 'If I have been unhappy enough to fall under the Board's displeasure, I most humbly beg the favour to resign the Lark and go to Chiltinham [Cheltenham] for recovery of my health, being violently afflicted with pain in my breast and some scurvy…' and he adds a postscript asking 'that Their Lordships will send down a better man to command in the Downes, for I am neither fond nor fit to be a Commodore.'

More letters written on the following days to the same recipient, Thomas Corbett, Secretary to the Admiralty Board, give details of his manning and outfitting operations in the Downs, and an offer to send his journal to the Board so 'the Board will be able to judge whether I have done my Duty', adding again 'I have a most violent soar throte and pain in my Breast'. On 1 August he repeats his request to resign the *Lark* 'as Their Lordships are pleased to say I am Disorderly Officer … for in this affair my character, which is Dear to me, is at Stake', signing himself off as 'Your Injured, Tho' Very Humble Servt . to Command Geo. Graham'.

Things did not improve, and the nadir seems to have been reached on 4 August, when the Captain writes:

> I am hon. with the Board's Commands without Loss of time to supply Captain West ('tis done), though I fear not to his satisfaction as he is a Young Gentleman of a Mighty odd Sort of Temper. As he is my Officer, I most Humbly Pray with all Submission that as he has in him the Genius of Command that I, who have not, may be permitted to attempt to Recover a Scorbutic Constitution at the Wells of Chiltingham [Cheltenham].

To this the Secretary's hand adds the dry superscription: 'Lord Geo. Graham Does not care to be under the command of Captn.West'.[9]

Told to stop bombarding the Board with express letters ('I acknowledge … you desire no more expresses'), the 8th of August finds him writing from Waldershare, near Dover, the seat of Lord Rockingham, and after this interval on shore things seem to calm down. Back on the *Lark* two days later ('10 August 1741. 8 am Saluted Lord Rockingham at his going Away with 13 guns')[10] in his letter of 14th August, written in the neat hand of his amanuensis and not his own wild scrawl, the Captain sounds almost apologetic:

> I am … much Beholding to Their Lordships' Indulgence. I shall make no bad use of favours. … Rest I really want, for none I've had for more than Fifteen months. If I have been too warm in any of my humble Remonstrances to Their Lordships, it proceeded from thinking that I had been injured by my Masters. I have but one Merit to plead, which is, I hope I am honest.

Further notes follow, still sounding angry and stressed, requesting to be discharged from active service on half pay, so that he can 'attempt to gain a Younger Brother's Bread amongst the Merchants'.

His resignation accepted, the last entry in the Captain's journal is on 27 August, and on 2 September, at Sheerness, the *Lark* is taken over by Captain George Lord

Forrester to undergo repairs. There follows a three-year gap in Captain Graham's naval career about which the biographers are silent, but which is probably highly relevant to this picture.

While absent at sea in 1741, Graham was elected (appointed would be a more appropriate word) Member of Parliament to his father's constituency of Stirlingshire, as an opposition Whig.[11] Apart from his limited activities in this role, little is known about him during this period. It does appear, however, that immediately upon going ashore, the Captain suffered some kind of a breakdown, perhaps even what we would now call a burn-out. Writing to Lord Lincoln on 18 September 1741, Horace Walpole describes Lord George Graham as deranged,[12] making it clear that 'mad' is not meant to be a rhetorical term: 'all England is mad! Lady Cowper, Mr. Skinner, Lord George Graham, and Tom Hervey are shut up', adding a lurid account of the self-immolation of the seriously demented Sir William Keyt at Norton a couple of weeks earlier. A slightly different spin was put on to it a few months later, after Graham's father, the 1st Duke of Montrose, had died in London on 7 January 1742. In March that year a newspaper reported:

> Yesterday the Right Hon. the Lord George Graham was so well recovered of his late indisposition (contracted by attending his father the late Duke of Montrose, during his late illness) as to be able to serve his country in Parliament.[13]

By July the Captain was leading a fairly normal life for a young man at a loose end. In a letter to Mann, dated 21 July 1742, Walpole recounts a horrendous incident, widely reported in the press, in which overzealous drunken constables locked twenty-eight Covent Garden vagrants and prostitutes, but among them also 'honest labouring women', into a minute cell in the St Martin's Roundhouse for the night, where several suffocated by the morning. Walpole adds:

> These same men, the same night, broke into a bagnio in Covent Garden, and took up Jack Spencer, Mr Stewart and Lord George Graham and would have thrust them into the Roundhouse with the poor women, if they had not been worth more than eighteen pence![14]

Whether the Captain ever fulfilled his stated intention of going to Cheltenham for a cure is not known, but its specific mention at this early date is interesting.

Although the purgative powers of Cheltenham waters were advertised as early as 1720, the wells' first modest pump room had only just been built in 1738, by a Captain Henry Skillicorne (1678–1763) of Bristol, after the wells had come into his possession by marriage. Skillicorne had been a successful merchant privateer for forty years and was evidently a born entrepreneur – he could 'do business in 7 tongues' and was never known to be intoxicated. He saw a niche market for the wells among the sea-going fraternity and set about promoting them as particularly effective cure for the scurvy, the bane of all seamen. As early as 1739, Admiral Sir George Forbes, 3rd Earl of Granard, declined a command on the grounds of his poor health, for which he had been 'advised to go and drink the waters at Cheltenham, Glos.'[15] It should be noted, if only for its rarity at this period, that the Earl was famously abstemious in his habits, a teetotaller, and that he was the father of Lady Mary Forbes, Captain Graham's intended, about whom more later.

In 1740 Cheltenham Wells had received a tremendous boost through the writings of Dr Thomas Short (*c.*1690–1772), a Scottish physician with a wealthy and highly regarded practice in Sheffield, when he published the second volume of his massive account of *The Mineral Waters of England* etc.[16] In it he describes Captain Skillicorne's activities in glowing terms and praises the waters of Cheltenham 'Spaw' as the perfect cure for 'all Scorbutic Habits', also for gravel, asthma, intermittent fevers, 'coldness of the Body', 'lowness of spirits', and all 'Nervous Diseases'. He writes that it never fails 'to give a keen appetite' and, when drunk fresh from the spring, 'great Life and Cheerfulness of the Spirits', adding, somewhat mysteriously, that 'the Water is a great Provoker of Venery'. He also claims that mineral waters in general 'have restored several who have been melancholy or maniac'. In less flowery terms, all of this seems to have been achieved simply by relieving the victims of constipation. It is no surprise to see Captain Henry Skillicorne in the subscribers' list, with six copies to his name. Dr Short also notes that Cheltenham waters are singularly clear, suitable for bottling, and that its salt 'is beyond any other … the Salts Crystalize presently like clear transparent Ice on the Pavers and the sides of the Well'. These salts soon became a great local industry, exported all over the world, to be mixed with pure spring water, or sprinkled over food for health-giving effect. Dr Short's recommendations, especially for nervous diseases, are eminently sensible: 'Exercise, Cheerful Company, frequent change of Ideas, chiefly of the pleasant sort' and 'abstinence,

Fig. 22 *Captain Lord George Graham in his Cabin* (detail)

temperance, a little light white meat, no spirits or malt'. In this he stands in line with his great seventeenth-century predecessor Dr Thomas Sydenham, who famously cured a patient 'in a pitiful state of hysterical upset' by ordering 'him a roast chicken and a pint of canary'. On the last item, however, they part company, for Dr Short denounced all alcohol as 'a Stygian poison'.

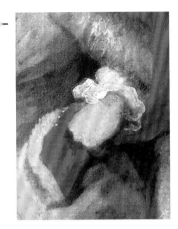

In the light of the above one can see that the Captain is manfully undergoing the recommended cure, his table swept clean of alcohol, his punch-bowl filled not with punch but with pure water, a huge salt-cellar displayed prominently next to his companion's plate, while a proudly smiling cook brings in a delicious roast fowl. It has been often stated that the cook is pouring the gravy down the neck of the man in black; in actual fact he is not only placed well back from the seated figure but he also holds a white napkin in such a way as to catch any spills. The overflowing gravy, however, makes a point, for it was the mark of a superlative cook that his roast should be 'swimming in its own Gravy' or be 'knuckle deep in luscious Gravy'.[17] Accordingly, the visual pun of placing the young man directly under the ship's crown compass marks him out as a prince among cooks (fig.22).

The Captain himself is wrapped warmly against any 'coldness of the Body' in a fur-lined robe of the kind worn by Ottoman court dignitaries (note the row of tiny buttons along the cuff, fig.23), no doubt a souvenir of his recent voyage to Turkey. His long pipe seems to be a form of the Turkish *chibouk*, that is, a pipe with a stem of varying length made of metal or jasmine wood that could be carried around in sections when travelling(fig.24). It was normally used for smoking tobacco, but this could be mixed with medicinal herbs like hashish, then regarded as an effective sedative and analgesic.[18] Whether the glowing embers in the pipe are medicinal or not is impossible to say, but it should be remembered that Dr Sydenham recommended another now suspect substance, opium, as the best God-given treatment against all types of pain.

Music has been praised as a cure for melancholy since ancient times, and it was recommended that it should go hand in hand with 'mirth and merry company'.[19] As presented here (fig.25), it is doing double duty, because its aim is not only to cheer up the Captain but it also carries the message of another cure, that 'that a man without a woman is no better than an ass', to quote an old Irish ballad. And an old Irish ballad it certainly is that is being sung by a red-haired singer,[20] for just readable on his song-sheet are the words, upside down, 'Arrah my Judy…'. A song of that title was performed by the Irish singer and freemason Michael Stoppelaer at Covent Garden in May 1741, and again at Masonic concerts in May and June 1742.[21] The text of this song is not known, but one can guess that it might be the ancestor of a popular Irish courting song that reached the printed page of ballad broadsheets by the mid-nineteenth century under the title of 'The Ol' Bog Hole'.

Fig. 26   A saucer from Lady Mary Forbes's set of china, bearing the Graham coat of arms with the Montrose motto 'NE OUBLIE', Private collection

Fig. 27   Artist unknown, *Portrait of Lady Mary Forbes*, c.1745, oil on canvas, 76.2 x 63.5 cm (sight), Private collection

In it a young man endeavours to persuade his Judy (a universal name for 'girl') to marry him, allaying her fears of being hitched to a layabout with promises that

> To keep you genteel I'll work at my trade,
> I'll handle the shovel the hook and the spade…

to repeated refrains of

> Arrah cushla mavorneen ('Come on, love of my heart'), will you marry me.

This fits in with the fact that by the time Graham wrote his will on 11 February 1745 he was apparently betrothed to Lady Mary Forbes (1712–97), daughter of the aforementioned admiral George Forbes, 3rd Earl of Granard, and sister of Graham's coeval and colleague, Captain (later Admiral) John Forbes (figs.26, 27). Although seated in Ireland, the family was of Scottish origin and retained some lands near Aberdeen. Naming her his sole executor and residuary legatee, Graham refers to her only as 'my dear and most Honoured Friend', perhaps in order to spare her the full widow-like mourning expected of the formally engaged in the case of his death. In the event, he did die before the marriage could take place, and Lady Mary ended her days quietly as the second wife of James Irvine of Kingcausie, near Aberdeen, devoting her time to gardening and French literature.[22]

Graham's table companion is plausibly identified by James Sambrook[23] as the Scottish poet and playwright David Mallet (1701/2?–65), tutor to the Captain and his elder brother William, later 2nd Duke of Montrose, from 1723 until 1731. Not only was he very much part of the Montrose household at Shawford, near Winchester, at Cley, Norfolk, and at Hanover Square, London, for eight years, but he also took the boys on a tour of Europe in 1727 and remained on friendly terms with them for life. Successful, well connected (he was under-secretary to the Prince of Wales) and newly widowed in 1742, Mallet lost no time in acquiring a new wife, fifteen years his junior, who came, moreover, with a dowry of £10,000. Lucy Elstob, described by Gibbon as a 'talkative, positive, passionate, conceited creature,' was said to take great care to see that her husband, a very short man, was always well-dressed, usually in black velvet. A man with so sanguine an outlook on life was well placed to take his despondent former pupil in hand, perhaps assuming (though only some thirteen years older than his charge) a paternal role after the old duke's death in January 1742, advising the young man to sort out his health, to get married, to resume his profession and to start filling in the empty pages of the captain's journal he is holding out to him. It stood to reason that in order to marry, the Captain had to have a decent income, and that was best gained by taking prizes (that is, capturing foreign ships) at sea. Mallet also collaborated extensively with musicians and composers of the theatre, and was a friend of the writer Aaron Hill, who composed (or was prompted to compose) a laudatory poem 'To Lord George Graham, on his Action, near Ostend, on 24th June 1745', in which Hill congratulates Mallet by name on having had so rewarding a pupil:[24]

Oh, Mallet, this was *he* – sweet heav'n fac'd boy!
Thy friend congratulates thy conscious joy:
Pride of thy care, thou led'st his earliest youth,
To court plain glory, white as robeless truth.

It would be fitting for the Captain to bequeath the picture to his brother William, now 2nd Duke of Montrose, as a memento not only of himself, but also of their former tutor. Unfortunately there are no known portraits of Mallet with which this image can be compared, but it is not inconceivable that Mallet, shown here with all the ingredients of his sound tutorial advice clustered around him, could have been the chief instigator of the picture.

Finally, as already noted by Paulson,[25] there is a Masonic connection between the Captain and Hogarth, and it is relevant to this picture. Lord George Graham and William Hogarth were both nominated on 30 March 1734 to be Grand Stewards of the Grand Lodge Dinners for the ensuing year. For professional reasons the Captain was unable to be present and was replaced by William Graeme.[26] This means that both were to become members of the distinguished Grand Stewards' Lodge, but that only Hogarth made it, thus putting him in a position where he could take up his Steward's staff and claim the privilege of presiding over a little ceremony for his 'Brother' Lord George Graham. By presenting himself as Master of Ceremonies, but in the guise of his signature pug, Hogarth deftly conveys a sense of amused fraternal ease without offending worldly rank. There is a tendency to identify every pug that appears in a Hogarth picture as representing the painter himself but, apart from the famous self-portrait in the Tate, this is the only instance where one can be fairly certain of this being so. The piece of paper in front of him could be a song-sheet, or a list of rules, but it may have also carried his signature – upside down.[27]

In his will Captain Graham refers to Hogarth respectfully as 'Mr.', leaving not only to his brother the Duke 'my Conversation Piece drawn by Mr Hogarth', but also 'to Captain Willoughby Merchant my own picture by Mr. Hogarth'. Captain Merchant (or Marchant, d.1763) of St Anne's, Limehouse, commanded the Levant Company's ship the *Thames* on the voyage to Turkey, but the picture of Graham bequeathed to him remains untraced.[28] Graham describes himself as a resident of the parish of St Paul's, Covent Garden, and must have had an interest in the theatre, for he leaves his gold watch to 'Mr. James Quin', a fellow freemason and celebrated actor, who was painted by Hogarth *c.*1739.[29]

More surprising, however, is Graham's bequest 'to Mr. Dodsley of Pallmall Bookseller my Seapiece and four small pictures in the Dining Room'. Robert Dodsley, by now a well established and highly regarded bookseller and publisher, was, for all his sober modesty, well received in the best society, and acquainted with practically all the writers of the day. As a bookseller, he would have certainly handled Dr Short's *Mineral Waters of England* and, having grown up in nearby Mansfield, may have even been acquainted with the famous Sheffield physician. There is nothing, however, in Dodsley's extensive known correspondence that otherwise connects him with Graham.

Fig. 28 William Hogarth, *James Quin, Actor, c.*1739, oil on canvas, 76 x 62.2 cm, Tate, London

Fig. 29 Sir Joshua Reynolds,
Portrait of Robert Dodsley, 1760,
oil on canvas, 75 x 63 cm,
Dulwich Picture Gallery, London

Having written his will, Graham presided a few days later, on 15 February, as one of six Stewards at the annual feast of the independent electors of Westminster at Vintners' Hall. By all accounts it was a great party, at which twenty-one formal toasts were drunk, including (toast no.6) 'That the fleet of England may be the terror of Europe' and (toast no.17) 'That all English ships may be commanded by independent officers'.[30] Immediately thereafter Graham resumed his naval career, having been offered the command of the 60-gun *Cumberland*. Significantly, he declined this in favour of the 24-gun frigate *Bridgewater*, as better suited, according to Charnock, 'to his active turn of mind', in other words, a friskier vessel better adapted for the taking of prizes. As already noted, in this he was spectacularly successful in the Channel off Ostend in June 1745, from which action he brought home two large captured Dunkirk privateers. He was soon promoted to the 60-gun *Nottingham*, with which he sunk the French privateer *Bacchus*, saving, it was noted, its entire crew bar the first lieutenant who was killed in action. He continued to patrol British waters, watching for French ships endeavouring to rescue Jacobites fleeing the country after the '45 rebellion, and engaged in several skirmishes. In these he showed a professional prudence and disregard for personal gain that earned him the praise of his masters, as shown in a report of 15 May 1746, sent to John Russell, 4th Duke of Bedford, first Lord of the Admiralty:

> I send you … a copy of [a letter] from Lord George Graham; though they contain no successes, the parties concerned seem to have acquitted themselves very well … poor Lord George is much to be lamented that he wanted strength to make an immense fortune and, considering the warmth of his complexion, much to be commended for not having thrown away the King's ships.[31]

Early that October Captain Graham was ashore and ill at Bristol, whence his brother the Duke of Montrose brought him to Bath.[32] Here, on 2 January 1747, the Captain died, aged 32 and unmarried.

Sometime between the second half of 1742 and the end of 1744, some of Captain Lord George Graham's well-wishers must have conspired in an effort to make him fit and healthy enough to resume the career in which he was meant to shine, to return him, in effect, to his natural environment of a captain's cabin in a ship of His Majesty's Navy. They went to work with all the tools available to them – a healthy regimen, curative mineral salts and waters, good food, merry company, jokes, songs, sensible advice and the promise of future happiness. The picture was presumably painted as a record of their success (albeit short-lived), and as an affectionate testimonial to their subject's 'invincible fund of good humour'. [33]

I am grateful to Roger Knight and Pieter van der Merwe for reading the above paper, for invaluable information and advice on all things naval and on Captain Graham in particular, and for guidance through the intricacies of the Admiralty records.

1 Oil on canvas, 68.5 x 88.9 cm (28 x 35 in) National Maritime Museum (Caird collection), cat. BHC2720.

2 R. Paulson, *Hogarth. Vol. 2: High Art and Low, 1732–1750*, Cambridge 1992, pp.176–77. Mary Webster (*Hogarth*, London 1979, p.134) suggests the possibility of an earlier date.

3 PCC PROB 11/752, 8 January 1747, written 11 February 1745.

4 First recorded when exhibited Glasgow 1888 (225); sold by the Duke of Montrose in 1932 to Sir James Caird, Bt., by whom presented to the Museum.

5 Pieter van der Merwe considers that it suggests a small ship without a stern gallery, perhaps the size of the *Lark*. Shown are three of four stern windows; the pier glasses between them were not standard and are a personal touch, suggesting a wealthy captain. The dark area behind the singer is probably the curtained entry into a quarter gallery, that is, the 'necessary place' which protruded out over the sea. This detail may be relevant to the hoped-for effect of Cheltenham waters, as described later.

6 National Maritime Museum, Admiralty Records/ Lieutenants' Logs L/L/27 and 28. The first volume includes the log of Lt. John Ferguson of the *Lark*, and, unusually, the second includes the journal of Captain Lord George Graham, one of a few captains' logs misplaced *ab origine* among the lieutenants' and not in the National Archives at Kew.

7 John Charnock, *Biographia Navalis*, vol.5, London 1797, pp.22–24.

8 National Archives, ADM 1/1828, Captains' Letters 1739-41G. All letters quoted are from this volume, where they are arranged in alphabetical order of the captains' names, and then roughly in date order.

9 This is presumably Captain Temple West (1713–57), later MP for Buckingham and vice-admiral. See R. Sedgwick, *The History of Parliament. The House of Commons 1715–1754*, 2 vols., London 1970, vol.2, p.531.

10 National Maritime Museum, Adm. Records/ Lieutenants'. Logs L/L28 (Capt. Lord George Graham's journal)

11 R. Sedgwick, *The House of Commons 1715–1754*, vol.2, p.75.

12 *Horace Walpole's Correspondence Vol. 30*, ed. W.S. Lewis and R.A. Smith, London 1961, pp.22–23. For Tom Hervey's mental problems see R. Halsband, *Lord Hervey. Eighteenth-Century Courtier*, Oxford 1973, p.280.

13 *The Daily Post*, Tuesday, 23 March 1742. I am particularly grateful to Pieter van der Merwe for this reference.

14 *Horace Walpole's Correspondence, Vols. 17–27, with Sir Horace Mann*, ed. W.S. Lewis, W.H. Smith, G.L. Lam and E.M. Martz, New Haven and London 1954–71, vol.17, pp.504–5. There is some satisfaction in reading that the following morning the Roundhouse was pulled down by an angry mob and that its keeper was in due course sentenced to death, commuted to transportation, for murder.

15 John Forbes, *Memoirs of the Earls of Granard*, ed. George-Arthur-Hastings, Earl of Granard, London 1868, p.155.

16 Thomas Short, *An Essay towards a ... history of the principle* [sic] *mineral waters ... Being the second volume of The Mineral Waters of England*, Sheffield 1740, pp.77–79, 142, 202, 211–13, 227, 269. Volume 1, on the mineral waters of northern England, had been published in 1734. See also his entry in the *Oxford Dictionary of National Biography*.

17 [Ned Ward], *A Compleat and Humorous Account of all the Remarkable Clubs and Societies in the Cities of London and Westminster*, first published 1709, cited 7th ed. London 1756, pp.320, 325.

18 G.G. Nahas, 'Hashish in Islam, 9th to 18th century', *Bulletin of the New York Academy of Medicine*, vol.58, no.9, December 1982, pp.814, 823ff. I am also grateful to D. Duco of the Stichting Pijpenkabinet, Amsterdam, for his helpful suggestions.

19 Robert Burton, *The Anatomy of Melancholy*, 1621. This edition with an introduction by William H. Gass, New York 2001, pp.115–19, 'Music a Remedy' and 'Mirth and merry company'.

20 Traditionally, wavy or curly red hair was a mark of the Irish, just as lank red hair was that of the Scots.

21 Philip H. Highfill, Kalman A. Burnim and Edward A. Langhans, *A Biographical Dictionary of Actors ... Vol. 14 S. Siddons to Thynne*, Carbondale, Illinois 1991, p.293. I am particularly grateful to Andrew Pink for pointing out a reference to this concert in *The Champion or Evening Advertiser*, London, for Tuesday, 22 June 1742, and for providing translations for the Irish words.

22 I am grateful to Henry Irvine-Fortescue for all information on Lady Mary Forbes, including the fact that there is still a youthful portrait of her, by an unknown hand, at Kingcausie, as well as some of her china, bearing the Graham coat of arms with the poignant Montrose motto 'NE OUBLIE'.

23 *Oxford Dictionary of National Biography*, article 'Mallet (formerly Malloch), David, 1701/2?–1765, poet'.

24 F. Dinsdale, 'Memoir', in D. Mallet, *Ballads and Songs*, new ed. London 1857, p.20.

25 R. Paulson, *Hogarth*, p.430 n38.

26 This was kindly pointed out to me by Ric Berman, quoting *Quattro Coronati Antigrapha*, Vol. X (1913), pp.240–41, which also notes (pp.301–2, 311, 315) that Graham served as Senior Grand Warden and acting Grand Master in 1738. Berman also notes a report in the *London Evening Post*, 1 June 1736, recording the presence of Lord George Graham, Lord Forrester and other members of the British Fleet at the constituting of the Masonic Lodge in Lisbon.

27 Close inspection of the picture in the National Maritime Museum Conservation Studio registered what might be the remnants of a capital 'H', but the traces are too faint to provide firm evidence. I am most grateful to Caroline Hampton, Roger Quarm and Elizabeth Hamilton-Eddy for all their help in examining the picture.

28 Unless one identifies it, purely on grounds of likeness, with the 'Unknown Man in a blue coat', dated 1739, in the Manchester Art Gallery.

29 E. Einberg and J. Egerton, *The Age of Hogarth*, London 1988, pp.98–101.

30 *Gentleman's Magazine*, vol.15, February 1745, p.107.

31 *The Correspondence of John, 4th Duke of Bedford* ed. Lord John Russell, vol.1 London 1842, p.103.

32 HMC (Astley papers) 1900, p.355, letter, dated 11 October 1746, at Bath, from Fanny Russell to Col. Charles Russell, saying that the Duke of Montrose, 'who has been to Bristol to fetch his brother, Lord George, who is ill', is about to leave for London.

33 John Charnock, *Biographia Navalis*, vol.5, p.24.

'ALL THE QUALITY OF HIS PICTURES EXCEPT THE COLOUR'
Richard Wilson's Drawings as Collectors' Items

Paul Spencer-Longhurst

Fig. 30   Richard Wilson, *The Castle of St Angelo, Rome,* 1752-56, black chalk on grey paper, heightened with white, 24.1 x 39.4 cm,
Tate, London N02438.
Formerly Paul Sandby and William Esdaile collections.

'ALL THE QUALITY OF HIS PICTURES EXCEPT THE COLOUR'[1]
Richard Wilson's Drawings as Collectors' Items

Paul Spencer-Longhurst

Late in his chequered career, Richard Wilson (1713–1782) was reduced to selling his drawings *en masse* to his 'good friend … in days of adversity'[2] Paul Sandby in order to survive financially. Yet Wilson was also the artist who in 1754 had been personally retained by William Legge, 2nd Earl of Dartmouth (1731–1801), to record the memorable monuments, sites and views of his grand tour in a breath-taking series of presentation drawings. Today Wilson's drawings survive in some number in major museums in Britain and America yet, as Brinsley Ford was the first to remark,[3] the stages of his career represented in these collections are very uneven, with the majority dating from his Italian period. This raises questions as to the purpose of drawings for the artist himself. Ford differentiated Wilson's graphic oeuvre into four types: studies, designs, sketches and compositions.[4] David Solkin went further in dividing the small number of drawings known from Wilson's stay in Venice (1750–51) into two distinct categories: views of local scenery, executed with relatively little regard for compositional niceties on the one hand and, on the other, purely imaginary designs strongly influenced by Francesco Zuccarelli's rococo style.[5] These were followed by the 'Lock tour' drawings, not meant to serve as finished views but commissioned or acquired by William Lock of Norbury (1732–1810) as quick souvenirs of noteworthy sites which he and Wilson passed on their way to Rome together.

Following Wilson's decision, taken in Venice, to devote himself to landscape came a prolonged burst of activity as a draughtsman, which gained momentum over the next few years. The artist slowly abandoned Zuccarelli's fantastic notion of landscape art in favour of focusing his attention on the outside world – Roman ruins and fragments of classical sculpture, individual trees and the occasional view of an identifiable site. These drawings in common with the other 'many excellent drawings and sketches left by Wilson'[6] were almost without exception executed in black chalk, often worked with stump, and heightened with white on blue- or grey-green paper – a practice which sets them apart from the majority of English landscape drawings of the period and suggests the influence of artists working at the French Academy in Rome. However, a small number in pen and ink, mostly imaginary compositions, are known from Wilson's later Italian period. His career as a draughtsman culminated in the resplendent Dartmouth set which, as Solkin observed, 'reveal a remarkable agility to digest complex natural data in front of the motif, together with a noteworthy capacity to anticipate the problems involved in transforming an immediate visual experience of a site into a highly polished design.'[7] After his departure from Italy, Wilson seems to have had surprisingly little use for draughtsmanship, which he must have regarded primarily as a way to record the various phenomena of nature for future reference in paintings. Very few securely datable drawings survive after 1757 although he did continue to produce some drawings of Italian subjects for sale, at least until 1760.[8]

In the Wilson historiography there has been little discussion of the drawings as collectors' items *per se* since Brinsley Ford's *The Drawings of Richard Wilson* (1951). It is the purpose of this essay briefly to survey some of the major private collections of the drawings made over the two centuries or so between Wilson's departure for Italy and the publication of Ford's seminal book, and to indicate how such private collections have created and nourished public ones in Britain and the USA.

The principal owners of Wilson drawings during his own lifetime are first mentioned by Joseph Farington, the egregious diarist and former pupil of Wilson, who on 2 May 1811 met Thomas Sandby at the opening day of Sandby's father's sale at Christie's, where together they looked over the numerous lots of drawings by Wilson.[9] PAUL SANDBY (1725–1809) had bought drawings directly from the artist (fig. 30). Best remembered for his watercolours and as the first British printmaker to use aquatint systematically, from the 1750s he had been involved in the campaign to found the Royal Academy and became the friend and supporter of Wilson, like him one of the Founder Members. Sandby bought up the drawings in Wilson's studio, initially with a view to selling them to his gentlemen pupils but for the most part keeping them himself.[10] As recorded in 1824 by Thomas Wright, Wilson's early biographer, 'When distress compelled Wilson to sell drawings which he had executed, at half a crown apiece, Paul Sanby [*sic*] paid him for a great number with a juster estimation of their worth, and with a liberality creditable to his memory and feelings as an artist.'[11] Many of the drawings featured in Sandby's own posthumous sale as 'An Invaluable Assemblage of near 70 Original Drawings by Wilson' offered over three days.[12] Among the numerous sketches, views, compositions or studies bearing Sandby's distinctive collector's mark, some are easily recognisable from the catalogue descriptions, such as *View of the Banks of the Dee in Cheshire*[13] and ... *an elaborate and faithful study, a portrait of the Arbra [sic] Sacra, on the borders of the Lake Nemi*.[14] As noted by Solkin, Sandby's pencil inscription on the verso of his own mount of the former casts an interesting sidelight on his role as a dealer in Wilson paintings: 'Banks of the Dee in Cheshire / I once had the picture of this / P.S./sold it to Sr S. Clarke / it was painted for a friend of Wilsons one Hughes an oil m... / ... [from] whom I bought it.'[15] The second drawing, now known as *The Arbra Sacra on the Banks of Lake Nemi* is highly finished and subtle in touch, clearly intended as an independent work of art rather than a preparatory study for any other composition. Four of the entries in the sale catalogue, listed as 'landscape models, designed to draw from', also give an intriguing but elliptical hint of Wilson's pedagogical practice.[16] Two of the drawings in the third day's sale were among those by various artists presented framed and glazed, implying particular significance to the owner.[17] The catalogue entries give an idea of their importance to Wilson himself and their role in the genesis of his paintings: '80. A drawing, the effect of a storm: It was from this sketch Mr Wilson took the idea of painting his celebrated picture of the *Niobe*. 81. A ditto, a fragment of rock: this study appears to have been greatly admired by Mr Wilson, who introduced it into several of his pictures.' Farington, who had been Wilson's pupil from 1763 to 1767, records that he 'recommended to Him [Sandby] to be careful in the sale of them, [and] told Him how few persons posessed [*sic*] drawings by Wilson – namely Lord Dartmouth, Mr. C. Bowles, myself – and Mr. W. Locke, & that it wd. be better to keep them together than to sell any of them at low prices.'[18]

Of those collections mentioned by Farington, the earliest was that of William Lock of Norbury Park, Mickleham, Surrey. Wilson seems to have met Lock shortly after his arrival in Venice about November 1750, and to have travelled in the young

Fig. 31   Richard Wilson, *The Cascade at Terni*, 1751-52, black chalk on white laid paper, 28.6 x 21.6 cm, Yale Center for British Art, Paul Mellon Collection, B1977.14.576.
Formerly Earl of Warwick and Iolo Williams collections.

grand tourist's carriage to Rome, where they arrived early in 1752. *En route* Lock employed him in 'taking sketches of the country through which they passed.'[19] This included stop-off points such as Ferrara, Ravenna, Rimini, San Marino, Ancona and Loreto. After that, when the itinerary turned inland via Spoleto and Narni, there is a gap in the visual record until the animated *Cascade at Terni* (fig.31).[20] As Ford noted, the sketches done on this journey form a distinct stylistic group, characterised by loose pencil work.[21] Each drawing possesses an immediacy and informality that clearly denotes its having been made on the spot and in many cases at speed. By the end of his life, Lock possessed 'a numerous assemblage of the works of R. Wilson, R.A.'[22] comprising 201 sheets, plus a twenty-sheet 'Scrap book containing Roman Views and Antiquities, *in bistre and black and red chalk*'.[23] These consisted mostly of small designs, sketches and *vedute* of landscapes, buildings, monuments and fountains in Rome and the Campagna, including 'Porta Pinciana, with the Artist designing'[24] and twelve 'Small circular Landscapes, Views in the Environs of Rome, *taken in the years* 1754 and 1756'.[25] Less predictably there were also twenty-two 'Varia Costumi Italia, *fine* [*sic*]'[26] which included the portrait of Thomas Jenkins (1722–1798, see fig.40), and nine framed and glazed drawings,[27] one of which was an intriguing 'capital Drawing, View of a Lake, with Mountainous Scenery, by Moonlight, *black and white chalk, in black and gilt frame* [*sic*]'.[28] Unlike Sandby, Lock did not use a collector's mark and records of his ownership might thus have been lost had not William Esdaile later noted their provenance on the versos.[29]

The DARTMOUTH series, executed in 1754–55, is generally agreed to include some of the finest eighteenth-century landscape drawings from any European school. Lord Dartmouth made the Grand Tour with Frederick North, arriving in Rome some time after August 1752 and returning to England by the end of May 1754. Executed in black chalk and stump on grey paper heightened with white, all the surviving drawings are signed and dated 1754, and nineteen of them are inscribed with a number. Each was similarly mounted by the artist onto a larger piece of white paper, then surrounded with a lilac wash border and an attached white *cartellino* identifying the scene (see fig.32).[30] With the exception of some pure landscapes and a few more contemporary views, such as St Peter's, they are mostly evocations of a timeless, classical Rome, although the artist seems also to have spent a period with his patron in the neighbourhood of Naples.[31] One surviving drawing portrays a purely imaginary scene, *Landscape with Banditti* – a Rosa-esque dramatisation of exotic banditry rather than a souvenir of classical antiquity – and there are two highly detailed studies of rococo fountains. These are presentation drawings *par excellence* and were the object of Farington's comment that 'The drawings he made at that period were so excellent that it may be justly said they have all the quality of his pictures except the colour.'[32] In further praise, the artist John Hoppner (*c*.1758–1810) later said 'they were such as the Greeks would have made, & put all others at a distance,'[33] and in 1809 Charles Long (1760–1838), the politician and connoisseur, later created Lord Farnborough, 'said they are admirable; & owned that He preferred them to His [Wilson's] pictures.'[34] Comprehensive assessment of

Fig. 32   Richard Wilson,
The Villa Borghese, Rome, 1754,
graphite, black chalk and stump,
heightened with white, 28 x 42 cm,
Private Collection, London.
Formerly Earl of Dartmouth
collection.

this magnificent commission remains impossible since of the sixty-eight drawings recorded by Farington[35] only the twenty-five rediscovered by Lady Dartmouth in a cupboard at Patshull House in 1948 are known today.[36] Having remained concealed for so long, the Dartmouth drawings were finally dispersed by the 8th Earl in 1954.[37] Many have since found their way into public collections although one still occasionally appears in the art market (fig.32).[38]

With a single exception all the surviving Dartmouth drawings belong to the sub-set of 'twenty drawings, views of the environs of Rome', designated as shortly to be finished in a letter by Thomas Jenkins, Lord Dartmouth's agent in Rome, dated 1 June 1754.[39] The multi-talented Jenkins (see fig.40) – artist, dealer, banker and *cicerone* to British grand tourists – was a fertile source of patronage for Wilson, the draughtsman as well as the painter. For example, thirty drawings by Wilson were shipped from Italy to England in February 1755 under Jenkins's supervision. In addition it was Jenkins who had introduced Wilson to Dartmouth, and to STEPHEN BECKINGHAM, of Bourne Park, Kent, who had embarked on the Grand Tour in 1751 and two years later purchased Wilson drawings through the agency of Jenkins. In a letter of 30 March 1755, Jenkins referred to the dispatch of two lots of Wilson drawings in a case shipped on the preceding 28 February, which included 'a portfolio with 30 of Mr Wilson's drawings …, the property of Mr Beckingham.'[40]

CHARLES OLDFIELD BOWLES (d.1862) was the only son of Wilson's admirer and patron, Oldfield Bowles (1739–1810), variously described as 'painter, musician, botanist and scientific farmer', and the owner of North Aston Hall, Oxfordshire. Bowles senior possessed several pictures by Wilson and himself painted in the manner of the artist under instruction from Wilson's pupil, Thomas Jones (1742–1803). He also possessed Wilson sketchbooks, one of which he gave in 1784 to his friend, Sir George Beaumont. It is unclear how or when Bowles came by these sketchbooks but he may well have been the 'gentleman' whom the portraitist William Beechey (1753–1839) took to visit Wilson just before he left London for retirement in Wales, and who 'bought all his sketchbooks' in order to provide the painter with the means for his journey.[41]

JOSEPH FARINGTON (1747–1821), diarist, painter and topographical draughtsman, was a pupil and assistant in Wilson's studio from 1763 to 1767, as well as an exhibitor at the Society of Artists from 1756 to 1773, and later at the Royal Academy, becoming a Royal Academician in 1785. Farington, who mentioned Wilson's drawings in his diary up until 1811, nowhere recorded the number in his own possession but some are known such as *Study for a Picture: Tivoli* (fig.33). As Ford remarked, Farington as Wilson's pupil had an unrivalled opportunity to acquire his master's drawings, yet there is relatively little solid evidence of his collection of them.[42] Among the surviving drawings known or said to have belonged to him, a few bearing his

Fig. 33   Richard Wilson, *A Study for a Picture: Tivoli with the Temple of the Sibyl and the Grand Cascade*, black chalk, heightened with white on grey paper, 25.2 x 18.7 cm, National Museum Wales NMW A 5752.
Formerly Joseph Farington, Lady Ford, John Deffett Francis and Thomas Woolner collections.

initials on the verso are to be found at the National Museum Wales. Yet at the sale of his drawings, papers and diaries in 1921, the only Wilson lots were his palette and the Memorandum Book now in the Victoria & Albert Museum.[43]

SIR GEORGE HOWLAND BEAUMONT, 7th baronet (1753–1827), the leading connoisseur, amateur painter and draughtsman of his day, was a close friend, admirer and promoter of Wilson.[44] Early in his career Beaumont owned at least three Wilson oils and went on to buy more, including the central work of the artist's career, *The Destruction of Niobe's Children* (formerly Tate Gallery, destroyed by enemy action in 1944).[45] Since learning the skills of draughtsmanship as a boy at Eton from Alexander Cozens (1717–86), Beaumont had become a drawing

Fig. 34   Richard Wilson, *Coast Scene, near Barmouth (?)*, graphite, 14.6 x 19.9 cm,
The British Museum 1867,1214.775. Formerly Sir George Beaumont collection.

enthusiast. He continued to take lessons while up at Oxford from John Baptist
Malchair (1731–1812), who set him to make copies of Wilson as well as of Old
Masters, including Claude. Beaumont owned one of Wilson's sketchbooks used by
the artist in Rome in 1754, which was given to him by Bowles on 2 December 1784
and which remained in the Beaumont family until 1963 (now Yale Center for British
Art).[46] This is largely devoted to sensitive and highly finished studies in chalk of
antique sculpture, copses and gnarled trees, together with recognisable views of
Rome and the Campagna. The existence of another sketchbook in Beaumont's
collection is recorded on a graphite drawing, *Coast Scene, perhaps near Barmouth*,
in the British Museum (fig.34). It is inscribed: 'This drawing was taken out of

Wilson's sketch book Novr 20th 1822. belonging to Sir G. Beaumont Bart. And given by him to me G. Arnald, who now gives it to his old friend Smith.' Beaumont owned other drawings from the same sketchbook, including *Box Hill, Surrey* (Yale Center for British Art), *Conway Castle* (National Library of Wales, Aberystwyth) and *Snowdon* (Huntington Library, San Marino, California). The British Museum also holds an intriguing double-sided study, the verso of which, *Prow of a Roman Galley*, is inscribed 'RWGB' which probably indicates a Beaumont provenance.[47]

BENJAMIN BOOTH (1732–1807), a Director of the East India Company and friend of Sir Joshua Reynolds, formed his Wilson collection at the Adelphi comprising at least fifty paintings and a small number of drawings. The latter included *Lake Scene by Moonlight* and *Tall Trees*, both *c.*1752–57 (Brinsley Ford Collection) and both inscribed verso, 'I purchased this drawing of Mercati, in Marylebone High Street, Oct. 1788. B.B. [and] Marianne.'[48] Booth's collection was briefly inherited by his son, the Rev. Richard Salwey Booth (1762–1807), then by his two daughters, of whom Elizabeth died in 1819, leaving the entirety in the hands of Marianne, who in 1794 had married Sir Richard Ford MP, sometime Under Secretary of State for Home Affairs and Chief Magistrate at Bow Street. Either LADY FORD or her son, RICHARD FORD (1796–1858), bought seventy-one drawings from the Lock sale of 1821. Richard Ford, author of the well-known *Hand-Book for Travellers in Spain* (1845), inherited half of this collection from her. He had 'many of Wilson's finest drawings from nature, which he principally made when studying at Rome; one of which is particularly interesting since it contains Wilson's own figure, seated on the ground in his bag-wig, making a drawing of Raffaelle's villa.'[49] The drawings passed via his son, Sir Francis Clare Ford (1828–1899), Ambassador to Spain – some to Captain Richard Ford (1860–1940), others to his brother, John Gorman Ford (1866–1917), and thence to his nephew, Sir Brinsley Ford (1908–1999). These eighty or so drawings, including two added by Sir Brinsley,[50] constitute far and away the most impressive and comprehensive private collection of Wilson drawings in the world today.

Wilson's sketches and studies appear to have been more popular among his fellow artists than with the buying public at large, who tended to prefer more finished drawings or, increasingly, the newly fashionable watercolours of Wilson's younger contemporaries. The portrait-painter THOMAS HUDSON (1701–1779) was also the leading collector of prints and drawings of his day and owned a number of Wilson's drawings, including *An Italian Landscape with a Bridge*.[51] Several

Fig. 35 Richard Wilson, *Lake of Nemi*, 1753, graphite and black chalk on grey paper, 27.7 x 42 cm, Tate, London T09302. Formerly Thomas Monro and Paul Oppé collections.

circular vignettes comparable to those belonging to William Lock, such as *Pastoral Landscape with a Tower* (*c*.1754–56, Rijksprentenkabinet, Amsterdam), were among those in the possession of the Irish painter NATHANIEL HONE (1718–1784), who acquired numerous drawings direct from the artist.[52] FRANCIS MILNER NEWTON (1720–1794), first Secretary of the Royal Academy, owned *A View of Hounslow Heath, London*, recently on the London art market[53] and the landscapist and scenery painter, JOHN INIGO RICHARDS (1731–1810), Royal Academy Secretary from 1788, owned Wilson's supposed *Portrait of Admiral Thomas Smith* (British Museum).[54] Unsurprisingly, Sir Joshua Reynolds (1723–1792), first President of the Academy, whose relations with Wilson were often strained, cannot be shown, from the evidence of his posthumous sales, to have owned any of his drawings.[55]

Dr THOMAS MONRO (1759–1833), whose famous 'academy' evening sessions of copying and supper provided a training in watercolour for Girtin and Turner, owned at least twenty-one Wilson drawings.[56] These included *Lake of Nemi* (fig. 35) and *The Roman Campagna with Peasants dancing* (Pierpont Morgan Library, New York). The connoisseur and amateur RICHARD PAYNE KNIGHT (1751–1824), a member of the Society of Dilettanti and a founder of the British Institution, was also a Trustee of the British Museum to which he bequeathed his collection of small bronzes, coins, gems, cameos and Old Master drawings in 1824. The latter comprised 1,144 drawings, including two albums of sketches by Gainsborough and John Hamilton Mortimer (as well as 250 drawings by Claude), and was certainly one of the major collections of this type formed in Britain to date. Wilson was disappointingly and rather unconvincingly represented by four uncharacteristically diagrammatic topographical works set in the Roman Campagna.[57]

In the first two decades of the nineteenth century reviving interest in Wilson was already traceable in the accounts of the artist's life by Hodges, Jones, Farington and Edwards.[58] It revealed itself most clearly in his presence with eighty-six paintings (from a total of 221) at the 1814 British Institution exhibition,[59] and drove the publication in 1811 by Robert Archer of *Studies and Designs by Richard Wilson*[60] – soft-ground etching facsimiles by John Whessell of some of Wilson's Roman drawings in the possession of Oldfield Bowles (including leaves from the sketchbook now in the Victoria & Albert Museum). This was followed in 1825 by another major graphic publication, when Thomas Hastings brought out his *Etchings from the Works of Richard Wilson*.[61]

Wilson the draughtsman came to be represented in several of the most prestigious collections of this period. The banker and collector WILLIAM ESDAILE (1758–1837) owned numerous drawings by the artist (in addition to two paintings)[62] which featured as part of his sixteen-day posthumous sale in 1838. Esdaile had begun by acquiring Old Master pictures but the pride of his collection evolved as prints and drawings, which were kept in special cabinets in his house

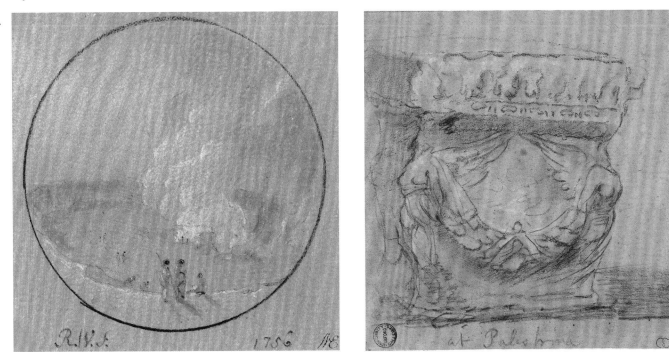

Fig. 36 Richard Wilson,
Landscape with a Volcano Crater,
probably Vesuvius, 1756 signed
'R.W.f.', black and white chalk on
prepared laid paper, 9.6 x 10 cm,
Royal Academy of Arts, London,
03/1876.
Formerly William Lock of
Norbury and William Esdaile
collections.

Fig. 37 Richard Wilson, *A*
Roman Altar at Palestrina, black
chalk heightened with white on
brownish-grey paper, 14.6 x 14 cm,
Ashmolean Museum, University
of Oxford, Inv. No. 1898.
Formerly Chambers Hall
collection.

on Clapham Common. Many of these came from previous great auctions in
London, including those of Lock and Sir Thomas Lawrence.[63] On 20 March 1838,
thirty-seven Wilson drawings were sold in thirty-five lots at prices ranging from
five shillings the pair to £3.15s.[64] Two of the most atmospheric were *Landscape with*
a Volcano, probably Vesuvius and *Landscape with a Volcano Crater, probably that of*
Vesuvius, both signed in monogram and dated 1756. Previously in the collection
of Lock, both are predictably monogrammed by Esdaile lower right (fig.36).[65] The
sixth day of Esdaile's sales, saw a further thirty-two Wilson drawings in twenty-
nine lots fetch prices ranging from five shillings to £7.15s.[66]

Mid-nineteenth-century sales attest to a sustained demand for the drawings
among leading collectors and dealers, which was indirectly to lead to their
increasing arrival in public collections. The banker and poet, SAMUEL ROGERS (1763–
1855), owned five drawings by Wilson, three of them in the uncharacteristic
coloured chalk medium,[67] in addition to at least three paintings. At the time of his
death, the dealer SAMUEL WOODBURN (1786–1853), at 134 Piccadilly, possessed a large

Fig. 38 Richard Wilson, *Head of an Italian*, black chalk heightened with white on grey laid paper, 36.2 x 26.7 cm, Victoria & Albert Museum, London, Dyce.637. Formerly the Rev. Alexander Dyce collection.

number of Wilson's drawings, of which about eighty featured in his posthumous sales.[68] These included the supposed *Portrait of Admiral Thomas Smith* which had formerly belonged to John Richards and was bought by the British Museum, as well as several from Esdaile's collection. Other professionals with Wilson interests included notably WALTER BENJAMIN TIFFIN (1795–1877), a print dealer and publisher based in the Haymarket, then the Strand, who acted as a very prolific agent for the British Museum (and through whom the purchase of *Admiral Smith* was made).

CHAMBERS HALL (1786–1855), a virtuoso and antiquarian best known for his collections of drawings by Francesco Guardi and for antiquities, also collected drawings by Wilson, including *A Roman Altar at Palestrina* (fig.37). In 1855 Hall gave his collection of twenty-one Wilson drawings to the Ashmolean, later to be described by Laurence Binyon as 'almost all of exceptional quality and interest'.[70] The Rev. ALEXANDER DYCE (1798–1869) owned only one landscape painting by Wilson but his collection of drawings, bequeathed to the Victoria & Albert Museum, included *Head of an Italian* (fig.38) and contained 'no less than twenty-eight sketches; most of them (it is true) very slight, but still possessing the same refinement of thought as his pictures. The most remarkable for poetic feeling in the series is certainly *Lake Nemi* of 1753; this is a gem of the brightest water for a student whose art education is advanced enough to comprehend it.'[71]

JOHN DEFFETT FRANCIS (1815–1901) was a portrait-painter, printmaker and collector who lived much of his life in Swansea. His munificence to public institutions included three presentations to the British Museum of drawings by or attributed to Wilson: in December 1873, August 1875 and, most notably, no fewer than seventy-four in December 1881. He was equally generous to the National Museum of Wales (and bequeathed a large collection of British drawings and watercolours to the Swansea Art Gallery, now the Glynn Vivian Gallery). From the collection of Deffett Francis came *Chelsea Old Bridge*, owned by the painter JAMES MCNEILL WHISTLER (1834–1903) and once in Joseph Farington's collection.[72] Whistler's brother-in-law, the leading etcher Sir FRANCIS SEYMOUR HADEN (1818–1910) owned a red chalk *View near London*. Among later nineteenth-century artists the Pre-Raphaelite sculptor THOMAS WOOLNER (1825–1892) also owned at least two Wilson drawings (as well as one painting[74]), one of them likewise presented by Deffett Francis and formerly in the Farington collection (see fig.33).[75] The colourful 'dentist, artist, patron, collector, dealer, curator, connoisseur, forger [and] propagandist'[76] JAMES ORROCK (1829–1913) of 48 Bedford Square, perhaps most

Fig. 39 Richard Wilson, *Banks of the Tiber*, 1757 signed 'R.W.F.', red chalk, heightened with white, on prepared paper, 16.8 x 21.9 cm, Museum of Art Rhode Island School of Design, Providence. Formerly Earl of Warwick and Charles Fairfax Murray collections.

charitably described as an omnivorous *marchand-amateur*, owned and dealt in large numbers of English pictures, especially by Constable and Wilson, including numerous drawings by or attributed to the latter.[77]

Most of the drawings in the prestigious collection of George Guy Greville, 4th Earl of Warwick (1818–1893), *aide-de-camp* to Queen Victoria, had been inherited from his uncle, Sir Charles Greville (1763–1822). At Warwick's posthumous sale much of this collection was dispersed, including seventeen drawings by Wilson in six lots,[78] among which *Banks of the Tiber* (fig.39) was bought by Charles Fairfax Murray (1849–1919). This polymath – artist, connoisseur, dealer and adviser to numerous private and public collections in Europe and the United States – included five Wilsons among the 1400 Old Master drawings that he in turn sold to

Fig. 40 Richard Wilson,
Portrait of Thomas Jenkins,
*c.*1752–53, black chalk and stump,
heightened with white on grey
paper, 27.4 x 19.7 cm,
The Pierpont Morgan Library,
New York, III.42.
Formerly William Lock of
Norbury and J. Pierpont Morgan
collections.

J. Pierpont Morgan in 1910. As a result of that transaction only two featured in his posthumous sale.[79] HERBERT PERCY HORNE (1864–1916), the poet, architect, typographer-designer and historian of Italian Renaissance art, was an enthusiastic collector of English drawings and owned a number by Wilson. Two of these, *Study of a Tree with an Artist drawing* and *Study of Trees with Landscape Study verso*, remain at the Museo Horne in Florence, the city where he spent the last decade of his life.[80] They were among a small number of British drawings retained by Horne after selling the majority of his collection to Sir Edward Marsh in 1904.

By the turn of the century wealthy American collectors were beginning to show an interest in Wilson drawings, often advised by dealers such as Knoedler's, New York.

The highly successful banker, international financier, and voracious collector J. PIERPONT MORGAN (1837–1913) bought vast amounts of heterogeneous material *en masse*, including the Fairfax Murray collection of drawings, which he kept in his mansions at Prince's Gate and Dover House, before transferring them to the USA (fig.40). The Pierpont Morgan Library was founded by his son John Pierpont Morgan Jr (1867–1943) in 1909 and holds a distinguished group of Wilson drawings such as *The Roman Campagna with Peasants dancing*, once in the Monro and Esdaile collections.[81] In Chicago WILLIAM F.E. GURLEY (1854–1943), a distinguished geologist, presented a number of Wilsons including *View of the Banks of the Dee in Cheshire* as part of the gift of about 4,000 Old Master, British and American drawings to the Chicago Art Institute in 1922 in memory of his mother, and a subsequent bequest of a further 6,000 which together now constitute the Leonora Hall Gurley Memorial Collection. Later in the century the banker, collector and anglophile philanthropist PAUL MELLON (1907–1999), founder and benefactor of the British Art Center at Yale University and the Paul Mellon Centre for Studies in British Art, London, showed a discriminating enthusiasm for Wilson the draughtsman. He bought mainly on the London art market, securing major examples such as two Dartmouth drawings, *The Via Nomentana* and *Temple of Minerva Medici*, formerly in the collection of Thomas Lowinsky, and through Colnaghi's the ex-Beaumont *Italian Sketchbook* of 1754. In due course these and others would help to form the nucleus of the outstanding graphic collections at the British Art Center.

In the twentieth century, the focus of collecting began to pass from private collectors to public institutions, though with dealers still playing a crucial role. Wilson drawings were routinely handled by Agnew, Colnaghi and Spink, and notable individuals involved in the trade included E. Parsons & Sons of Brompton Road and their trainee, F.R. MEATYARD ('Honest Fred') of High Holborn and later 32 Museum Street. Meatyard sold numerous Wilson drawings over the years, notably to the British Museum and the National Museum of Wales. PERCY MOORE TURNER (1905–1952), dealer, writer and principal adviser to Samuel Courtauld also owned and handled Wilson drawings, while in the 1950s a number passed through the hands of BERNARD MILLING, of the Squire Gallery, Baker Street. One such was *A Skirmish in Rowing Boats in the Bay of Baiae, an Island Beyond*, which formed part of the collection of Sir JOHN WITT (1907–1982), son of Sir Robert (q.v.inf.).[82]

Fig. 41 Richard Wilson, *Study of Figures for 'A View of the Campagna'*, *c*.1755, black chalk heightened with white on blue laid paper, 19.4 x 27.1 cm, Yale Center for British Art, Paul Mellon Collection, B1977.14.6060. Formerly Thomas Lowinsky and Paul Mellon collections.

As noted above, Captain RICHARD FORD of Ennismore Gardens, had inherited a large collection of Wilson paintings and drawings via his ancestors Marianne (Lady Ford) and Richard Ford. In his drawings sale at Christie's in 1929 a folio of forty-one drawings in nineteen lots was sold. His son, JOHN FORD sold four more at Sotheby's in 1947 but three of these were bought back by his son BRINSLEY FORD and remain in the family collection.[84] Sir Brinsley, the pre-eminent exponent of Wilson's drawings in the first half of the century, fought against the prevailing trend and successfully retained intact his inherited collection of them. His friend, the portraitist and narrative painter THOMAS ESMOND LOWINSKY (1892–1947), best remembered for his book illustrations, was also a major connoisseur, collector and enthusiast for Wilson drawings (fig.41). Lowinsky 'confined himself to the British School but bought with remarkable distinction'[85] and secured a number of Wilsons from the sale of Captain Ford. His wife retained these drawings after his death and they were finally sold by his son, Justin Lowinsky, to Paul Mellon through Colnaghi's in 1963.

Henry Scipio Reitlinger (1882–1950), an art historian and collector of Old Master drawings, Oriental porcelain and Renaissance ceramics, whose publications included *Old Master Drawings, a Handbook for Amateurs and Collectors* (1922), left much material – ceramics and drawings – to the Fitzwilliam Museum, Cambridge. His posthumous sale included a version of *The Gypsies*, formerly in the Fairfax Murray collection, *A Road near the Ramparts of a Town*, from the Sandby collection, and four other drawings by Wilson.[86] The City solicitor, collector and joint founder of the NACF, Courtauld Institute and benefactor of the Witt Library, Sir Robert Witt (1872–1952) bequeathed the renowned collection of almost 4,000 drawings assembled by himself and his wife to the Courtauld Institute, including twelve by Wilson. Another regional gallery to benefit from a private collector's generosity was Birmingham Museum and Art Gallery, which in 1953 received two Wilson drawings, *Landscape near Rome* and *Stone Archways* as part of the handsome bequest of over 400 English works on paper by the Midlands manufacturer J. Leslie Wright (1862–1953).[87]

Witt's contemporary, Sir Edward ('Eddie') Marsh (1872–1953), was a civil servant in the Colonial Office, a confidant of Winston Churchill, and a collector, scholar, aesthete and patron. In 1900 he acquired *The Summit of Cader Idris* (Tate Britain) but oil paintings were the exception in his collection and four years later he bought the Horne collection of 200 British drawings, including Cozens, Cotman, Girtin and a group of Wilsons of which his adviser Robert Ross declared, 'I know of no such set of Wilsons in private hands.'[88] Wilson drawings from the Marsh collection may now be found at the National Gallery of Scotland, the Victoria & Albert Museum, the Ashmolean Museum and the British Museum, which holds the highly uncharacteristic study, *Still-life with Flask*, formerly in the Warwick collection (fig.42). This must have been one of the 'special drawings … hung for refreshing contemplation at strategic points on his [Marsh's] staircase, where he would pause for breath on the way up.'[89]

Other notable collectors of Wilson drawings (and paintings) included Colonel Maurice Harold Grant (1872–1962), author of the landmark *Chronological History of the Old English Landscape Painters*[90] and Iolo Aneurin Williams (1890–1962), author of the monumental *Early English Watercolours* of 1952. Museum

Fig. 42 Richard Wilson, *Still Life with a Flask*, *c.*1752–53, black chalk and stump, 21.6 x 17.8 cm, The British Museum 1953,0509.5. Formerly Earl of Warwick and Sir Edward Marsh collections.

correspondent of *The Times* from 1937, Iolo Williams was an avid collector of British works on paper, including Wilson's *Cascade at Terni* (see fig.31) from the Warwick Collection. In 1960 he gave twenty-four drawings to the British Museum and at his death left sixty-five more, though these included none by Wilson as he was anxious to fill gaps in the museum's collection. Several, however, were bought by Paul Mellon and are now at Yale. Contemporaries of Grant and Williams whose collections of Wilson drawings have benefited the British Museum and other institutions include ARTHUR MELVILLE CHAMPERNOWNE (1871–1946), of Dartington Hall, Totnes, LEONARD G. DUKE (1890–1971), who owned *A View of the Roman Colosseum* (Metropolitan Museum, New York [91]) and G. BELLINGHAM-SMITH (active 1915–1931).

Fig. 43 Richard Wilson, *'Idea': Travellers marooned on a Rock in a River*, signed 'R.W.f.' and inscribed 'Idea', black chalk, 20 x 26 cm, Huntington Library and Art Gallery, San Marino, California 63.52.297. Formerly Sir Bruce Ingram collection.

Sir BRUCE INGRAM (1877–1963) was a leading journalist and long-standing editor of the *Illustrated London News*. In collaboration with the dealer D.C.T. Baskett he acquired about 5,000 drawings during the last thirty years of his life, of which over half were of the English School. Ingram owned the tantalising *'Idea': Travellers marooned on a Rock in a River* (fig.43), acquired at his death by the Huntington Library and Gallery, San Marino, California, and the charming *Study of a Dog*.[92] One hundred drawings by Wilson and others, covering a period of four centuries, were purchased from his collection by the Ashmolean Museum in 1963.[93]

PAUL (A. P.) OPPÉ (1878–1957), Deputy Director of the Victoria & Albert Museum 1910–1913 and a founder member of the Walpole Society, began collecting English watercolours in 1904. By the time of his death his collection comprised 3,000 works from the seventeenth to the early twentieth centuries, including drawings, oil-sketches and prints (see fig.35). Many of his Wilson drawings have impressive pedigrees, having passed through the hands of Sandby, Lock, Hone, Esdaile, Warwick and even John Constable.[94] Most of this distinguished collection is now at Tate Britain, which acquired it in 1996 with the assistance of Heritage Lottery Fund and the NACF following the death of his son, Denys Oppé.[95] It includes no fewer than twenty-seven drawings by and two attributed to Wilson.

The Tate's acquisition of the Oppé Collection may be seen as a culmination of the twentieth-century enrichment of British national institutions with the drawings of Richard Wilson. Today the most extensive and representative public collections of his graphic work are to be found in London at the British Museum, Tate Britain and the Victoria & Albert Museum. Pre-eminent collections further afield include those at the Ashmolean Museum, Oxford, National Museum Wales, Cardiff, which houses over twenty drawings by or attributed to the artist, and the National Gallery of Scotland, Edinburgh. Smaller collections are to be found at such institutions as the Cecil Higgins Museum, Bedford and the Whitworth Art Gallery, Manchester. In the United States the leading collections remain those at the Yale Center for British Art, the Metropolitan Museum and Pierpont Morgan Library, New York, the Art Institute of Chicago and the Huntington Library and Gallery, San Marino, California. On the basis of such splendid holdings, it is fervently to be hoped that the exhibitions and publications planned for the approaching tercentenary of Richard Wilson's birth will focus attention on his drawings and their provenances, thereby enhancing the artist's reputation not only as a painter but also as a draughtsman.

Collectors of Richard Wilson drawings are marked in the text by the use of small caps.

This essay could not have been undertaken without constant reference to the pioneering work of the late Sir Brinsley Ford on Richard Wilson and his drawings. I am likewise deeply indebted to the researches of the late Professor W.G. Constable and Professor David Solkin. In addition I am most grateful for the kind assistance of Charlotte Brunskill, Emma Floyd, Francis Ford, Emmeline Hallmark, Elspeth Hector, Dr Kim Sloan, and colleagues at the British Museum, Tate Britain, Victoria & Albert Museum, National Museum Wales, and Yale Center for British Art.

The essay is dedicated to Professor Brian Allen in gratitude for his establishment and encouragement of the Wilson Research Project to celebrate the tercentenary of the artist's birth. It could not have been written without the support and understanding of Sue, Rose and Flora Spencer-Longhurst.

1 See note 32.

2 William T. Whitley, *Artists and their Friends in England*, vol.1, London 1928, p.169.

3 B. Ford, *The Drawings of Richard Wilson*, London 1951, p.11. This seminal book is hereafter referred to as 'Ford 1951'.

4 Ford 1951, p.26.

5 David H. Solkin, *Richard Wilson: The Landscape of Reaction*, exh. cat., London 1982, p.132.

6 Edward Edwards, *Anecdotes of Painters ...*, London 1808, p.86.

7 Solkin, *Richard Wilson*, p.153.

8 A drawing entitled *View near Rome* was no. 129 at the Society of Artists exhibition in 1760.

9 Christie's, Pall Mall, 2–4 May 1811. In addition to Sandby's own drawings and watercolours, this included architectural designs by his brother, Thomas Sandby, the drawings by Wilson, shipping drawings by 'Vanderveldt', and drawings by Marco Ricci, Goupy and a few other contemporary artists.

10 J.T. Smith, *Nollekens and his Times*, vol.1, London 1828, p.130.

11 Thomas Wright, *Some Account of the Life of Richard Wilson, Esq, R.A.*, London 1824, p.77.

12 According to the catalogue entries the number of individual drawings should total ninety-five. However, six are described as 'body colour on pannel' (Second Day's Sale, 3 May 1811, lots 106–110) and there may have been inaccuracies or last minute changes in the distribution of the drawings among the lot numbers.

13 Christie's, Second Day's Sale, 3 May 1811, part of lot 97; now Chicago Art Institute.

14 Christie's, Second Day's Sale, 3 May 1811, lot 101; now Yale Center for British Art.

15 David H. Solkin, 'Some new Light on the Drawings of Richard Wilson', *Master Drawings*, vol.16:4 Winter 1978, p.408.

16 Christie's, Second Day's Sale, 3 May 1811, lots 102–105.

17 Christie's, Third Day's Sale, 4 May 1811, lots 80 & 81.

18 J. Farington, *Diary* (2 May 1811), ed. K. Cave, vol.11, New Haven and London 1983, p.3922.

19 Anon. [William Hodges], 'An Account of Richard Wilson, Esq., Landscape Painter, F.R.A.', *The European Magazine and London Review*, vol.17, June 1790, p.403 [–5].

20 Yale Center for British Art, B1997.14.5746.

21 Ford 1951, p.19.

22 Sotheby, 3–9 May 1821, *A Catalogue of the Valuable Collection of Prints and Drawings of the late W. Lock, Esq...*, title page.

23 *Ibid.* 3 May 1821, lot 397 (original italics).

24 *Ibid.* part of lot 385.

25 *Ibid.* lot 386.

26 *Ibid.* lots 387–9.

27 *Ibid.* lots 407–414.

28 *Ibid.* lot 407.

29 Ford 1951, p.46.

30 A further six survive on different coloured mounts and without any inscriptions.

31 [William Hodges], 'An Account of Richard Wilson, Esq.', p.403. The 1752 sketchbook shows that he visited Naples that year.

32 J. Farington, *Biographical Note*, c.1805, published in *Exhibition of Works by Richard Wilson*, exh. cat., Ferens Art Gallery, Hull 1936, p.12.

33 J. Farington, *Diary* (1 June 1806), vol.7, 1982, p.2775.

34 J. Farington, *Diary* (24 June 1809), vol.9, 1982, p.3495.

35 J. Farington, *Diary* (9 June 1806), vol.7, 1982, p.2781: 'Lord Dartmouth's I went to in the morning to see the drawings by Wilson, the number of them 68. ...'

36 For further details of the discovery and the Dartmouth collection of drawings by Wilson, see Brinsley Ford, 'The Dartmouth Collection of Drawings by Richard Wilson', *Burlington Magazine*, vol.90, no.549, December 1948, pp.337–343, 345.

37 Christie, Manson & Woods, London, 29 January 1954, lots 4–28.

38 On 14 July 2010 *The Villa Borghese, Rome* was sold at Sotheby's London to a private collector for just under £100,000 (lot 57).

39 Ford, 'The Dartmouth Collection of Drawings by Richard Wilson', p.338.

40 Cited by Ford, 'The Dartmouth Collection of Drawings by Richard Wilson'. Beckingham also acquired four large landscapes paintings by Wilson, of which only two have been identified.

41 Whitley, *Artists and their Friends*, vol.1, p.380.

42 Ford 1951, p.47.

43 Puttick & Simpson, London, 9 December 1921, *Catalogue of the Joseph Farington, R.A. (1747–1821) Collection of Drawings, Papers and Diaries bequeathed to the late Miss M.L.E. Tyrwhitt of Northwood Lodge, Wallington, Surrey* [and others], lots 152–249. The palette was lot 166 and the Memorandum Book [V&A P.94–1921] part of lot 248.

44 Wilson's early biographer, Thomas Wright, claimed that Beaumont was a pupil of Wilson, but cultural and social constraints make this unlikely in any literal sense.

45 He later also owned *Lake Avernus* (National Museum Wales NMW A 5191), which he presented to John Constable in 1812.

46 Yale Center for British Art, B1977.14.4719.

47 BM 1881,0212.44.

48 For a discussion of Booth's collection and its descent in the Ford family, see W.G. Constable, *Richard Wilson*, London 1953, pp.122–25; and for the drawings in particular, *The Walpole Society*, vol. LX, 1998, pp.14, 20–21, BB 47–50.

49 J.T. Smith, *Nollekens and his Times*, vol.1, p.130; see also *Walpole Society*, vol. LX, 1998, pp.68–73, nos. RF57–RF107.

50 *Walpole Society*, vol. LX, Part II, pp.265–66, nos. RBF569 and RBF570.

51 Christie's London, 2 March 1976, lot 99. None however were listed individually in his posthumous sale catalogue, Langford, London, 15–27 March 1779.

52 None were listed individually in his posthumous sale catalogue, Hutchins, London, 7–15 February 1785.

53 Christie's, 5 July 2011, lot 119.

54 BM 1854,0628.18; Squibb's auction room, 12 March 1811, lot 133. Although believed to be Wilson's study for a portrait of Admiral Smith until 1971, the drawing has since been convincingly re-attributed to Sir Godfrey Kneller as a study for a lost portrait of the engraver, Peter Vandrebanc [Vanderbank], dating from c.1695–97.

55 Phillips, London, 5–26 March 1798 and Christie's, London, 16–17 May 1821 [Dowager Marchioness of Thomond]. Wilson is not mentioned by name in the catalogues, though they do include folios of unidentified drawings.

56 Christie & Manson, 1 July 1833, lots 140–146.

57 BM OO,04–7.

58 [William Hodges], 'An Account of Richard Wilson, Esq.', 1790; Thomas Jones, 'The Memoirs of Thomas Jones', finished 1798 (published *Walpole Society*, XXXII, 1951); Joseph Farington, *Biographical Note*, c.1805 (published in *Exhibition of Works by Richard Wilson, R.A.*, exh. cat., Ferens Art Gallery, Hull 1936); and Edward Edwards, *Anecdotes of Painters*, 1808.

59 *Catalogue of Pictures by the late William Hogarth, Richard Wilson, Thomas Gainsborough and J. Zoffani [sic] exhibited by the Permission of the Proprietors in Honour of the Memory of those distinguished Artists and for the Improvement of British Art*, British Institution, London 1814, pp.16 and 18–22.

60 *Studies & Designs by R. Wilson, done at Rome in the year 1752, Caffe delle Inglesi*, etched by John Whessell, Oxford 1811, published by Robert Archer, Oxford …

61 T. Hastings, *Etchings from the Works of Ric. Wilson, with some Memoirs of his Life, etc.*, London 1825.

62 The paintings were sold at Christie's, 24 March 1838: lot 49, *The Summit of Cader Idris* and lot 68, *A River on the Bank of an Italian Lake*.

63 No Wilson drawings were identified as such in Lawrence's posthumous sale catalogues, Christie's, 20–21 May and 17–19 June 1830.

64 Christie's, 20 March 1838, lots 614–648. A similar number of drawings by Gainsborough fetched prices ranging from 12s. to £6.

65 Royal Academy London, Inv. Nos. 03/1876 & 03/1877 respectively.

66 Christie's, 21 March 1838, lots 761–789.

67 *Cader Idris* (black and white chalks); *Tivoli – Sunset* (coloured crayons); *The Campagna and St Peter's* and *The Tiber*, both in coloured crayons; and '*The Temple of Peace* – Indian ink heightened with white. Very fine with the engraving': Christie's, Samuel Rogers's Sale, Tenth Day, Thursday 8 May 1856, Drawings, lots 1235–1238.

68 Christie & Manson 19–20 June 1854, lots 231–232, 238, 751–757, 976–998, 1237–1251, 1500–1510; Christie, Manson & Woods, 14 June 1860, lots 1610–1614.

69 BM 1854,0628.18.

70 *The Vasari Society*, 2nd series, part IV, 1923, p.11, no.18.

71 [W.M.:] *South Kensington Museum Art Handbooks: The Dyce and Forster Collections*, Chapman and Hall, London 1880, p.43. *Lake of Nemi in 1753* is DYCE.643.

72 National Museum Wales, NMW A 3989. An inscription on the mount reads 'Yours / My dear Whistler / J.D.F.'

73 NMW A 10913, 'bought at Mr F. Wilson's sale, 25 July, 1863,' [or 1865], according to an inscription on the verso.

74 *River Scene*, which had formerly belonged to J.M.W. Turner.

75 National Museum Wales NMW A 5752. An inscription on the verso reads in part: 'I have much gratification in begging my friend Thomas Woolner's RA acceptance of it. J. Deffett Francis.'

76. Edward Morris, title of article in *Visual Culture in Britain*, vol.6:2, 2005, pp.85–98. See also Byron Webber, *James Orrock, R.I., Painter, Connoisseur, Collector*, London 1903.

77 However, his sale of 4 and 6 June 1904, while including twenty-four Wilson paintings, offered no drawings.

78 Christie Manson & Woods, 20 May 1896, lots 442–447. A further four were sold by the 6th Earl , Sotheby & Co., 17 June 1936, lot 152.

79 Christie Manson & Woods, 30 January 1920, lot 60, *A View near Rome*, and 2 February 1920, lot 231, *Banks of the Tiber*, see Fig. 39.

80 Inv. Nos. n.5991 & n.6098 respectively. See *Il paesaggio disegnato: John Constable e I Maestri Inglesi nella Raccolta Horne*, Florence, Museo Horne, 24 October 2009–30 January 2010, exh. cat. by Elisabetta Nardinocchi and Matilde Casati, nos. 7 & 8. I am indebted to Professor David Solkin for kindly drawing this exhibition to my attention.

81 Pierpont Morgan Library, New York, Acc. No. III, 40.

82 Sotheby's, London, 19 February 1987, *Drawings and Watercolours from the Collection of the Late Sir John and Lady Witt*, lot 49, catalogued as *River Landscape with a Tree in the Foreground*, sold again at Christie's, London, 5 July 2011, lot 118.

83 Christie Manson & Woods, 17 June 1929, lots 1–19. Captain Ford's 18 paintings were sold at Christie's on 14 June 1929, lots 7–24.

84 Sotheby & Co., 19 March 1947, lots 87–90. The fourth drawing, lot 88, was bought by Villiers David.

85 Monica Bohm-Duchen, *Thomas Lowinsky*, exh. cat., Tate Gallery 1990, p.17.

86 Sotheby & Co., 27 January 1954, *The H.S. Reitlinger Collection*, Part II, lots 256–261.

87 Inv. Nos. P441,53 and P442,53 respectively.

88 Christopher Hassall, *Edward Marsh – Patron of the Arts*, 1959, p.112.

89 Hassall, *Edward Marsh*, p.666.

90 M.H. Grant, *A Chronological History of the Old English Landscape Painters in Oil from the XVIth Century to the XIXth Century*, 3 vols., 1926–47. Grant owned, *inter alia, Stone Archways*, later in the J. Leslie Wright collection (BMAG P442,53).

91 Inv. No. 64.45.

92 Sotheby's, 5 June 2008, lot 197.

93 See exhibition catalogue, Ashmolean Museum, Oxford 1963, *Exhibition of English Drawings purchased from the Collection of the late Sir Bruce Ingram*, Introduction [unpaginated]; see also Luke Herrmann and Michael Robinson, 'Sir Bruce Ingram as a Collector of Drawings', *Burlington Magazine*, vol.105, May 1963, pp.204–7.

94 *Tree Study* (Tate Britain T09307)

95 See further A. Lyles, R. Hamlyn et al., *British Watercolours from the Oppé Collection*, exh. cat., Tate Britain, 1997.

LOCATION, LOCATION, LOCATION
Reynolds, Gainsborough and the View from Richmond Hill

Martin Postle

Sir Joshua is now building a very beautiful house at Richmond, where he intends to go often in the summer, and from there it is a very fine prospect.[1]

James Northcote,
21 December 1771

Fig. 44   *Previous page:* Photograph of Wick House
Fig. 45   View from the Dining Room, Wick House

LOCATION, LOCATION, LOCATION
Reynolds, Gainsborough and the View from Richmond Hill

Martin Postle

Reynolds's villa, known as Wick House, still stands on the brow of Richmond Hill (fig. 44).[2] Recently, it was on offer on the local housing market, for seven million pounds. As the estate agent's brochure notes, situated in 'one of Richmond's premier locations', this 'Grade II listed house enjoys one of the most outstanding views in England' (fig. 45).[3] Wick House is significant for a number of reasons. It is Reynolds's only remaining residence, all trace of his other homes having disappeared.[4] It is also situated in a striking landscape, which has remained remarkably unchanged since the eighteenth century. Finally, Richmond Hill is among the most culturally resonant places in the British Isles; a modern Arcadia for poets, artists and writers for several hundred years. The sale of Reynolds's house, some 240 years after its creation, provides an opportune moment to consider the role of Wick House in the evolution of Reynolds social, cultural and artistic life at the very time he was assuming a far more public role as President of the Royal Academy. It also provides an opportunity to consider a rather less celebrated house on Richmond Hill, which has long since gone; the residence of Reynolds's great artistic rival, Thomas Gainsborough.

From the fourteenth century Richmond's rise to prominence was predicated by its significance as a location for the Court. At that time, the Manor of Shene was transformed into a Royal palace, while in 1501 Shene was renamed Richmond by Henry VII after his home in Yorkshire. As the court became established, landed estates and hunting grounds were developed and extended, culminating in the 1630s with the enclosure of Richmond Park by Charles I. By the late seventeenth

Facing page

Fig. 46 Leonard Knyff, *The Terrace and View from Richmond Hill*, *c.*1720, oil on canvas, 59 x 120 cm, Ionides Collection, Orleans House Gallery, on loan to Museum of Richmond, Richmond

Fig. 47 Peter Tillemans, *View of the Thames from Richmond Hill*, *c.*1720–23, oil on canvas, 109 x 230 cm, UK Government Art Collection

Above

Fig. 48 Antonio Joli, *A View from Richmond Hill Looking South-West*, *c.*1750, oil on canvas, 63 x 121cm, On loan to Marble Hill House, Twickenham

century, Richmond Hill was established as a place for polite assembly, not least since it commanded an unrivalled prospect of the Thames and surrounding countryside. From this time onwards the view from Richmond Hill began to achieve canonical status. Among those artists who painted the view was the Dutch topographical painter, Leonard Knyff (1650–1722), who painted the *View of Richmond from the Hill Walk* in 1720 (fig. 46). Another artist closely associated with Richmond was the Flemish-born Peter Tillemans (*c.*1684–1734), among whose most impressive paintings is his panoramic view of the Thames from Richmond of around 1720–23 (fig. 47).[5] In 1733 Tillemans, who suffered from asthma, moved to Richmond 'for the Air and his health'.[6] He died the following year during a visit to Suffolk. His house, close to Richmond Hill, still stands.[7]

By the mid-eighteenth century Richmond Hill had became a mecca for artists and engravers, as a plethora of images of Richmond, Twickenham and the surrounding area were produced to cater to its increasing fashionability.[8] They included the Italian, Antonio Joli (1700–1777), who not only painted a view of the Thames from Richmond (fig. 48), but also provided a series of capriccios for John James

Fig. 49   James Mason after Augustin Heckel, *A View of Richmond Hill from the Earl of Cholmondelly's*, 1749, etching, 29.3 x 45.5 cm, The British Museum

Fig. 50   John Wootton, *View from Richmond Hill, near the 'Star and Garter' Tavern*, c.1750, brush drawing in grey wash over graphite, 27.4 x 45 cm, The British Museum

Heidegger, the opera impresario, at his house in nearby Maids of Honour Row. Less well known, but perhaps more significant in the present context, was Augustin Heckel (1690–1770), a German-born gold chaser who turned to making topographical views of the area when he moved to a house on Richmond Hill during his retirement (fig. 49).[9] The view from Richmond Hill down river included major landed estates, such as Syon, the seat of the Duke of Northumberland. Up river, among the most significant points of interest by the mid-eighteenth century was Twickenham, by that time confirmed as a popular retreat for artists and writers. Its kudos stemmed from a decision by Alexander Pope to establish a riverside villa and garden nearby in the 1720s.[10] By the mid-eighteenth century the neighbourhood, known as Cross Deep, was also inhabited by a number of leading artists. They included Samuel Scott and Thomas Hudson, who established a handsome riverside Palladian villa there in the 1750s, together with a Gothic summer house.[11] Hudson's villa, which Reynolds must have known well, also functioned as a museum, where he displayed his collection of old master paintings, drawings, and engravings.[12] According to Reynolds's biographer, Charles Robert Leslie, 'Many years later, when Reynolds had built a house on Richmond Hill, and Hudson occupied one on the opposite side of the Thames, the latter made some remark on the circumstance, and Sir Joshua replied, "I never expected that I should look down on you, Sir"'.[13] Yet, by the time that Reynolds entered the property market, Twickenham was already quite congested and much of the land was already parcelled up.

We know, from a passing remark made by Dr Thomas Percy, that in 1763 Reynolds was renting a house in Twickenham, where he invited Samuel Johnson to lodge for several weeks in November that year to work on his edition of Shakespeare.[14] Reynolds himself also made frequent social visits to friends' houses in the vicinity of Richmond and Twickenham during the 1760s. They included the country retreat of Richard Owen Cambridge, author of the *Scribleriad*, who in 1750 had acquired a Thameside villa named Twickenham Meadows.[15] Another close associate in the vicinity was Heaton Wilkes, brother of the politician John Wilkes, then exiled in France.[16] As well as visiting Wilkes at his home in Teddington, Reynolds also met up with him at the Star and Garter, a popular inn established in 1738 close to the entrance of Richmond Park, and which features in John Wootton's view of Richmond Hill from around 1750 (fig. 50). By the end of 1767 Reynolds may have been taking serious interest in acquiring a second home in Richmond, noting in his pocket book on Sunday 15 November, 'Richmond to see a h'. In the event he decided against renting a house in Richmond and instead decided to build one.

Once Reynolds had assumed the Presidency of the Royal Academy, his desire to acquire a permanent country residence evidently became more urgent, and in July 1769 he acquired a cottage with a small parcel of land on the estate of the Earl of Dysart, Lord of the Manor of Petersham, a hundred yards or so to the east of the Star and Garter. It was situated on the far edge of the Petersham estate, where it abutted Richmond.[17] At the time Reynolds's villa was being erected, a new map of Richmond was commissioned by the King's newly appointed Surveyor General, Peter Burrell.[18] The map provides a detailed record of land and properties in and around Richmond (fig. 51). Although his house had yet to be completed, it is significant that Reynolds is mentioned by name on the map, his presence being regarded as a boon to the Manor, and presumably to the map's creator. Reynolds's choice of site was dictated by the location, for in other respects it was not propitious. The house was situated to the west of the fashionable Terrace Walk on Richmond Hill, which had recently been rebuilt.[19] However, the entrance façade faced north, away from the hill, and the house backed directly onto a scrubby and vertiginous piece of grazing land, adjacent to a few hovels and a ramshackle public house, the Bull's Head.[20] The entrance to the property, as it was built, stood upon the public road, which led to the Park and the common land. The appearance of the hill before Reynolds's built his villa can be seen in Charles Grignion's

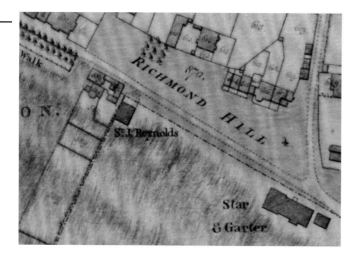

engraving, after Augustin Heckel, 'West view of Richmond from the Star and Garter' of 1752 (fig. 53). As well as his villa, Reynolds established a small garden. At the bottom stood a small row of almshouses and to the immediate left a pigsty.[21] It is not surprising that Reynolds's niece remained unimpressed by Reynolds's choice of location. 'A place, to tell you the truth, I hate; for one has all the inconveniences of town and country put together, and not one of the comforts: a house struck upon the top of a hill, without a bit of garden or ground of any sort near it but what is as public as St. James's Park'.[22] By this time, as characterised in William Bunbury's satirical view of Richmond Hill (fig. 52), the constant tourist traffic ensured that residents enjoyed little privacy.

Reynolds's villa was designed by fellow Academician, William Chambers, an experienced and accomplished architect in townhouse and suburban villa design, who had created a series of country residences near London for aristocrats and successful professionals. They included Parksted, Roehampton for the 2nd Earl of Bessborough, Teddington Grove for the wealthy London merchant, Moses Franks, as well as various garden buildings and a residence for George III at Kew.[23] Since the early eighteenth century villa culture had been proliferating along the Thames. Daniel Defoe observed in 1724: 'From Richmond to London, the river sides are full of villages, and those villages so full of beautiful buildings, charming gardens, and rich habitations of gentlemen of quality, that nothing in the world can imitate it'.[24]

Fig. 51 'Plan of the Royal Manor of Richmond, otherwise West Sheen, in the county of Surrey, Taken under the direction of Peter Burrell Esq. His Majesty's Surveyor General in the year 1771 by Thomas Richardson in York Street, Cavendish Square, London' (detail), Museum of Richmond, Richmond

Fig. 52 William Dickinson after William Bunbury, *Richmond Hill*, 1782, engraving, 46.5 x 76 cm, The British Museum

Fig. 53 Charles Grignion the Elder after Augustin Heckel, *A West View of Richmond etc., in Surrey from the Star and Garter on the Hill*, 1752, coloured engraving, 26 x 40 cm, UK Government Art Collection

As Giles Worsley has noted, the suburban villa had a very different function to the country house situated on landed estates. 'They did not generally make political or ancestral statements, or have a dominant social or economic role in their neighbourhoods'.[25] In 1760 the writer and socialite Mrs Henrietta Pye observed: 'The Genius of the inhabitants inclines not towards Commerce, Architecture seems their chief Delight; in which if any one doubts their excelling, let him sail up the River and view their lovely Villas beautifying its Banks'.[26] And yet, the villa was only an option for those with inherited wealth or were successful in commerce. Reynolds's villa was both a conspicuous sign of his burgeoning social status and his commercial success in the metropolis.

Wick House was, in architectural terms, a modest affair, even though Solomon Brown, 'bricklayer to his Majesty' and the builder of Chambers's Pagoda at Kew, and the distinguished plasterer Francis Engleheart (father of the miniaturist, George Engleheart) were employed in its construction.[27] In truth, with negligible architectural pretensions, Reynolds's projected villa presented little opportunity for Chambers to demonstrate his flair for villa design. James Northcote, at that time a pupil of Reynolds, noted that Chambers was the architect 'not because it was intended to make any display of taste in the building, for convenience alone he was consulted in it'.[28] In Sir John Soane's Museum is a ground-floor plan for Wick House made by Chambers's office (fig. 55).[29] This plan, presumably, represents Chambers's initial design, showing a modest entrance hall and staircase, with three adjoining rooms. Yet, as Chambers's correspondence with Reynolds reveals, and as the subsequent layout of the house indicates, Reynolds opted for a grander residence than originally envisaged.

Fig. 54   The bow window in the dining room of Wick House

Work probably began on the house in 1770. On 29 September 1771, Reynolds noted in his pocket book a visit to Richmond, almost certainly to inspect the building works. However, as Chambers's correspondence with him reveals, progress was slow, partly due to structural problems, and problems with contractors.[30] Eventually, in October 1772, the house was completed and Chambers was able to present Reynolds with a final bill for £1655 1s. 4½ p. He also summarised the issues which had complicated the design and building process:

> You may remember that your 1st Intention was to have one large room which was to be on the Parlour Floor & only to have atticks over it. You then desired to have the large room up stairs & an eating Room upon the Parlour floor &c: this was done & attended wth some additional Expense when finished. However your friends thought there was not Elbow Room enough, so a good part of what was done was demolished & a large Eating room wth a Bow Broke out was made at considerable expense. Your little Garden wth the Pales that enclose it has likewise cost something & as the Ground was all a very stiff Clay the digging part, of which there was a good deal, exceeded what I expected & I was under the necessity of making a new Sewer of a considerable Length to take off the water as the one wʰ runs by your Building was not deep enough to drain it.[31]

The costly and problematic bow window had been incorporated into the ground floor dining room and in the drawing room on the floor above (fig. 54).[32] Reynolds, although he was parsimonious in his approach to the project, was clearly intent upon making the most of the view. Below ground, Chambers had also provided extensive brick vaults for which Reynolds had to obtain an annual

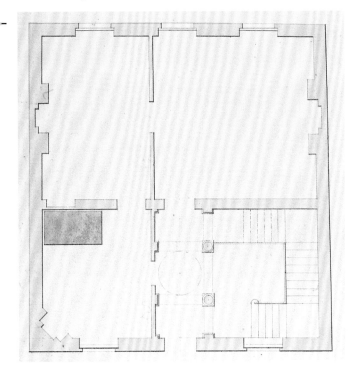

Fig. 56 Artist unknown, *The Wick and Wick House, c.*1785, pen and watercolour, 33 x 52.1 cm, location unknown (photograph Museum of Richmond)

Fig. 55 Sir William Chambers, *Floor Plan for Wick House, Richmond, c.*1770, Sir John Soane's Museum

licence, as they encroached onto the adjacent manor, under the public road at the front of the house.[33]

Among the few paintings made during Reynolds's lifetime to feature Wick House is a watercolour, presently unlocated, attributed variously to Paul Sandby and John Inigo Richards (fig. 56).[34] The view is towards the park, showing in the foreground the posts and turnstiles, which formed part of the new public walk, called the Queen's Terrace, which led from the existing Terrace to the Park. Reynolds's villa is towards the centre of the composition (the second house from the right). It is situated behind 'The Wick', a house built in 1775 for Lady St Aubyn by Sir Robert Mylne, upon the site of the old Bull's Head tavern.[35] To the left and behind Wick House is The Star and Garter, and in the background, to the left of the entrance to the park, Ancaster House, constructed in 1772 for Peregrine Bertie, 3rd Duke of Ancaster. Reynolds was familiar with his new neighbours, having painted the portraits of the Duke and Duchess of Ancaster and their children, as well as the recently widowed Lady St Aubyn, her husband and son.[36] As depicted here, Wick House, which has a modest pedimented portico entrance, is composed of three storeys on the street façade. It was unpretentious yet reasonably spacious, being described in 1794 as comprising 'Dining and Drawing Room, 30 feet by 18, looking towards the River; four best beds, and four Servants' beds'.[37]

Reynolds made use of Wick House from the early 1770s onwards, particularly in the summer months when he socialised with friends and family. As a local property owner, he was named in 1772 among the trustees appointed under the Petersham Highways Act to repair and light the road between Kingston and Richmond, and in 1775 attended a Vestry meeting in his capacity as a local ratepayer.[38] A review of his surviving sitter books over the period 1773 to 1789 indicates that Reynolds entertained at Wick House, on average, between two and four times a year, mostly on Sunday, between the months of May and September. Generally, Reynolds only spent the day at Wick House, entertaining select parties of around a dozen guests for, as Samuel Rogers later observed, 'he always wanted to get back to town among people'.[39] Towards the end of his life, in the summer of 1789, when his health was poor and his sight was failing, he spent time there with his niece, Mary Palmer.[40] He also sometimes stayed there after dinner parties, as he did one night in August 1775. Among the guests on that occasion was Reynolds's nephew Samuel Johnson, a young schoolmaster at Mr Hobden's Academy for Young Gentlemen in nearby Hounslow. He was invited by his uncle to stay the night, although he declined since he had to be at school early the next morning.[41] Reynolds's sister Frances, who also stayed at Wick House that night, was in the habit of residing there for extended periods; and increasingly so, as her relationship with her brother deteriorated and her role as housekeeper in Leicester Square was superseded by their niece, Mary Palmer.[42]

In 1781, by which time Reynolds and his younger sister were estranged, Fanny suggested that he should transfer ownership of Wick House to her. Reynolds penned a sarcastic response, which deserves to be quoted in full:

> Dear Sister
> I am very much obliged to you for your kind and generous offer in regard
> to the house at Richmond not only giving me leave to use it occasionally but

even as long as I live provided I will give it to you, but as I have no such thoughts at present I can only thank you for your kindness – tho I am much older than you I hope I have not yet arrived to dotage as you seem to think I am, voluntarily to put myself in the situation of receiving the favour of living in my own house insteed [*sic*] of conferring the favour of letting you live in it

> I am your most affectionate
> Brother
> J Reynolds

Shortly afterwards she left Reynolds's household to lodge with the translator John Hoole, and after Reynolds's death, upon receiving an inheritance from him, moved to a large house in Queens's Square.[43] Despite his apparent harsh treatment of his sister on this occasion (she had clearly overstepped the mark), Reynolds could be hospitable, offering to accommodate his friend John Parker, 1st Lord Boringdon at Wick House, following the death of his wife in 1775.[44] Reynolds was also a generous host on the occasions that he invited friends to dine there.

Typically, Reynolds's guests would set off from London in the late morning, the main group travelling in his coach, an ostentatious vehicle by all accounts, which had formerly belonged to a lord mayor of London.[45] Their host sometimes joined them or travelled by horse or in a post chaise (a fast, light carriage). Reynolds's sister Frances, acting as housekeeper, would on occasion leave early in the morning ahead of the main group, at times travelling on foot.[46] The party would travel west from central London through Kensington and Chelsea, crossing the Thames at the toll bridge linking Fulham and Putney. They would then proceed through the villages of Barnes and Mortlake, travelling along Sheen Lane, and up towards Richmond Hill via Black Horse Lane (now Queen's Road) across Pesthouse Common; a journey of around an hour or more. The visit would invariably include a promenade to take in the view from Richmond Hill. This social ritual would be followed by a convivial dinner at Wick House, after which the party would return to town around eight in the evening.[47] On various occasions, guests included members of Reynolds's immediate family, as well as friends such as Samuel Johnson, James Boswell, Edmund Burke, David Garrick, Edward Gibbon, Fanny Burney, and the Thrales. Fellow artists were also occasionally welcomed, including Benjamin West and Joseph Wilton, who visited with their wives.

A number of Reynolds's guests gave accounts of their visits. In August 1773, on a fine summer's day, the Scottish philosopher and poet James Beattie described an enjoyable day out at Wick House, dining with Reynolds and various friends on a haunch of venison, presumably from the nearby deer park.[48] Hannah More recalled an occasion in 1776 when the party included Burke, Garrick and Gibbon. 'There was hardly a person in company that I would not have chosen as eminently agreeable …We had a great deal of laugh, as there were so many leaders among the patriots, and a good deal of attacking and defending, with much wit and good humour.'[49] In 1778, Frederick ('Fritz') Robinson told his brother Thomas, Lord Grantham that he had dined at Wick House with friends and family from Devon, including his sister Anne ('Nanny'), his brother-in-law John Parker, Edward Eliot (later Baron Eliot of St Germans), and no less than 'three Mr. Bastards'. Reynolds's house, he noted, had 'two very good rooms with delightful views'. The following summer he visited Reynolds in Richmond again, taking with him 'a basket with peaches, nectarines, grapes and melons' gathered in a friend's kitchen garden in Putney.[50]

Not everyone enjoyed their visit to Wick House. Mrs Thrale was characteristically scathing:

> Mr Garrick was sick, and Lady Rothes was troublesome; She brought two Babies with her both under six Years old, which though the prettiest Babies in the World were not wanted there at all, they played and prattled and suffer'd nobody to be heard but themselves … The Wits wanted to be talking & could not be heard, The Family folks fretted – but Langton and his Wife with a triumphant Insensibility kissed their Children and listened to nothing with Pleasure but what they said.

In order to restore some semblance of order, Reynolds's sister Fanny directed a maid to take the Langton children out for a walk, 'very little to the Satisfaction of the Parents'. Garrick, who was clearly nauseous, sat alone at a table by the open window. At this point the children returned. 'Lady Rothes [Mrs Langton], who did not much like that they should lose their dinner so … directed them to go to Mr. Garrick's Table, and eat fair. He was sick before, and I actually saw him change colour at their approach.'[51] Reynolds, we can assume, merely turned a deaf ear.

Early in 1782 Fanny Burney visited Wick House. Reynolds had been introduced to Fanny, daughter of his friend Charles Burney, in September 1778, shortly after the publication of her hugely popular debut novel, *Evelina*, a book he admired intensely and promoted assiduously, along with its attractive young author. On their first meeting, Fanny recorded in her journal that Reynolds had been particularly attentive, 'though he did not *make Love*!'[52] Given the otherwise surprising nature of the remark, it is probable that 'dear little Burney', as Reynolds referred to her, knew already of a plan hatched by Mrs Thrale and Mrs Montagu to matchmake her with the fifty-five year bachelor.[53] Shortly afterwards, to her intense mortification, Fanny's name was also romantically linked with Reynolds in a satirical 1778 pamphlet by George Huddesford, who was himself a friend and former pupil of Reynolds.[54]

Fanny Burney, who in 1782 was still evidently being courted by Reynolds, journeyed from London to Wick House in Reynolds's carriage. She was accompanied by her father, Reynolds, Mary Palmer, and Edmund Boyle, 7th Earl of Cork and Orrey ('ugly and unpleasing').[55] 'Sir Joshua's house', observed Burney, 'is delightfully situated, almost at the top of Richmond Hill'. Following a walk along the Terrace with the rest of the party, Fanny and Reynolds spent some time alone, 'Tête à Tête', in the first floor saloon, where 'the *Knight of Plympton* was desiring my opinion of the prospect from his Window, and comparing it with Mr Burkes'.[56] Reynolds's reference was presumably to Gregories, near Beaconsfield in Buckinghamshire, an opulent mansion set in 600 acres, for which Edmund Burke had paid £20,000 in 1768 – the implication being, perhaps, that Reynolds's view was much finer and had been achieved at a fraction of the cost. Shortly afterwards, Reynolds and Fanny were joined in the room by Dr Shipley, Bishop of St Asaph and his daughter, Georgiana, whom Fanny found insufferable, wearing 'almost a constant smile, – but not of softness, nor of insipidity, but of self-sufficiency, and internal satisfaction'.[57] They were followed by Mary Palmer, Edward Gibbon, Edmund Burke's wife and son, together with a third gentleman, whom she had not seen before. Was he, Fanny surmised, '*The* Burke'? The party at that point made their way downstairs to the dining parlour, Fanny being unable to speak to Mary Palmer concerning her speculations about the stranger's identity. It was only then that Reynolds, who was clearly enjoying the game, brought them together, announcing 'Mr Burke! – Miss Burney! –'[58] Unfortunately, at that point Miss Shipley insisted that Edmund Burke should sit next to her, compelling Fanny to take a seat next to Burke's son.

Throughout 1782 Fanny Burney and Reynolds continued to socialise. However, a severe attack of paralysis suffered by Reynolds in November 1782 put an end to any talk of marriage between them. 'How, my dearest Susy', she told her younger sister, 'can you wish any wishes about Sir Joshua and me? A man who has had two shakes of the palsy! What misery should I suffer if I were only his niece, from terror of a fatal repetition of such a shock! I would not run voluntarily into such a state of perpetual apprehension for all the wealth of the East'.[59]

Visitors to Richmond Hill relished the view. When the trustees of the late William Hickey sold off the parcel of land adjacent to Reynolds's house in 1774, upon which Lady St Aubyn's house was to stand, it was described in the advertisement as the location 'most justly acknowledged to be the finest in Europe'.[60] And when the German essayist Carl Philipp Moritz visited in the summer of 1782, he stated that the Terrace 'does assuredly afford one of the finest prospects in the world'. 'Here it was', he wrote, 'that Thomson and Pope gleaned from nature all those beautiful passages with which their inimitable writings abound!'[61] Even so, to the tutored eye, Richmond Hill offered a great deal more than an excellent 'prospect' of the Arcadian countryside, or a fond recollection of Pope and Thomson. As Fanny Burney enjoyed the view from the dining parlour at Wick House, Reynolds had drawn the attention of his guests towards a white house further down the hill belonging to Lady Diana Beauclerk, prompting a conversation on her recovery following the recent death of her abusive husband.[62] As Reynolds's friend and protégé Ozias Humphry observed a decade or so earlier:

> From this Terrace one looks down upon the Thames, a sublime translucent Mirrour, on the other side of which are the beautiful meadows of Twickenham, judiciously arranged and adorned by Mr Owen Cambridge their Proprietor, in which is situated his Hospitable Mansion. On the Hill near the Park Gate is a villa of the Duke of Ancaster's and beyond it within the Park the Lodge of Princess Amelia. Under the Hill to the westward, in a rich Dell, is one singularly beautiful of the Duke of Montague. Over this villa are the woods of Petersham, a seat belonging to the Earl of Harrington. Beyond this again are the Earl of Dysart's Groves at Ham.[63]

Reynolds was familiar with all these powerful local magnates and had painted portraits of a number of them. It was this 'political' as well as poetic landscape that Reynolds relished, and to which he wished to be affiliated. Richmond was to London what Tivoli had been to Rome; a sophisticated country retreat where the nation's movers and shakers could, from the comfort of their Thameside villas, take pride in their status and success in the city. Richmond was by now resolutely cosmopolitan. Horace Walpole, who had no love for London, even referred to Richmond as 'my metropolis'.[64]

Reynolds does not appear to have used Wick House as a studio; not least because he rarely spent more than a day at a time in Richmond. On one occasion, a Richmond-based astronomer, William Gardiner, suggested that, since he was too infirm to travel to London, Reynolds should become his '*Magnus Apollo*' and paint his portrait upon his 'next Retreat to our little *Alps*'.[65] Reynolds did not comply. Reynolds did however paint the view from Richmond Hill (fig. 57) although, according to Boswell, it was not done 'very well'.[66] When it was first engraved in 1788 by William Russell Birch (1755–1834) (fig. 58), for *Delices de la Grande Bretagne*, a series of thirty-six landscape views after contemporary British painters, it was entitled a 'View from Sir Joshua Reynolds's House Richmond Hill', suggesting that the vantage point was Wick House.[67] Reynolds's picture is undated, but was completed by 1784, when it was exhibited by the Society for Promoting Painting and Design, Liverpool. Various influences have been suggested for the picture, including *The Return of the Ark* of 1659 by Sébastien Bourdon (London; National Gallery), which Reynolds had purchased in 1775 and which he mentions in the fourteenth *Discourse*.[68] A more compelling comparison, however, can be made with another picture in Reynolds's collection, Rubens's *Landscape by Moonlight* (fig. 59). Reynolds's painting, which is almost the same size as Rubens's *Landscape*, was produced, I would argue, as a 'companion' piece: a practice which he advocated in his *Discourses* and which he resorted to frequently in his portraits and fancy pictures.[69] In the eighth *Discourse* of 1779, he praised Rubens's *Landscape by Moonlight* for its artifice in departing from literal nature: 'he might, indeed, have made it more natural, but it would have been at the expense of what he thought of much greater consequence, the harmony proceeding from the contrast and variety of colours'.[70] Certainly, Reynolds's own landscape of the Thames from Richmond could have been more natural, had he not been less concerned with the view itself than its potential as a means to explore, with the example of Rubens before him, the visual language of the old masters.

Fig. 58 William Russell Birch, *View from Sir Joshua Reynolds's House, Richmond Hill*, 1788, engraving, 15 x 17.4 cm, The British Museum

Fig. 57 Sir Joshua Reynolds, *The Thames from Richmond Hill*, 1788, oil on canvas, 69.8 x 90.8 cm, Tate, London

Reynolds's only known artistic conversation relating to the view from Richmond Hill was with the landscape painter, Richard Wilson. It appears in *An Essay on the Picturesque* by Uvedale Price, first published in 1794. Price states:

> Sir Joshua Reynolds told me, that when he and Wilson the landscape painter were looking at the view from Richmond Terrace, Wilson was pointing out some particular part; and in order to direct his eye to it, 'There', said he, 'near those houses — there! Where the figures are.'—Though a painter, said Sir Joshua, I was puzzled: I thought he meant statues, and was looking upon the tops of the houses; for I did not at first conceive that the men and women we plainly saw walking about, were by him only thought of as figures in the landscape.[71]

The exchange, as Reynolds admits, suggested a fundamental difference in how he and Wilson looked at the real world. Wilson, who often painted the Thames in and

Fig. 59   Sir Peter Paul Rubens,
*Landscape by Moonlight, c.*1635–
40, oil on panel, 64 x 90 cm,
The Courtauld Gallery, London

around Richmond, appears to have transformed what he saw before him into the visual language of a Claudian classical landscape. Reynolds, despite his acute understanding of the visual and poetic associations of this particular prospect, was accustomed to look at the view from Richmond Hill in a far more literal manner.

⁎ ⁎ ⁎

By the mid-1780s, by which time he had been appointed Principal Painter to the King, Reynolds was not the only artist able to enjoy the view from Richmond Hill in the comfort of his own home. Thomas Gainsborough, who enjoyed much more cordial relations with the Court, also lived there. In his will Gainsborough bequeathed to his daughter Margaret, among other things, 'my house in Pall Mall as at Richmond'.[72] Until recently the whereabouts of Gainsborough's house in

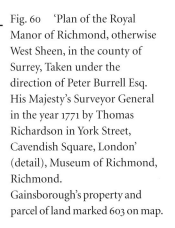

Fig. 60 'Plan of the Royal Manor of Richmond, otherwise West Sheen, in the county of Surrey, Taken under the direction of Peter Burrell Esq. His Majesty's Surveyor General in the year 1771 by Thomas Richardson in York Street, Cavendish Square, London' (detail), Museum of Richmond, Richmond. Gainsborough's property and parcel of land marked 603 on map.

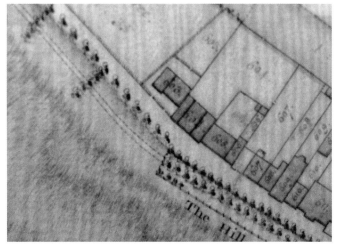

Richmond was unknown. However, painstaking research by Richmond's leading local historian John Cloake, among Land Tax Returns and associated archival documents, has revealed its precise location (fig. 60). We also know, owing to Cloake's research, that before he established a house in Richmond he also had a house in Kew, which still survives (fig. 61).[73]

Gainsborough moved from Bath to London in 1774, setting up home at Schomberg House, Pall Mall, close to St. James's Palace and Buckingham House.[74] During this time he courted Royal patronage and by the early 1780s was preoccupied with a number of important Royal commissions, including full-length portraits of the King and Queen and fifteen separate oval portrait of the King and Queen and the royal children.[75] Gainsborough also gravitated towards Kew, which was not only a residence of the Court but an enclave of artists with courtly connections, including his friend Joshua Kirby and the miniaturists Jeremiah Meyer and George Engleheart.[76] In the summer of 1783 Gainsborough wrote a letter inscribed 'Kew Green, Sunday Morg / Church time'.[77] It has been speculated that the letter was written from the home of Kirby's widow, Sarah, who lived at what is now 61 Kew Green.[78] However, Cloake has established that in 1783 and 1784, a 'Miss Gainsborough' was paying rates of 15 shillings a year on a house assessed at an annual value of £30. Land tax returns for Kew indicate that the owner was rebuilding the house in 1780, but that from 1781 to 1783 'Mr Gainsborough' was the tenant. In 1784 the land tax return stated 'Mr. Gainsborough – empty' and in

Fig. 61 Gainsborough's house, 25 Kew Green

Fig. 62 Attributed to John Boydell, *The Thames at Richmond*, c.1744–49, oil on canvas, 59.4 x 108 cm, Richard Green

1785 'empty', indicating by that time Gainsborough had given up the property completely.[79] The 'Miss Gainsborough' referred to in the rate list was presumably Gainsborough's unmarried daughter Margaret, her sister Mary having in 1780 entered into a brief and unsuccessful marriage with the court oboeist Johann Christian Fischer. Gainsborough's residence has been identified by Cloake as the present 25 Kew Green, an unpretentious three-storey brick terraced house on the south side of the Green, adjacent to Kew Palace.

In 1785 Gainsborough swapped his house in Kew for a residence in Richmond. From this year until 1791 Gainsborough (who had died in 1788) is listed in the land tax returns as the occupier of a house situated on the brow of Richmond Hill. The property had been converted in the early 1770s by the owner, Charles Pearce, a London tailor and aspiring property developer, from two adjoining cottages into single dwelling.[80] Gainsborough paid a comparatively modest annual rate of £20 for the house and £9 for the garden.[81] In 1779, when the property changed ownership, it was described as ' two Tenements with the Yard and Garden thereunto belonging containing by the map and Survey lately taken of the said Manor about twenty three Perches situate [*sic*] upon Richmond Hill within the Manor aforesaid … abutting South West upon the Highway there leading beyond Richmond Hill to Petersham' (see fig. 60).[82] The cottages are identifiable in a painting of Richmond Hill from the

Fig. 63 Attributed to John
Boydell, *The Thames at
Richmond* (detail)

Fig. 64 Leonard Knyff, *View of
Richmond from the Hill Walk*
(detail of fig. 46 showing
Gainsborough's house, directly
behind the inn sign)

late 1740s (figs. 62 and 63), attributed here, tentatively, to the young John Boydell.[83]
They are also just visible in Leonard Knyff's earlier view of Richmond Hill and the
Terrace (fig. 64), tucked immediately behind the Roebuck Inn. As the map of 1771
shows, Gainsborough's property was very close to Wick House.

   Gainsborough's decision to establish a home in Richmond was probably
motivated by his desire to acquire a house with a view of the Thames and in a
salubrious area. It may also have been related to concerns about patronage and his
public profile. Reynolds was President of the Royal Academy and Principal Painter to
the King. Even so, he gained little in the way of patronage from him. By contrast, the
King was fond of Gainsborough and even visited his home on Richmond Hill, where,
amongst other things, he admired 'a picture by Vandervelde' belonging to the artist,
which featured subsequently in his studio sale.[84] There may have been other reasons

Fig. 65   Henry Birche after
Thomas Gainsborough,
Cottage Children, 1791,
engraving, 57.9 x 39.1 cm,
The British Museum

for the King to visit Gainsborough in Richmond at this time. In October 1785, shortly after Gainsborough had established a house on Richmond Hill, Henry Bate-Dudley stated in the *Morning Herald* that Gainsborough was to make a new painting for the King, 'the landscape, Richmond Water-walk, or Windsor – the figures all portraits'.[85] Richmond water-walk was a fashionable promenade, and it is known that Gainsborough made a number of drawings at this time which may relate to such a project. While such drawings may well have been made in his London studio, if Gainsborough was indeed contemplating a painting of Richmond water-walk he would also have wished to have a physical presence in Richmond.

Far more than Reynolds, Gainsborough derived inspiration for his art from Richmond and its environs; not least in relation to his fancy pictures, which were then a major focus of his energies. According to Henry Bate-Dudley, the boy and girl who featured in his *Cottage Children with the Ass* (fig. 65) were tenants in a cottage near Richmond, 'where Mr. Gainsborough has a house'.[86] A number of his drawings of poor children, dating from the mid-1780s, were probably made in and around Richmond, near Gainsborough's house. Prominent among these children was John, or 'Jack', Hill – who may be identified as 'John Thomas Hill', baptized in Richmond Parish church on 16 December 1781.[87] Hill was clearly regarded with great affection by Gainsborough's family, including his daughter Margaret, who wished to adopt him. In 1790, following Gainsborough's death, at which time he was around eight years old, Hill was sent to be educated at Christ's Hospital.[88]

Gainsborough was clearly attached to his house in Richmond, regarding it as a place of respite and a means of escaping the pressures of his portrait practice in the city. In the spring of 1788 a swelling in his neck, of which he had been conscious for several years, was causing him considerable pain. He was dying from cancer. Towards the end of May, he went to stay at his house in Richmond in the hope of recuperation.[89] In June he left Richmond for the last time, and returned to London. He died in Schomberg House, Pall Mall, on 2 August. Eight days later, on 9 August, his body was conveyed to the churchyard of St Anne's, Kew, a stone's throw from his former house on Kew Green. The six pall-bearers were fellow artists, Francesco Bartolozzi, William Chambers, Samuel Cotes, Benjamin West, Paul Sandby and Joshua Reynolds. Gainsborough was interred beside his friend, Joshua Kirby. A few months later Jeremiah Meyer was laid to rest beside them.[90]

Gainsborough's Richmond home remained in his family's possession for a few years after his death, when it was sublet. Soon, however, it passed into other hands.[91] Any trace of the house has long since disappeared. It was rebuilt as a mansion in the 1820s, enlarged as a hotel in the 1830s, and subdivided once more into two separate properties in the 1850s. The 'footprint' of the house is the present 124–126 Richmond Hill.[92] The Roebuck tavern, which stood next to Gainsborough's house, still survives.

Fig. 66   Joseph Constantine Stadler after Joseph Farington, *From Richmond Hill down the River*, 1793, hand-coloured etching and aquatint, 20.9 x 31.6 cm, Private Collection

Fig. 67   Robert Havell Snr after William Havell, *A View from Richmond Hill*, 1815, aquatint, 21 x 30.5 cm, UK Government Art Collection

* * *

While memory of Gainsborough's time in Richmond faded, in the years immediately following Reynolds's death, his Richmond residence became something of a landmark. A number of views of Richmond Hill, looking down river, incorporated Reynolds's house. It is prominent in the aquatint, *From Richmond Hill down the River*, by J.C. Stadler, after Joseph Farington, which was published in 1793 by Boydell's Shakespeare Gallery (fig. 66) and formed part of Boydell's *History of the River Thames*. It occupies a similar position in Robert Havell's aquatint of 1815 (fig. 67).[93] In 1804 Richard Cooper (*c.*1740–1814) exhibited at the Royal Academy a 'view of the Thames; taken from Richmond Hill, with a part of the late Sir J. Reynolds's house in the foreground'. A sepia watercolour by Cooper, in the Government Art Collection (fig. 68), shows a view of Richmond Hill with part of a house to the left. However, the house in question is not Wick

Fig. 68 Richard Cooper Jnr, *The Thames at Richmond*, c.1804, sepia wash on paper, 57 x 89 cm, UK Government Art Collection

Fig. 69 Richard Cooper Jnr, *The Thames at Richmond*, c.1804, sepia wash on paper, 19.5 x 32 cm, Abbott & Holder JV

House but the neighbouring property to its right, The Wick.[94] In a related but less finished drawing (fig. 69) Cooper included Wick House. This drawing was possibly a compositional sketch for the work exhibited at the Royal Academy in 1804 – assuming that the finished view was not the picture presently in the Government Art Collection. Yet, if Cooper had perhaps been confused over the identity of Wick House and The Wick, he was not alone. In 1826, *The Mirror of Literature, Amusement, and Instruction* featured an engraving of Reynolds's house on Richmond Hill, based upon 'an original drawing, made in 1817' – although, again, the house in question is clearly The Wick.[95] Perhaps the confusion arose over the fact that, of the two houses, The Wick was rather more architecturally distinguished than its neighbour, and therefore may have appeared to be a more likely country residence for the former President of the Royal Academy.

Reynolds bequeathed Wick House, along with the rest of his estate, to his niece Mary Palmer. Although Mary agreed to sublet the Richmond house, she informed Reynolds's executor Philip Metcalfe that she did not wish to sell the furniture, perhaps because of its personal associations.[96] In 1794, two years after Reynolds's death, Wick House was advertised to let 'Furnished, for Six to Sixteen Months'.[97] Two years later, in the spring of 1796, the house was again advertised to let, although the furniture was now offered for sale.[98] By this time, Mary Palmer, who had in 1792 married Murrough O'Brien, 5th Earl of Inchiquin, had given up any interest in Wick House, which was sold to Francis Henry Proby, younger son of Captain Charles Proby, a commissioner of Chatham Dockyard, the uncle of Reynolds's friend, John

Joshua Proby, 1st Earl of Carysfort.[99] In 1803 the house was sold to a Mrs Lyell, who successfully petitioned for the removal of the poor houses at the bottom of the garden, and the removal of the adjacent pig sties.[100] From at least the 1830s, Wick House was subject to redevelopment.[101] By 1863 a large extension had been added on the left side of the property by the new owner, with canted bays at the front and back. Over the next few decades the house became virtually unrecognisable, through the addition of Victorian mouldings, balconies and verandahs, while the canted bay at the front was transformed into a five-storey tower, complete with an octagonal smoking room (fig. 70).[102] In 1883 the property was sold by auction. No mention was made of its previous association with Reynolds, perhaps because it was hard to conceive how this cluttered Victorian pile was once a neat Georgian villa.[103]

By the 1920s Wick House operated as a hotel. And, in 1937, in the name of progress, the Ministry of Health sanctioned its demolition, along with The Wick, which was to be replaced by a block of flats; presumably in an attempt to democratise the view.[104] Mercifully, The Wick was reprieved when it was purchased privately and restored. In 1950 it became the home of the actor John Mills, and subsequently the Rolling Stones guitarist Ronnie Wood. It is presently owned by the rock musician Pete Townshend; an affirmation of the way in which Richmond Hill, once the playground of the Georgian glitterati, continues to court celebrity.

Wick House was saved from demolition by the outbreak of the Second World War, when troops were billeted there. After the war it was purchased by the Star and Garter Home, and converted into a hostel for its nursing staff. At this time the Georgian façade was partially restored, although not to its original appearance (fig. 70).[105] Wick House was sold in 2006 by the Star and Garter to a private individual, and was on the property market again in 2011. Sadly, its interior has been gutted. Reynolds's dining room, where Fanny Burney first encountered Edmund Burke, and intellectual giants such as Johnson and Gibbon conversed, is currently in a sorry state (fig. 71). None the less, against the odds, Wick House has survived into the twenty-first century. In some measure, its survival has depended on its continued association with Reynolds. On the other hand, as Reynolds was the first to realize when he purchased a hovel on a pocket handkerchief of land in order to enjoy the view from Richmond Hill, this unprepossessing plot offered the perfect location, location, location.

Fig. 70 Photographs of Wick House, above in the later 19th century and below in 1950, Richmond Local Studies Collection

Fig. 71   The Dining Room,
Wick House, in 2011

I would like to thank local historian John Cloake and Jane Baxter, Local Studies Librarian, Richmond upon Thames, for their guidance and expertise in the preparation of this essay.

1   James Northcote to Samuel Northcote, 21 December 1771, Royal Academy of Arts, MS. NOR/7. See also William T. Whitley, *Artists and their Friends in England 1700–1799*, 2 vols., London 1928, vol. 2, pp. 286–87. Northcote suggested in the same letter that his brother, an instrument maker, might make a telescope for Reynolds, to help him to enjoy the view and to promote his own skills.

2   It is not known when the villa was named 'Wick House', but it was probably sometime during the nineteenth century, possibly to distinguish it from the neighbouring house, which was by the 1860s known as 'The Wick'. See Richard Crisp, *Richmond and Its Inhabitants from the Olden Time. With Memoirs And Notes*, Richmond 1866, p. 290. The name 'Wick' may have referred originally to a dairy farm, or simply a hamlet, and was related, perhaps, to the cluster of buildings which stood on the brow of Richmond Hill, prior to the building of 'Wick House' and 'The Wick' in the 1770s.

3   'Wick House Richmond Hill, TW10 6RN'. http://residential search.savills.co.uk/content/assets/search/247696/HQBrochure

4   Reynolds's house at 5 Great Newport Street, where he lived from 1753 to 1760, was demolished in 1766–67. His house at 47 Leicester Square was demolished in 1937. For further details see F.H.W. Sheppard., ed., *The Survey of London, The Parish of St Anne Soho*, London 1966, vol. 34, pp. 346, 508–12; Derek Hudson, *Sir Joshua Reynolds. A Personal Study*, London 1958, pp. 50, 73, 256, n. 1.

5   See Robert Raines, 'Peter Tillemans, Life and Work, with a List of Representative Paintings', *The Walpole Society*, 1980, vol. XLVII, pp. 53–54, no. 56.

6   Raines, *The Walpole Society*, 1980, p. 26.

7   Tillemans's house, presently named 'Halford House', is situated at 27 Halford Road, Richmond. It was purchased in 1954 by the Richmond Christian Fellowship.

8   For a comprehensive catalogue of the relevant engravings see Bamber Gascoigne, *Images of Richmond. A Survey of the topographical prints of Richmond in Surrey up to the year 1900*, Richmond 1978; Bamber Gasgoigne and Jonathan Ditchburn, *Images of Twickenham, with Hampton and Teddington*, Richmond 1981.

9   For Heckel see Stephen Pasmore, 'Augustin Heckel and Richmond Hill', *Richmond History*, No. 2, 1981, pp. 19–13; John Cloake, '*Prospects about Richmond*': mid-eighteenth century drawings and prints by Augustin Heckel, exhibition, Museum of Richmond, 12 October 1993–19 February 1994.

10   See Morris R. Brownell, *Alexander Pope's Villa. Views of Pope's villa, grotto and garden: a microcosm of English landscape*, exhibition catalogue, Marble Hill House, London 1980.

11   See Anthony Beckles Willson, *Mr Pope & Others at Cross Deep, Twickenham in the 18th Century*, Richmond 1996, pp. 104–15.

12   See Joel-Henrietta Pye, *A Short Account, of the Principal Seats and Gardens, in and about Twickenham*, London 1760, pp. 28–30.

13   Charles Robert Leslie and Tom Taylor, *Life and Times of Sir Joshua Reynolds: with notices of some of his contemporaries*, 2 vols., London 1865, vol. 1, pp. 85–86.

14   Walter Jackson Bate, *Samuel Johnson*, London 1978, p. 392.

15   There are references to 'Mr Cambridge' in Reynolds's sitter book on 27 April 1766, 19, 27 April and 12 July 1767, 8 January, 25 June, 9 July 1769. All these dates were Sundays. Boswell also records a visit to Cambridge's villa, with Reynolds and Johnson on 18 April 1775. See George Birkbeck Hill and L.F. Powell, eds., *Boswell's Life of Johnson*, 6 vols., Oxford 1934–50, vol. 2, p. 361. Although Reynolds was a good friend of Cambridge, he did not paint his portrait.

16   There are several references, giving directions to Wilkes's house, in Reynolds's sitter books. He notes, for example, opposite the week beginning 16 August 1765: 'Mr Wilks first go to Teddington Church / 2d turning on the right after left the Church / 1st House on the right / Stephens farmer at Hampton Wick'. On Saturday 24 August 1765 he notes '9 Mr Wilks Hampton Wick', and on Thursday 29 August '3 ½ Mr. Wilks. Second Turning beyond Teddington Church'. It has been suggested that these entries refer to clandestine meetings with the exiled John Wilkes, who was also a friend of Reynolds, although this is evidently incorrect. See Leslie and Taylor, *Life and Times of Sir Joshua Reynolds*, vol. 1, p. 250 and note 2. See also Arthur H. Cash, *John Wilkes. The Scandalous Father of Civil Liberty*, New Haven and London 2006, p. 192 and note 70.

17   In 1750, the Earl of Dysart, Lord of the Manor of Petersham, had granted to Anne Edwards land measuring four by two rods upon which a cottage was built. In 1758 the property passed to Patrick and Isabella Johnson. On 2 July 1769 Patrick Johnson surrendered the land and cottage to Reynolds. The conveyance of the land was carried out by Reynolds's friend, the lawyer, Joseph Hickey (1712–94). See Alfred Spencer, ed., *Memoirs of William Hickey*, 4 vols., London 1913, vol. 1, p. 309, note; Derek Hudson, *Sir Joshua Reynolds. A Personal Study*, p. 108. There are numerous appointments with Hickey in Reynolds's sitter book during the early 1770s, when Reynolds was also painting his portrait. See David Mannings, *Sir Joshua Reynolds. A Complete Catalogue of his Paintings*, New Haven and London 2000, vol. 1, pp. 256–57, no. 902.

18   'Plan of the Royal Manor of Richmond, otherwise West Sheen, in the County of Surry; in Grant to Her Majesty. Taken under the Direction of Peter Burrell Esq: His Majesty's Survr Genl in 1771, by Thos Richardson in York Street, Cavendish Square'. A hand-coloured impression of the map is on display at the Museum of Richmond.

19   John Cloake, *Cottages and Common Fields of Richmond and Kew*, Chichester 2001, pp. 218, 286–87.

20   See John Cloake, 'The Wick and Wick House', *Richmond History*, No. 5, 1984, pp. 4–5.

21   On 23 August 1803, Petersham Vestry noted that the then owner of Wick House, Mrs Lyell, had applied to take in part of the common land and remove the poor houses to the rear of Wick House. On 20 March 1804 the inhabitants of the poor houses were instructed to move hog sties from near Wick House, which were considered a nuisance. Four months later the poor houses were demolished and a portion of the common land was sold to the owner of Wick House for £250. See Charles D. Warren, *History of St. Peter's Church Petersham, Surrey*, London 1938, p. 88.

22 Leslie and Taylor, *Life and Times of Sir Joshua Reynolds*, vol. 2, p. 542.

23 See John Harris, *Sir William Chambers. Knight of the Polar Star*, London 1970, p. 245, no. 122, p. 249, no. 135. See also pp. 32–39, 40–61.

24 Roy Porter, *London. A Social History*, London 1994, p. 119.

25 John Harris and Michael Snodin, *Sir William Chambers. Architect to George III*, New Haven and London 1996, p. 79.

26 Pye, *A Short Account, of the Principal Seats*, p. 52.

27 See John Harris, *Sir William Chambers*, p. 242.

28 James Northcote, *The Life of Sir Joshua Reynolds*, 2 vols., 1818, vol. 1, p. 304.

29 Sir John Soane's Museum, Drawings by Sir William Chambers, Drawer 43 Set 4/ 22. See also John Harris, *Sir William Chambers*, p. 242. Two architectural drawings of windows for Wick House are in the Fitzgerald Kenney albums in the National Gallery of Ireland, MS 22016. They are inscribed 'for Sir J.R. Copy sent Jany 30th 1778', and 'Finishing for Windows in Bed Room at Sir J.R.'. See Edward McPartland, *James Gandon. Vitruvius Hibernicus*, London 1985, p. 210.

30 For Chambers's correspondence concerning the construction of Wick House see British Library: BL Add.MS 41133, 55–55V, 64, 71, 85V, (13 Oct. 1771–15 Oct. 1772), cited in John Harris, *Sir William Chambers*, p. 242, no. 118. The RIBA Journal, 24 Aug 1893, contains abstracts of the correspondence. For a summary of the principal issues, with extracts from Chambers's correspondence, see Derek Hudson, *Sir Joshua Reynolds. A Personal Study*, pp. 109–10.

31 Hudson, *Sir Joshua Reynolds. A Personal Study*, p. 110.

32 When the house was sold by Christie's in 1803 it was described as comprising 'a dining room and drawing room, each 30 feet long by 18 feet wide, with spacious bow, convenient secondary apartments and domestic offices. The premises are in the neatest repair and condition, and well suited for the occupation of a Man of Fashion, or a small genteel Family'. News clipping, Richmond Local Studies Collection. Early views of Reynolds's house, including those by Farington and Havell (figs. 67 and 68) clearly show a double bow window on the garden façade, although it was later replaced with a canted bay window, probably when the house was radically remodelled in the later nineteenth century. An anonymous watercolour of Wick House, dated 1787 shows the house with four storeys, although the evidence of other dated works, suggests that it was either made at a later date or is incorrect. See also E. Beresford Chancellor, *The History and Antiquities of Richmond, Kew, Petersham, Ham, &c.,* Richmond 1894, p. 194, and note 1, which includes a reproduction of the watercolour.

33 12 August 1772, 'Licence to enlarge vaults to Sir Joshua Reynolds', Court Rolls of the Manor of Richmond, vols. 7–8, 12 p. 1972. Richmond Local Studies Collection. Reynolds paid an annual rent of one shilling for the ground occupied by his cellars.

34 *Bygone Richmond 1562–1846. A Loan Exhibition of Paintings, Drawings and Prints in aid of Finland*, Streatham House, Sheen Road, Richmond, 1940, no. 21. See also Christopher Hussey, 'The Wick, Richmond, Surrey', *Country Life*, 1 February 1941, p. 100, fig. 1 (where it is attributed to Paul Sandby); Gertrude Stirling, 'Sir Joshua Reynolds at Richmond', *Country Life*, 27 October 1950, p.1426, fig. 1; John Cloake, *Richmond Past. A Visual History of Richmond, Kew, Petersham and Ham*, London 1991, p. 63, fig.103.

35 See Hussey, 1941, p. 100; John Cloake, 'The Wick and Wick House', pp. 8–10. Mylne's designs for The Wick were sold at Christie's, 30 November 1983 (29).

36 See Mannings, *Sir Joshua Reynolds. A Complete Catalogue*, vol 1, nos. 163–171, and 1708–1710.

37 *The True Briton*, Monday 14 July 1794. The dimensions of the dining room and drawing room today, excluding the bays, are the same as those cited in 1794.

38 Charles D. Warren, *History of St. Peter's Church Petersham*, pp. 87–88.

39 Rogers also noted, 'Fox said that Sir Joshua Reynolds never enjoyed Richmond, – that he used to say the human face was his landscape'. Samuel Rogers, *Table Talk*, London 1856, p.86.

40 Leslie and Taylor *Life and Times of Sir Joshua Reynolds*, vol. 2, p. 542.

41 Susan M. Radcliffe, *Sir Joshua's Nephew. Being letters written, 1769–1778, by a young man to his sisters*, London 1930, pp.162–64.

42 On 6 October 1772 James Northcote told his brother, Samuel, that 'Miss Reynolds had been at Richmond for some time'. Royal Academy of Arts, ms NOR/12. See also William T Whitley, *Artists and their Friends in England*, vol. 2, p. 292. Fanny Reynolds was also staying at Wick House in September 1775, where she received a letter from her nephew. See Radcliffe, *Sir Joshua's Nephew*, p. 172. Mary Palmer moved in to Reynolds's home in Leicester Square on a permanent basis in 1773.

43 See Richard Wendorf and Charles Ryskamp, 'A Blue-Stocking Friendship. The Letters of Elizabeth Montagu and Frances Reynolds in the Princeton Collection', *The Princeton University Library Chronicle*, vol. XLI, no. 3, Spring 1980, pp.181–82.

44 'He has sent to Mr. Parker to desire he will come up and live at his house at Richmond as long as he pleases, as he is now at a lonely house where no person has lived these five and twenty years.' James Northcote to his brother Samuel, 3 January 1776, Royal Academy of Arts Archive, NOR/15.

45 Stephen Gwynn, *Memorials of an Eighteenth-Century Painter (James Northcote)*, London 1898, p. 245. See also James Northcote, *The Life of Sir Joshua Reynolds*, London 1818, vol.1, pp. 102–3; Ernest Fletcher, *Conversations of James Northcote, R.A.*, p. 204. For Reynolds's own reference to his coach see Malcolm Cormack, 'The Ledgers of Sir Joshua Reynolds', *The Walpole Society*, 1968–70, vol. XLII, pp. 106–7.

46 See Radcliffe, *Sir Joshua's Nephew*, p. 162. Frances Reynolds's nephew noted that she had left for Richmond that day at 8 a.m.

47 See the entry in James Beattie's diary for 15 August 1773, in Ralph S. Walker, ed., *James Beattie's London Diary*, Aberdeen 1946, pp. 54, 82.

48 See Walker, *James Beattie's London Diary*, p. 82.

49 William Roberts, *Memoirs of the life of Mrs. Hannah More*, London 1839, abridged, p. 39.

50 Correspondence between Thomas Robinson (1738–1786), 2nd Baron Grantham (1770), and his brother, Frederick [Fritz] (1746–92). Bedford and Luton Archives and Record Service, ms. 1778 n.d.; L30/14/333/213, 1 June 1779. The 'Bastards' almost certainly included Reynolds's friend from Devon, William Bastard (1727–82). The fruit in question was gathered from the Putney garden of John Dunning, 1st Baron Ashburton (1731–83).

51 Mrs Thrale, 13 August 1777. Katharine C. Balderston, *Thraliana. The Diary of Mrs. Hester Lynch Thrale (Later Mrs. Piozzi) 1776–1809*, 2 vols., Oxford 1942, vol. 1, p. 108, and note 3. Mary Leslie, Countess of Rothes (d.1820), following the death of her first husband, John, 10th Earl of Rothes, married Bennet Langton (1737–1801), in May 1770.

52 Lars E. Troide and Stewart J. Cooke, *The Early Journals and Letters of Fanny Burney. Volume III. The Streatham Years. Part I. 1778–1779*, Oxford, 1994, p. 143.

53 See Leslie and Taylor, *Life and Times of Sir Joshua Reynolds*, vol. 2, p. 224 and 239. It has been suggested that Reynolds had described Fanny to Huddesford as 'dear little Burney', a pet name given to her by Johnson. See Troide and Cooke, *The Early Journals and Letters of Fanny Burney. Volume III*, p. 224, note 39.

54 *Warley: A Satire addressed to the First Artist in Europe*, London, 1778. For Fanny Burney's reaction see Troide and Cooke, *op. cit.*, p. 194f, p. 220f.

55 Frances Burney, *Journal and Letters*, selected with an introduction by Peter Sabor and Lars E. Troide, with the assistance of Stewart Cooke and Victoria Kortes-Papp, London 2001, pp. 180–81.

56 Burney, *Journal and Letters* (2001), p. 181.

57 Burney, *Journal and Letters* (2001), p. 181.

58 Burney, *Journal and Letters* (2001), p. 182.

59 Charlotte Barrett, ed., *Diary and Letters of Madame D'Arblay, Volume 1, 1778 to 1784*, London 1846, pp.491–92.

60 *The Public Advertiser*, 10 December 1774.

61 Charles P. Moritz, *Travels, chiefly on foot, through several parts of England, in 1782. Described in letters to a friend*, London 1795, pp. 104–5.

62 Burney, *Journal and Letters* (2001), p. 183.

63 Ozias Humphry, ms. memoir, Royal Academy of Arts, HU/1/40.

64 Horace Walpole to Mary and Agnes Berry, 26 November 1790, in W.S. Lewis ed., *Horace Walpole's Correspondence*, 48 vols., 1937–83, vol. 11, p. 152.

65 William Gardiner to Joshua Reynolds, 2 May 1773, in Frederick W. Hilles, ed., *Letters of Sir Joshua Reynolds*, Cambridge 1929, Appendix III, p. 241.

66 Frederick W. Hilles., ed., *Portraits by Sir Joshua Reynolds*, London 1952, p. 21.

67 John Thomas Smith also noted that the picture, which then belonged to Samuel Rogers, was a 'view Sir Joshua painted from the window of his villa at Richmond'. John Thomas Smith, *Nollekens and his Times*, 2 vols., London 1828, vol. 2, p. 295.

68 For the suggestion of Bourdon see Derek Hudson, *Sir Joshua Reynolds. A Personal Study*, pp. 56–57.

69 See Martin Postle, *Sir Joshua Reynolds. The Subject Pictures*, Cambridge 1995, pp. 123–25.

70 Sir Joshua Reynolds, *Discourses on Art*, ed., Robert R. Wark, New Haven and London 1975, p. 161, lines 514–17.

71 Uvedale Price, *An Essay on the Picturesque, as Compared with the Sublime and Beautiful, and, on the Use of Studying Pictures, for the Purpose of Improving Real Landscape*, London 1794, p.339.

72 The Last Will and Testament of Thomas Gainsborough Esq., 5 May 1788. Public Record Office, The National Archives, Prob 11/1169.

73 John Cloake, 'Thomas Gainsborough's House at Richmond', *Richmond History. Journal of the Richmond Local History Society*, 2004, No. 25, pp. 24–26.

74 In Gainsborough's day, the house was numbered 87–89 Pall Mall, and Gainsborough occupied no. 87, the west wing, later numbered 80. The facade of no. 87 (80) is all that remains of Gainsborough's house. The facades of 87 and 88 (80 and 81) largely survived demolition in 1955, but from an early date no. 89 (82) suffered from subsidence. The facade had been already lost but was replaced in matching brickwork after the 1955 demolition of all the buildings behind. I am grateful to Dr Susan Sloman for the above information.

75 See Christopher Lloyd, *Gainsborough & Reynolds. Contrasts in Royal Patronage*, The Queen's Gallery, Buckingham Palace, London 1994, pp. 44–45, 50–51, 60–64, cats. 13, 16, 23.

76 Both Engleheart, who lived at Denmark House, Kew Road, and Meyer, who had a house on Kew Green, are buried alongside Gainsborough in the churchyard of St. Anne's, Kew. According to the beadle of St. Anne's church, Gainsborough was in the habit of visiting Meyer at Kew. See M.V. Jones, 'St Anne's at Kew, and Its Graveyard', *Surrey Magazine*, 1907, in 'Richmond Notes', Barkas Files, vol. 6, p. 82, Local Studies Collection, Richmond upon Thames.

77 Thomas Gainsborough to William Pearce, in John Hayes, ed., *The Letters of Thomas Gainsborough*, New Haven and London 2001, p. 153.

78 Hayes, *Letters of Thomas Gainsborough*, p. 154, note 2. See also William T. Whitley, *Thomas Gainsborough*, London 1915, p.251, who suggests that the letter was probably written from the house of Kirby's sister.

79 Cloake, 'Thomas Gainsborough's House at Richmond', p. 25. The only rate lists that survive are for 1783 and 1784.

80 Pearce had acquired the property in 1757, and continued to rent it out for the next fifteen years. In 1771, the two cottages, numbers 124 and 126 Richmond Hill, were rated separately. By 1774 they had been converted into one house by Pearce. See John Cloake, 'Richmond Rates 1726–1771. An Analysis of the Rate Books', ms. notes, Richmond Local Studies Collection. For further information on Pearce and his property speculation see John Cloake, 'Who built Downe House?', *Richmond History*, 2003, no. 24, pp. 43–46.

81 See Richmond Land Tax Records, 1780–96, microfilm, Richmond Local Studies Collection.

82 'The Commissioners in a Commission of Bankrupt against Charles Pearce and another to The Asignees Bargain and Sale. 2nd July 1779'. Land Revenue Court Rolls. LR3/92, f.404, National Archives, Kew. The house formed part of the property seized from Charles Pearce, a tailor and aspiring property developer, of Castle Street, Leicester Fields, who had been declared bankrupt. The occupier and subsequent owner of the house, who also became Gainsborough's landlord, was John Clementson. For Pearce see also John Cloake, 'Who built Downe House?', no. 24, pp. 43–66.

83 For a detailed account of the topography of the painting, there attributed to Joseph Nickolls, see John Cloake, 'A View of Richmond Hill in the late 1740s', *Richmond History*, 2004, no. 25, pp. 16–23.

84 Whitley, *Thomas Gainsborough*, p. 252.

85 *The Morning Herald*, 20 October 1785. See also John Hayes, 'Gainsborough's "Richmond Water-walk", *The Burlington Magazine*, vol. 111, no. 790, January 1969, pp. 28–31.

86 Whitley, *Thomas Gainsborough*, p. 251.

87 John Thomas Hill was the only child of that name baptized in Richmond parish church during the relevant period. He was the son of George and Elizabeth Hill.

88 Hill was admitted to Christ's Hospital on 2 September 1790. *Christ's Hospital Presentation Papers*, MS.12, 818A, 61, Guildhall Library, London. See also G.W. Fulcher, *Life of Thomas Gainsborough, R.A.*, London 1856, p. 132.

89 Whitley, *Thomas Gainsborough*, p. 305; John Hayes, *The Letters of Thomas Gainsborough*, p. 170.

90 Whitley, *Thomas Gainsborough*, p. 309.

91 Cloake, 'Thomas Gainsborough's House at Richmond', p. 24.

92 Cloake, 'Thomas Gainsborough's House at Richmond', p. 25.

93 Plate 1 from 'A Series of Picturesque Views of Noblemen's & Gentlemans's seats: with historical and descriptive Accounts. Engraved in aquatinta by R. Havell & Son (after designs by William Havell and others)', London 1823.

94 Cooper's drawing is one of several hundred landscape sketches by the artist, preserved by his daughter in an album. The album is now in the possession of Abbott and Holder JV, London. I am grateful to Tom Edwards for drawing my attention to the album, and discussing its contents.

95 *The Mirror of Literature, Amusement, and Instruction*, Saturday, 11 February 1826, No. CLXXXII, vol. VII, p. 31. The engraving accompanied an excerpt from a poem of 1807, lauding Reynolds and the view from Richmond Hill, by the Reverend Thomas Maurice (1754–1824), an oriental scholar and Assistant Keeper at the British Museum.

96 Mary Palmer to Philip Metcalfe, 23 June 1792. Philip Metcalfe, 1735–1818. MS Papers concerning the Sir Joshua Reynolds estate. Series I: Reynolds estate correspondence, 1792–1798 (11), Houghton Library, Harvard University.

97 Advertisement in *The True Briton*, Monday 14 July 1794.

98 *The True Briton*, Saturday 12 March 1796. The property was advertised several times in *The True Briton* until 7 May 1796. See also William T. Whitley, *Artists and their Friends in England*, vol. 2, p. 197.

99 *Filkin's Notes*, Richmond Local Studies Collection, vol.6, p.725. The last mention of Reynolds by name in the Petersham Land Tax records is on 22 June 1793, where he is recorded as the 'late Sir Joshua Reynolds', and taxed as £10 2s. The Land Revenue rent book for 1794 is missing. In 1795 the proprietor and occupier is listed as Proby. 'Mr Proby' must have been Francis Henry Proby (1769–1834), since his only brother, Charles Proby, was then rector of Stanwick, Northamptonshire.

100 Dated 23 August 1803. Petersham Vestry Books, Barkas Files, *Richmond Notes*, vol.19, p.883, Richmond Local Studies Collection. See also Warren, *History of St. Peter's Church Petersham*, p. 88.

101 Crisp, *Richmond and Its Inhabitants from the Olden Time*, p.290.

102 These alterations were carried out under the ownership of Alexander Tod, who purchased the property around 1860. See also Barkas Files, vol.11, p.414, citing a report in the *St James' Budget*, 25 May 1894, Richmond Local Studies Collection.

103 'Valuable Freehold Property free of land tax and tithe, comprising a family residence occupying one of the choicest positions on the Terrace and close to Richmond Park, known as "The Wick House"', sold by A. Chancellor, Tokenhouse Yard, Bank, 14 June 1883.

104 The Ministry of Health decided in 1937 to demolish Wick House and leave the plot vacant. See *The Times*, 2 July 1937. Occupants of Wick House, cited in Richmond street directories, are: 1861–90, Alexander Tod; 1891, Hon. William Tollemache; 1898–1912, H Schilleer; 1916, Mrs L Hooker; 1922, Mrs Willder (residential hotel with house); 1923, Mrs Hocker; 1924, Mrs D'Hondt; 1929–39, Richmond Hill Hotel Annex. Information from Richmond Local Studies Collection.

105 See Cloake, 'The Wick and Wick House', 1984, p.12.

Some Artists' Studios Described in 1785

Hugh Belsey

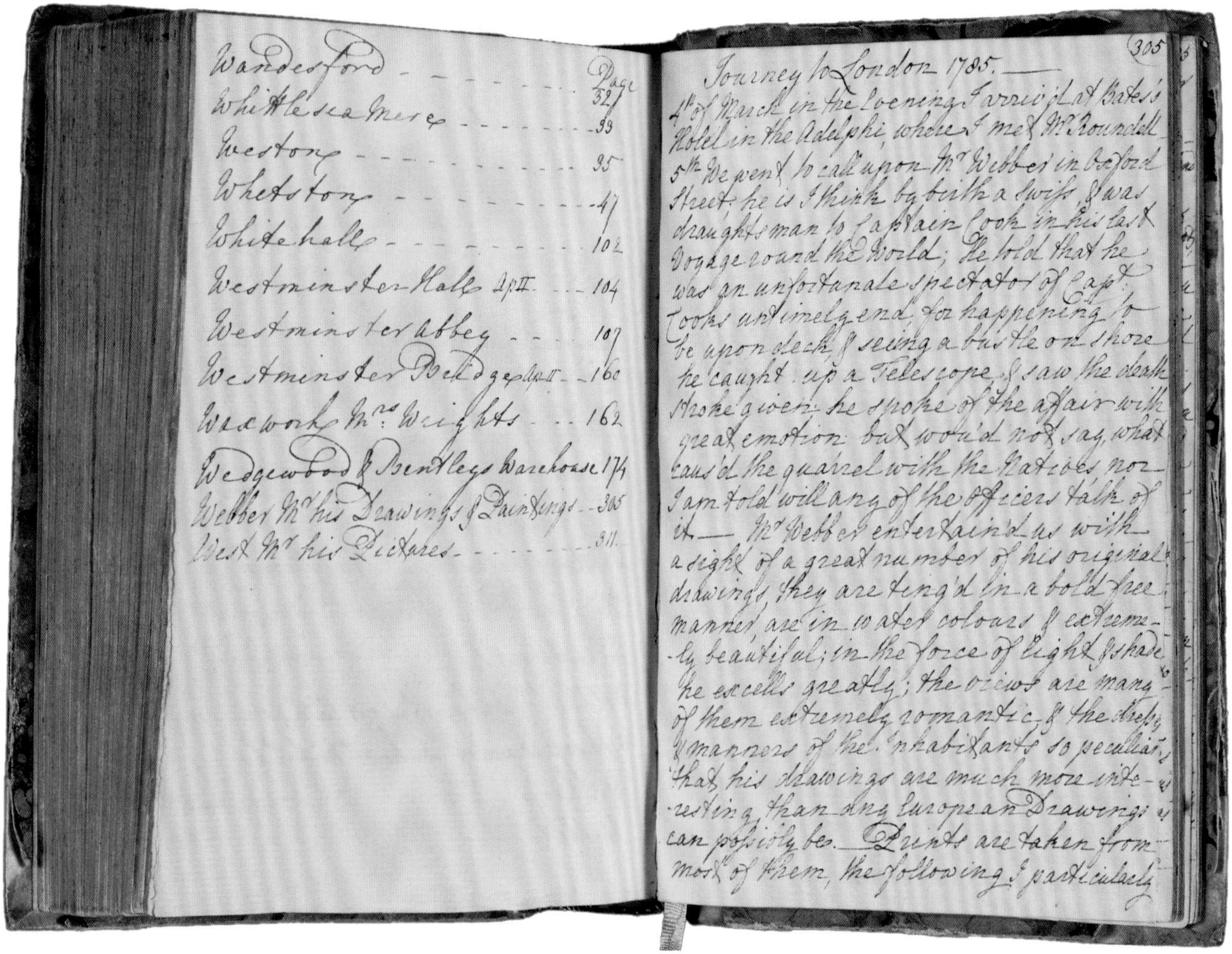

Fig. 72 Dorothy Richardson, Journal of Tours to London in 1775 and 1785, The John Rylands University Library, The University of Manchester, Eng Ms 1124, fols. 304–5

Some Artists' Studios Described in 1785

Hugh Belsey

Students of Dorothy Richardson's writings have long admired her dogged antiquarianism, her tenacious observations and her use of sources to add support to her own writing. These characteristics are outside the norm of travel writing by an eighteenth-century woman and, as a result, interest has focused on the snippets of her manuscript that hint at the author's character, her family background and her brush with academia. Although she was nervous of competing in a man's world, Miss Richardson has emerged as a bluestocking and her expansive notes include observations that go beyond the usual gambit of the travel writer.[1] Rather than focusing on the author, this essay returns to the writer's purpose and examines the content of her journals. It highlights just one aspect of her writings, a series of visits to artists' studios in London in March 1785.[2]

Dorothy Richardson (1746–1819) was born into a family of intellectuals who possessed one of the most comprehensive libraries in the north of England, she had a generous income, she was unmarried and so she was unencumbered by family responsibilities. This unusual combination of circumstances together with her innate energy and curiosity provided her with the means to travel and the desire to record the things she saw around her. A set of eight quarto notebooks are now in the John Rylands University Library in Manchester: five record tours in Yorkshire, Lancashire, the Midlands, Oxford, Bath and London; two are full of antiquarian notes; and another is a transcription of the memoirs of a seventeenth-century Royalist, Sir Henry Slingsby, 1st Bart.[3]

Dorothy Richardson was the daughter of Revd Henry Richardson (1710–78), Rector of Thornton-in-Caven, a parish midway between Burnley, Lancashire and Skipton, Yorkshire. She was the eldest in a family of two boys and two girls. Her sister Mary married Revd William Roundell, who following his father-in-law's death looked after the living until his son and namesake Henry (1754–84) finished his degree at Oxford. The elder Henry Richardson was a learned man, classically educated at both the universities of Oxford and Cambridge, with a sizeable income derived from his marriage to Mary (1717–1800), the daughter and heiress of a merchant from Oldham, Benjamin Dawson. After her father's death Dorothy moved with her mother to the village of Gargrave, five miles north of Thornton and close to Eshton Hall, the seat of her niece, Frances Mary Richardson Currer (1785–1861), the posthumous daughter of her brother Henry. Eshton Hall contained a distinguished library, some of which had been collected by Dorothy's great-grandfather, the physician and botanist Richard Richardson D.D. (1604–56) at Brierley Hall near Bradford.[4] Dorothy Richardson received an allowance from her niece that boosted her income and with such rich library resources at her disposal, she was able to prepare her trips thoroughly.[5] On the road she took extensive notes wherever she went and some time later transcribed her detailed descriptions into the journals preserved in Manchester. Like those of William Gilpin, whose works she studied, the manuscript journals were circulated to selected members of her family and to friends.[6] In later life she developed her antiquarian interests, studied botany and created a garden where one visitor was amazed by 'the beauty and rarity of its flowers'. She died in 1819.[7]

In many respects Richardson's journals are typical of the genre. They describe the varied landscape through which she travelled, the local antiquities, the ancient architecture, its historical associations and the contents of the grander country houses she visited. Reflecting the concerns of the late eighteenth century, she records with pride manufacturing and contemporary architecture. What is remarkable, as noted already, is the analytical detail she employs and her patience in peppering her writings with quotations from the relevant literature.

Although the majority of her trips were in the north of England, Dorothy Richardson occasionally ventured south and in 1770 she made a tour to Bath and then returned to Yorkshire via Oxford.[8] In the journals Bath only attracts the briefest mention and a thorough account of her experiences is written in the back

Fig. 73 Paul Sandby, *Demolition of Old Somerset House*, *c*.1776, watercolour, 21.6 x 24.1 cm, Museum of London

of a copy of *The New Bath Guide* that she had no doubt bought in the city. These endnotes include descriptions of the studios of Thomas Gainsborough and William Hoare of Bath that have been published elsewhere.[9] One of the journals now in Manchester is dedicated to two visits to London, the first in the summer of 1775 and, squashed into the back of the volume, an account of a subsequent tour to the capital in March 1785 (fig.72).

On 26 June 1775 Dorothy Richardson left Leeds with her Richardson aunt and uncle and a Mr Worthington and his son and daughter. Two days later they arrived at lodgings owned by a Mrs Renauld 'in Old Bond Street the back part looking on to Burlington Gardens'.[10] The tour is not recorded chronologically; instead it is given a geographical slant and focuses on the arrangement and growth of the city around a series of squares, and details most of the architectural and antiquarian sights. It begins with descriptions of the Adelphi, mentions Old Somerset House 'being in a very ruinous condition ... [which] they are beginning to pull ... down & propose upon the ground to build public offices' (fol.52; fig.73) and refers to major buildings along Strand, Whitehall and The Mall. Richardson's party was admitted to Devonshire House and the journal provides detailed descriptions of the rooms and their contents (fols.61–82) and on 19 July, immediately before the party returned to Yorkshire, they gained rare permission to tour Buckingham House (fols.83–101). Although not permitted to take notes, Richardson's memory served her well and she was able to supply descriptions of each room. She was particularly impressed by the Raphael cartoons in the saloon which were shown hanging above modern history pieces by Benjamin West.

Apart from her visits to Devonshire House and Buckingham House there were two other opportunities for her to list pictures. During a hurried visit to the picture dealer Gerard van der Gucht (1696/7–1776) in Brook Street she mentions stock attributed to Reni, Correggio, Claude and Lely (fols.114–15) and she draws up a similar list when she visited the Foundling Hospital (fols.126–33). The trip was balanced by visits to Mrs Wright's waxworks off Pall Mall (fols.162–67) and to the British Museum where Richardson was guided round the collection by Dr Daniel Charles Solander, the assistant librarian, who showed the party 'the greatest civility' over two days (fols.178–252).[11]

Dorothy Richardson's interest in manufacture did not pall in London and she records visits to another Mrs Wright, an embroiderer, who was making a particularly elaborate set of bed hangings for the Queen (fols.170–73). She also went to Wedgwood and Bentley's showrooms in Greek Street where she saw a variety of wares though, in comparison with the vases in the British Museum, she felt that Wedgwood 'cannot come up to the ancients, in lightness, or fineness of Metal' (fols.174–77). The trip concluded with pleasurable excursions to Kew, Richmond, Ranelagh and a crowded Vauxhall Gardens (fols.256–304). The party returned to Brierley immediately after their visit to Buckingham House on 19 July.

Ten years later Dorothy Richardson visited London again but the second tour had a sharper focus. She visited a number of museums, similar in character to her visit to Mrs Wright's waxworks in 1775. Sir Ashton Lever's museum in Leicester House was an eclectic group of natural history specimens, antiquities and anthropological exhibits where the eye was 'so bewilder'd, that it is almost impossible to know where to fix' and she was beguiled 'by the beauty & gaiety with which you are surrounded' (fols.320–21). Like the British Museum, which she had described in great detail during her 1775 trip, the collection had recently acquired exhibits from Captain Cook's ill-fated expeditions (fols.328–29). Her visit to Dr William Hunter's museum was compromised by the appearance of some of the

Fig. 74 Valentine Green and Francis Jukes after Frederick George Byron, *A Representation of Mr Lunardi's Balloon, as Exhibited in the Pantheon*, 1784, engraving/aquatint, 41 x 54 cm, The British Museum

Keeper's friends and she wrote that she 'had not the courage to take out my pocket Book to make minutes'; and, as a female, she was not inclined to look at some of the more extreme anatomical exhibits on display, so instead she wrote about the coin collection of Matthew Duane purchased by Hunter in 1776 (fols.336–38).[12]

Richardson was as attuned to architecture as she had been during her earlier visit and she described important public buildings that had only recently been completed. She admired the Pantheon in Oxford Street and visited it several times (fols.314–18). She writes that it 'was begun in 1772 … and is very striking even when it is empty; fill'd with company it must be infinitely grander' (fol.315). She was so impressed by the construction that she made a sketch plan of the building (fol.314) and during one of her visits she happened to meet the architect, James Wyatt, who was surprised by her analytical curiosity and helped her record the details (fols.317–18). During her time in London the Pantheon was used to exhibit Vincenzo Lunardi's balloon (fig.74) which had been taken on its maiden flight the previous autumn. Unsurprisingly it fascinated her and she enjoyed discussing its merits with its creator (fols.318–19).

The other building of merit was William Chambers' new Somerset House. Having noted the demolition of the Old Somerset House in 1775, Richardson was obviously attracted by the 'magnificent New Buildings' that by 1785 were not entirely fitted out though they were complete enough for her to provide an architectural analysis of the exterior (fols.332–33). The Royal Academy had moved into the north wing facing Strand and, like her earlier descriptions of both Devonshire House and Buckingham House, she wrote about each of the rooms and listed its contents.[13] Having toured the first floor Richardson's party, 'Ascending a second flight of steps, reach'd the Exhibition Room, which is very large & high; & lighted round the cov'd part of the Ceiling'. She added 'as there were no Pictures in it, the Exhibition not being begun this year, it look'd most dreary; A large rais'd Chair & a great number of Benches stood upon the Floor, lectures being read here to the Students, every Monday night' (fols.335–36).

Although Richardson's party included the usual sites, museums and public buildings as she had done before, her second trip to London had a different emphasis. She chose the time of year carefully and, rather than join the crush at the Royal Academy exhibition which opened in late April, she travelled to London a month or so earlier when artists' studios would be full of potential exhibits and gossip was full of plans for the exhibition.[14]

Richardson already knew the form as she had visited the studios of Gainsborough and William Hoare in Bath in 1770, and it is perhaps surprising that artists' 'shew' rooms had not been part of her London agenda in 1775. It seems probable that in London visits to artists' studios were restricted to those who intended to sit for their portraits and that people who intended to do little else but view the works on display were less welcome. However, the popularity of Copley's exhibition of *The Death of the Earl of Chatham* in May 1781 (which attracted more visitors than the Royal Academy's exhibition), while regarded as unwelcome competition, not only demonstrated that entrance fees were a useful addition to an artist's income but also showed that the public had an appetite for displays other than those at the Royal Academy. As well as following Copley's initiative, the opening up of studios was perhaps a measured response to the Academy's expansion, engendered by its move to new and grander premises; and, as Gainsborough had expressed in his vocal defection from the Academy in 1784, a stand against the institution's attempt to smother the individual. It became a growing trend for artists to display their work during the Academy's exhibition and within the space of three years the press were reporting the changing fashion. On 4 May 1787 the *Morning Herald* reported, 'At no period do we remember so many Exhibitions at one time as are now open. In every street, the word Exhibition, in great letters, admittance one shilling, strikes the eye – and at every exhibition we see company.'

In the previous September a German visitor to London, Sophie v. la Roche, recorded her trip in a conversational journal that replaced Richardson's intellectual rigour with more theatre, music and other social activity. With the curiosity of a foreign eye she built up a description of the city by examining the famous historic sites, visiting museums and making excursions to Windsor, Kew and Greenwich. Interestingly, she was also visiting artists' studios and on the morning of 13 September 1786 she saw the 'shew' rooms of Reynolds, Gainsborough, West, Stuart and the engraver Valentine Green.[15] She also took the opportunity to visit the workshops of the sculptors John Bacon and Joseph Nollekens and, as well as seeing Joseph Boydell's printshop, she visited Francesco Bartolozzi in his studio in Fulham.[16] Lacking Richardson's interest in detail, La Roche's descriptions are tantalising rather than informative and seem to reflect the conversations she had in each studio. The great merit of Richardson's account is her ability to appreciate the significance of what she saw, so her descriptions can usually be linked to known paintings and those that are unidentifiable provide reliable evidence of lost works. Such thorough comment about the public face of artist's studios has not been published elsewhere and Dorothy Richardson's observations provide a series of snapshots that no doubt mirror the unrecorded experiences of many other visitors.[17]

Richardson must have followed Captain Cook's expeditions to the South Seas with interest as her descriptions of the artefacts displayed in the British Museum and Lever's Museum are particularly animated. Given this concern it is hardly surprising that amongst her priorities in London was a visit to John Webber's studio. It must have been an extra bonus that she met him and was able to discuss his part in the last expedition (fig.75). Her choice of other artists is less surprising. She toured the main 'shew' rooms of the most successful portraitists – Gainsborough, Reynolds and Romney – and also visited the main practitioners of history painting, Copley and West. Nonetheless, beside her positive comments about Gainsborough's landscape painting, she appears to have lacked interest in

Fig. 75 John Webber, *James Cook*, 1776, oil on canvas in feigned oval, 44 x 35.4 cm, National Portrait Gallery, London

the work of his competitors in landscape. She failed to visit Paul Sandby at 4 St George's Row, Bayswater or Philip de Loutherbourg at Lisle Street. It is also interesting that the sculptor John Bacon, who was living at 17 Newman Street a few doors away from Benjamin West, was also overlooked.

Each description of a studio provides striking contrasts as well as new historical evidence. Whereas Webber's arrangements for viewing his studio seem informal, by comparison Gainsborough's appears rather impersonal. Her report of Reynolds's reputation as a skilled child portraitist is unexpected, and the large number of works displayed in Romney's studio reflects his considerable industry. Her observations on the number of paintings that were returned to various studios to be reworked, shipped elsewhere, or had been left in the studio by sitters for a lengthy time is also of considerable interest, as are the marked differences between the studios of portraitists and history painters. There were relatively few works displayed in Copley's studio, perhaps reflecting his preference for exhibiting a single history piece for a fee, but West appears to display a number of paintings that had been in his studio for some time. Having been exposed on her earlier travels to the work of Thomas Gainsborough in Bath and Benjamin West at Buckingham House, it is of interest to gauge the changes in her opinion of their work. She presumably referred back to her earlier tour journals and reminded herself that in 1775 at Buckingham House she had written of West: 'having heard him complimented with the name of the American Raphael', her 'expectations were much rais'd for I had never seen any of his works; but must own myself greatly disappointed. – his colouring is glaring, his composition in general too crouded & I think he never enough particularizes the principal Figure except in the Death of General Wolf ' (fols.93–94). In the light of these comments it is perhaps surprising that she chose to look at his work again but by 1785 her opinion had changed, no doubt in part influenced by the conversation she had with the artist himself. And, despite the various selling techniques employed by different artists, to this northern lady traveller it was the professionalism of Boydell's print gallery that proved most impressive – clearly a shop that exploited every aspect of salesmanship.

Richardson's studio visits provide interesting details about individual paintings and it is worth highlighting three fragments of information that expand, enhance or confirm our knowledge of late eighteenth-century art. She must have been following a recommendation to visit the miniaturist Dorman (or Dolman as she records), as he can hardly have enjoyed a reputation beyond London's artistic inner circle, and her comments expand our understanding of his work. Her description of Gainsborough's portrait of Mrs Sheridan reflects the length of gestation of this complex work. And her mention of the portrait of the Duchess of Rutland in Romney's studio confirms an important addition to the artist's canon of works.

Richardson's journals prove to be a rich source of information, for architectural historians and, with their detailed descriptions of paintings in collections up and down the country, for those with an interest in collecting. But it is in her 1785 London journal, a transcription of which follows, that we get a vivid sense of the workplaces occupied by some of the most celebrated artists working in London in the late eighteenth century.

A Journal containing notes taken by Dorothy Richardson of visits to London
in June/July 1775 and March 1785
(John Rylands University Library, Manchester Eng MSS 1124, fols.305–39).

[fol.305; Friday] 4th of March [1785] in the Evening I arriv'd at Bates's Hotel in the Adelphi, where I met Mr Roundell[18]

[Saturday] 5th We went to call upon Mr Webber in Oxford Street; he is I think by birth a Swiss, & was draughtsman to Captain Cook in his last Voyage round the World;[19] He told that he was an unfortunate spectator of Capt. Cooks untimely end, for happening to be upon deck, & seeing a bustle on shore he caught up a Telescope, & saw the death stroke given; he spoke of the affair with great emotion; but wou'd not say, what caus'd the quarrel with the Natives, nor I am told will any of the officers talk of it — Mr Webber entertain'd us with a sight of a great number of his original drawings, they are ting'd in a bold free manner, are in water colours & extremely beautiful; in the force of light & shade he excells greatly; the views are many of them extremely romantic, & the dresses & manners of the inhabitants so peculiar that his drawings are much more interesting than any European Drawings as can possibly be. — Prints are taken from most of them, the following I particularly [fol.306] recollect; The War Boat of Otaheite. — A Boat rising on the Sea.[20] — The Morie when a dead body lies in state; a bundle of white linnen at the feet, appears a mourner in the most elegant attitude, but this Mr Webber said was accidental.[21] — A Woman of Kamscatsci.[22] — A Winter Sledge drawn by Dogs.[23] — Inside of a Summer Hut at Kamscatsci,[24] Inside of a Winter Hut.[25] — A Dancing Girl of Otaheiti, a most elegant figure.[26] — An Oil painting of a woman of Otaheite ½ length & large as life, with white flowers for earrings; tho her complexion is copper colour, she is extremely handsome & graceful (fig.76).[27] — three Oil Landscapes, one of them a view in China, another in Otaheite, with a Hut, & a plantation of Cabbage Trees.[28]   —   Mr Webber excels equally in Oil, & in watercolours —

Fig. 76 John Webber, *Portrait of Puadua, Daughter of Oreo, Chief of Ulaietea*, signed and dated 1785, oil on canvas, 144.3 x 92.7 cm, Private collection

[Monday] 7th March we had a sight of Mr Gainsboroughs Pictures in [Schomberg House, 80] Pall Mall. — Mr Gainsboroughs forte is Landscape, in which I believe he stands unrival'd, we saw three very large & beautiful ones, & a small one with a View of St James's Park, with many very picturesque figures.[29] — Portraits, Mrs Sheridan sat upon a bank, with a French Dog at her feet the face beautiful & expressive the Landscape part, a River & Cascade.[30] — The Duke & Dutchess of

Fig. 77 Thomas Gainsborough,
*Edward and William
Thomkinson, c.*1784, oil on
canvas, 211.8 x 152.1 cm,
Taft Museum of Art,
Cincinnati, Ohio

Cumberland full lengths, unfinish'd.[31] — [fol.307] Mrs Siddons ½ length in blue
& white stripd drapery, a fox muff upon her lap, & a black spanish Hat with
feathers; her features not handsome, but very expressive.[32] — Mr. Tomkinson's
Son & Nephew full length (fig.77),[33] The Three eldest Princesses, two standing, &
one sat they look handsome chearful, fat Women.[34] — Mr Gainsborough's
Portraits are colour'd with great force but I think his pencil rather too rough for
the face of a beautiful Woman; in Men he excels. —

Fig. 78 Joshua Reynolds, *Jane,*
Countess of Harrington, with her
Sons the Viscount Petersham and
the Honorable Lincoln Stanhope,
1784–87, oil on canvas, 143 x 113cm,
Yale University Art Gallery

We next went to Sr Joshua Reynolds's in [47] Leicester Fields; his paintings are in
a large Room lighted from the top. The following I recollect Genl. Fawcet full length
in Regimentals;[35] Lady Dashwood with a Child in her arms, which she appears
going to kiss, a Kitcat highly finish'd, & extremely beautiful.[36] Mr Chas Fox ¾ a
good likeness.[37] — Mr Thos Wharton ¾ the Laureat.[38] — Omiah full length, in a
white dress, I believe Turkish, as it did not appear the dress of his Country.[39] —
Lady Harrington & two of her Children ½ length (fig.78).[40] — The Dutchess of
Devonshire ¾.[41] A Scotch Lord full length, the Head only finish'd, with a highland
Bonnet & Feathers finely executed.[42] Count LeLippe[43] — The Duke of Hamilton
& his Dutchess on Horseback.[44] — The Dutchess of Devonshire full length. Lord
Spencer Do[45] — Lord Bute & Chas Jenkinson full lengths in their hands, the

Articles of the Peace of 1773. — This Picture was some years at the Queen's Palace, but the King has now given it to Ld Mount Stewart.[46] — A Sleeping Venus & Cupid in the stile of Titian, this is call'd Sr Joshua's Masterpiece, & is indeed a wonderful Picture[47] —   I was disappointed with his Portraits; I have been Told he has particular pleasure in taking Children, & in those I think he most excels —

[fol.308] From Leicester Fields we bent our way to St. James's Street, & took a view of Mr Dolmans miniature Pictures. He paints both in miniature, & wash full lengths, as well as Heads; the colouring beautiful & delicate, his prices from 7 to 15 Guineas. I recollect The Dowager Lady Albemarle, a very old woman. & Col. Tarlton ½ length in his Cap & regimentals with the Head of his favourite White Horse, this is a most animated Picture.[48] — . . .

Being joined by Mr Roundell, our next excursion was to Mr Boydell's in Cheapside. He is the greatest Print dealer, I believe in Europe, & has already rais'd a large fortune, & encouraged by him, the art of engraving has within this few years arriv'd at great perfection. — At the very top of the House we were shewn into a very large long Gallery, the wall entirely cover'd with drawings in Gilt frames, they are chiefly in Black & white chalk but some few coloured. These drawings are I believe chiefly taken from pictures, & are those the prints are engraved from. — At the farther end of the Gallery is a square Room lighted from the top, & separated from the Gallery by a Glass Door, here are hung the most valuable drawings, very elegantly fram'd and many pictures — The Portraits of the Painters are capital — Sr Joshua Reynolds Kitcat, in black. — Mr West Kitcat. — the others I have forgot.[49] — Opposite to the Door hung a prodigious large & Elegant Gilt Frame; the top adorn'd with military trophies & laurel, in the center of the top an Oval [fol.310] Portrait of Mr Copley, at one end a portrait of Mr Boydels Nephew, at the other Mr Miller the engraver. This Frame belongs to Mr Copleys celebrated painting of the death of Major Pearson, & we were greatly disappointed to find it empty, the picture being taken out to have a drawing made from it (fig.79).[50] — In this Room were also a large old Picture of Shipping & It[s] companion the Destruction of the Gun Boats at Gibraltar. — A Drawing of the last window of New College Chapel Oxford fram'd exactly like the

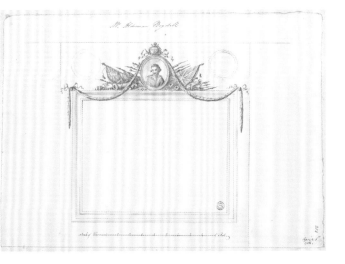

Fig. 79 Robert Adam, *Design for the Frame of The Death of Major Peirson by John Singleton Copley*, dated 'April th' 1784, Watercolour, 54.2 x 38.4 cm, Sir John Soane's Museum

Window, the design by Sr Joshua Reynolds; the bottom row of Figures are Prudence, Justice, Faith Hope & Charity.[51] — Miniature Oil Copies of Mr Wests Hanibal. The Death of General Wolf. Departure of Regulas. — & Mark Anthony haranguing over the Body of Cæsar.[52] —

[fol.311] From the British Museum we proceeded to Mr West's in [14] Newman Street Oxford Road. And were conducted down a long Gallery furnish'd with drawings into a large square Room lighted from the Roof & fill'd with paintings. Over the Chimney two very fine figures which the Servant calld Harriett & Joseph.[53] — The Transfiguration, with Isaiah on one side and Jeremiah on the other.[54] — The Last Supper very large.[55] — The Ascension likewise very large.[56] — Christ Healing the sick.[57] — Elisha raising the Widow's child.[58] — Belshazzar with the Writing upon the Wall.[59] — Prince Octavius in the Clouds, & an Angel conducting Prince Alfred to him; two Boy Angels above, below Windsor in a thick gloom; this is a most charming picture, & belongs to the Queen, it was sent to have some trifling alterations.[60] — The Cave of Despair with many figures.[61] — Portrait of Mr West in an Oval.[62] — Five Indian Chiefs who were in England.[63] — A Prince who fell in love with his step Mother.[64] — The destruction of the Gun Boats at Gibraltar[65] — Two Beautiful Female Figures & many others[66] — The Door into an inner Room being left a little open, Mr Webber who was with Mr West heard

Fig. 80   Benjamin West, *A View in Windsor Forest in Windsor Great Park*, 1785, oil on canvas, 152.4 x 215.3 cm, The Royal Collection

our voices, came to us, & introduc'd us into Mr Wests Painting Room. Here we saw a very large Landscape with a view of Windsor Forest in the Foreground a Hut & a wood cutters Family with Pigs &c, 2d distance the King hunting; & in the background Windsor Castle (fig.80).[67] — Mr West was painting a very large Picture for the King's Chapel there, the Subject St Peter preaching, the audience large; a harsh featur'd Man was sat by the [fol.312] fire almost smother'd with wollen drapery from whom Mr West was painting one of the figures[68] Mr West has lost the Bricky hue he gave his pictures some years ago; the colouring is now rich and mellow & the drawing delightful.[69] This room is also lighted from the top. . . . He is a tall thin Man not handsome, but has a most penetrating look. — We next went to Mr Romneys in Cavendish Square a passage fill'd with pictures leads into a room lighted from the top, in which the principal Pictures are plac'd. — The following I particularly remember. — Serina (from Haleys triumph of temper) sitting in white, so beautiful & expressive, that I cou'd scarcely persuade,

Fig. 81 George Romney, *Portrait of Edward Wortley Montagu (1713–76)*, 1775, oil on canvas, 141 x 108 cm, Sheffield Galleries and Museums

myself it was [fol.313] not real life.[70] — Serina reclin'd on a Couch equally pleasing.[71] — a Bacchanti with a Dog.[72] — The Dutchess of Rutland sitting in black full length,[73] Wortley Montagu in a Turkish dress & Black Beard ½ length, taken at Venice (fig.81).[74] — Mr Cumberland the author ½ length.[75] Sr William Hamilton Do.[76] Mr Christian full length with a Horse. — Mrs Christian Do in white, a very pretty woman; the background to her picture is a view of her House upon the Island on Windermere.[77] — St Cecilia full length[78] Lord Thurlow Do,[79] Mr Charles Yorke's daughter in a Hat ¾ very beautiful.[80] — The Duke of Marlborough full length,[81] Admiral Rowley ¾[82] Mrs Robinson (the celebrated

Fig. 82   George Romney, *Portrait of Emma Hamilton in a Straw Hat*, c.1785, oil on canvas, 76.2 x 63.5 cm, Huntington Library and Art Gallery, San Marino, California

Perdita) ¾ in an ugly cap, a Black Cloak & Muff, & I think by no means handsome.[83] Mrs Thornhill ¾ very handsome.[84] — Mr Edward Burke Do.[85] Miss Gunning Do.[86] Mr Charles Greville Do[87] A Lady in a Black Hat tied under her chin & a white Handkerchief, the Hat throws a beautiful shade upon the face (fig.82).[88] — Mr Romney is a most pleasing Painter, & I think his delicate pencil wou'd make any woman handsome All his portraits have wonderful Grace. —

From Cavendish square we proceeded to Mr Copleys in [25] George Street Hanover square. Here we pass'd thro' a passage with Pictures into a Room lighted from the top. — And were immediately struck with a most noble picture of Lord Chatham fainting in the House of Lords, the innumerable Heads are finely group'd & most of

Fig. 83 John Singleton Copley,
The Copley Family, 1776/1777, oil
on canvas, 184.1 x 229.2 cm,
National Gallery of Art,
Washington

them portraits; the attitudes & expression in the countenances of his children [fol.314] who surround him are admirable; a very particular account of this celebrated Picture is in print.[89] Brook Watson bathing in the Harbour of the Havannah & seiz'd by a Shark, which bit off his Leg; a Boat behind, with Men rescuing him this is a fine picture.[90] — Mr Copley, his Wife, two children & her Father Mr Clark, rather in miniature (fig.83).[91] — Mr Laurence the American sitting[92] Do. Lord & Lady Westcote & their Daughter[93] Do. Mr Pennant playing with a Dormouse very fine.[94] — Mr & Mrs Islip rather Miniature.[95] — Mr Copleys colouring it [*sic*, is] rich, & his grouping Extremely fine as a History painter he has infinite merit. — …

[fol.339] We left London [Tuesday] 15th of March

It is with great pleasure that I write this note for Brian Allen. I am most grateful for the valued support and encouragement he has given me during his time at the Paul Mellon Centre. I should also like to thank those that have helped me with this article: John Hodgson, Keeper of Manuscripts at the John Rylands University Library, Joanna Cobb, and Alex Kidson who kindly made many corrections and improvements to my notes on the paintings in Romney's studio.

1   Marcia Pointon, *Strategies for Showing: Women, Possession and Representation in English Visual Culture 1665–1800*, Oxford 1997, pp.89–130. For an alternative approach see Zoë Kinsley, 'Considering the manuscript travelogue: the journals of Dorothy Richardson (1761–1801)', *Prose Studies*, vol.26 (3), December 2003, pp.414–31. Richardson's journals are compared with the patterns of other female travel writing in Zoë Kinsley, *Women Writing the Home Tour, 1682–1812*, Aldershot 2008.

2   A similar approach to the present author is taken by Karen Lynch in 'Taking Great Notice: Dorothy Richardson's Account of Ornamental Buildings on the Boynton Estate, East Riding of Yorkshire', *The Follies Journal*, vol.7, Winter 2007, pp.1–22. A section of Richardson's description of West's studio (fols.311–12) is transcribed in Kit Wedd, Lucy Peltz and Cathy Ross, *Creative Quarters: The Art World in London 1700–2000*, exh. cat. Museum of London 2001, p.70.

3   The travel journals in the John Rylands University Library (hereafter abbreviated as JRUL) are Eng MSS 1122 West Riding of Yorkshire, Lancashire, Derbyshire and Nottinghamshire (1761–75); Eng MSS 1123 Oxford and Bath (1770); Eng MSS 1124 London (1775, 1785); Eng MSS 1125 North Riding of Yorkshire, Lancashire (1779); Eng MSS 1126 East Riding of Yorkshire (1801–2). The antiquarian notes are JRUL, Eng MSS 1127, 1128 and the memoirs of Slingsby are JRUL, Eng MSS 1129.

4   Information about the Richardson family appears in Dorothy Richardson's only known publication dated 23 December 1815 in J. Nichols, *Illustrations of the Literary History of the Eighteenth Century . . .*, 6 vols., London 1817–31, vol.1, pp.225–52.

5   Her interest in books was active. It is worth noting that during her tour to London in 1785 Richardson visits a bookseller, a Mr Edwards of Pall Mall, examines his stock and goes with him to the preview of the auction of books and manuscripts from Mr Askew's library (JRUL, Eng MSS 1124, fols.308–9).

6   This relationship is examined in Zoë Kinsley, 'Dorothy Richardson's Manuscript Travel Journals (1761–1801) and the Possibilities of Picturesque Aesthetics', *The Review of English Studies*, vol.56, 2005, pp.611–31.

7   The visitor was Richardson's great nephew Roundell Palmer, 1st Earl of Selborne who described the gardens of Gargrave in his *Memorials*, 4 vols., London 1896–98, vol.1, p.49. The best biographical synopsis of Richardson's life is in Lynch, 'Taking Great Notice', pp.1–2.

8   JRUL, Eng MSS 1123, fol.65.

9   *The New Bath Guide* was published annually. The edition used by Richardson was published by R. Cruttwell in 1770 and in May 1987 the volume was presented to Gainsborough's House, Sudbury (1987.003). For a transcription of a section of the text see Hugh Belsey, 'A Visit to the Studios of Gainsborough and Hoare', *Burlington Magazine*, vol.129, February 1987, pp.107–9 and for the subsequent history of the volume see Hugh Belsey, *Gainsborough at Gainsborough's House*, exhibition catalogue, Agnew's, London 2002, pp.104–5, no.51 repr. col. This was not the only occasion Richardson added a manuscript account to a published guide. During her visit to London in July 1775 she wrote notes on the Tower of London 'with the printed account of it' and her 'remarks upon Westminster Abbey' were similarly added to a printed pamphlet about the building (JRUL, Eng MSS 1124, fols.134, 161).

10 JRUL, Eng MSS 1124 fols.1, 49.

11 Daniel Charles Solander (1733–82). Richardson revisited the museum in 1785 when she 'greatly regretted' the death of Solander as he had given her 'the utmost attention, & . . . seem'd to have particular pleasure in communicating knowledge to those who shew'd the least Curiosity'. In 1785 she was shown round by Joseph Planta (1744–1827) who 'was either very ignorant, or extremely inattentive for he woud scarce answer a question we asked him; & hurried us thro' the rooms as fast as possible' (fol.310). See D. M. Wilson, *The British Museum: a history*, London 2002, pp.42, 56, 389, 391.

12 Pointon, *Strategies for Showing*, pp.98–100. See also Helen McCormack, 'Housing the Collection: The Great Windmill Street Anatomy Theatre and Museum' in *'My Highest pleasures': William Hunter's Art Collection*, ed. Peter Black, Glasgow and London 2007, pp.101–16. See also the description in Sophie v. La Roche, *Sophie in London 1786*, translated by Clare Williams, London 1933, pp.111–15.

13 A description of the rooms in 1780 appears in *A Candid Review* 1780, pp.10–11. This pamphlet was printed to mark the move to Somerset House.

14 For a study of eighteenth-century artists' studios see Giles Walkley, *Artists' Houses in London 1764–1914*, London 1994, pp.1–28.

15 La Roche, *Sophie in London 1786*, pp.151–54.

16 La Roche, *Sophie in London 1786*, pp.230–34, 237–39, 243–45.

17 Pointon quotes Richardson's description of West's studio to illustrate a literary point about the manuscript. She also transcribes details concerning Captain Cook's death and the personnel at the British Museum (*Strategies for Showing*, pp.109, 110).

18 Dorothy Richardson's brother-in-law, William Roundell, was married to her sister Mary. Richardson had seen the newly built Adelphi in 1775 and she probably chose to stay there for its central location with views up and down the river. 'The Royal Terrace commands one of the most striking views that can be imagin'd; The River immediately below, as great breath, with innumerable boats upon it of different sizes: Southwark upon the opposite shore with a range of distant Hills beyond; the first objects up the river, are Westminster Abbey; & almost opposite on the Surrey side, tho' rather higher the Arch-Bishop of Canterbury's Palace at Lambeth, an old brick Building. Next is Westminster Bridge . . . Black Friars Bridge is lately built under the direction of Milnes [William Mylne (1734–90)] the architect . . . the next object is the Monument, & below that as far as the eye will carry the Tower almost lost in smoke' (JRUL, Eng MSS 1124, fols.51–52).

19 On 10 March Richardson and her companion were shown round the British Museum by Joseph Planta (see note 11 above). There she found items given by Cook, 'all ticketed by Mr Webber' which she recorded as an addendum to her earlier notes made when she visited the museum in 1775 (fols.253–54).

20 Several drawings and watercolours of boats are published by Rüdiger Joppien and Bernard Smith, *The Art of Captain Cook's Voyages*, 3 vols., New Haven and London 1988, but none can be associated with Richardson's description.

21 Richardson may have mis-recorded the title. Webber formulated the title, 'A Chief Lying in State, Matavi Otahaite', for his soft-ground etching in 1789. The watercolour is in the State Library of New South Wales, Sydney (Dixson collection DG 28). See Joppien and Smith, *The Art of Captain Cook's Voyages*, vol.3, catalogue pp.352–35, nos.3.94, 3.95A repr.

22 A pencil drawing by Webber is in the National Library of Australia, Canberra (Rex Nan Kivell collection NK 52/F) and it was made into a print in 1784. See Joppien and Smith, *The Art of Captain Cook's Voyages*, vol.3, catalogue p.574, nos.3.350, 3.350A repr.

23 A drawing in pen and wash dated 1779 is in the National Library of Australia, Canberra (Rex Nan Kivell collection NK 52/C) and was made into a print in 1784. See Joppien and Smith, *The Art of Captain Cook's Voyages*, vol.3, text p.134, pl.161, catalogue pp.562–63, nos.3.336, 3.336A repr.

24 Webber's drawing, recorded in the collection of Francis P. Farquhar, does not appear to have been engraved. See Joppien and Smith, *The Art of Captain Cook's Voyages*, vol.3, text p.133, pl.160 catalogue pp.585, no.3.363 repr.

25 Webber's drawing in the National Library of Australia, Canberra was engraved in 1784. See Joppien and Smith, *The Art of Captain Cook's Voyages*, vol.3, text p.133, pl.159 col., catalogue p.559, nos.3.333, 3.333A repr.

26 The drawing is in the State Library of New South Wales, Sydney (Dixson collection, Pe 216) and was published in an engraving dated 1784. See Joppien and Smith, *The Art of Captain Cook's Voyages*, vol.3, text p.58, pl.66 col., catalogue p.361, nos.3.104, 3.104A repr.

27 The portrait is known in three different versions: National Maritime Museum (L.36-6), National Library of Australia, Canberra (Rex Nan Kivell collection NK 5192) and third, signed and dated 1785, appeared at Christie's 2 December 2008 (27) repr. col. It seems likely that this version was the one seen by Richardson and the one shown at the Royal Academy in 1785 (392). See Joppien and Smith, *The Art of Captain Cook's Voyages*, vol.3, text p.68, pl.79 col., catalogue pp.402–3, nos.3.149–51 repr.

28 The landscapes are probably the *View in Macao near the Canton River* of 1784 (National Maritime Museum, Greenwich), *A View of Otahaite Peha* of 1783 (Art Gallery of New South Wales, Sydney) and the *View at Cracatoa* of 1784 (National Maritime Museum, Greenwich) See Joppien and Smith, *The Art of Captain Cook's Voyages*, vol.3, text p.141, pl.170 col., catalogue pp.346, 591, 614, nos.3.87, 3.372, 3.410 repr.

29 *The Mall*, now in the Frick Collection, New York, is first recorded in November 1783 and remained with the artist until his posthumous studio sale in 1792 (John Hayes, *The Landscape Paintings of Thomas Gainsborough*, London 1982, pp.516–20 repr.). It seems likely that the large landscape given by the artist's daughters to the Royal Academy in 1799 was amongst those that Richardson saw in the studio (Hayes, *op. cit.*, pp.502–5 repr.). Her impression of Gainsborough's landscapes remained unchanged. In 1770 she wrote that Gainsborough 'excells most in Landscapes' and opined that they were 'very fine' (Belsey, 'A Visit to the Studios of Gainsborough and Hoare', p.109).

30 Richardson mistook the identity. The full-length portrait she describes is of Mary 'Perdita' Robinson now in the Wallace Collection (E.K. Waterhouse, *Gainsborough*, London 1958, p.87 (579), pl.238). The portrait of Mrs Sheridan now in the National Gallery of Art, Washington DC (1937.1.92; John Hayes, *British Paintings of the Sixteenth through Nineteenth Centuries: National Gallery of Art, Washington*, Cambridge 1992, pp.103–6 repr. col.) may have been exhibited at Schomberg House at the time of her visit and this may explain her confusion.

31 Royal Collection. Both portraits were left unfinished and were only sold after the artist's death. Both canvases were subsequently cut down (Oliver Millar, *Pictures in the Royal Collection: Later Georgian Pictures*, 2 vols, London and New York 1969, p.39, nos.795, 796, pls.65, 69).

32 National Gallery, London (683). See Judy Egerton, *National Gallery Catalogues: The British School*, London 1998, pp.114–19 repr. col.

33 The sitters are William (b. 1772), seated, the son of Edward Tomkinson (b. 1743) and his cousin, Edward (1773–1819), standing, the son of Henry Tomkinson (1741–1822). The portrait may have been commissioned by the sitter's grandfather, James Tomkinson (1711–94) and it is now in the Taft Museum, Cincinnati (1931.412).

34 The portraits were originally full length and the canvas was cut down about 1840; the original composition is recorded in Gainsborough Dupont's mezzotint published on 2 September 1793. The fragmentary canvas remains in the Royal Collection at Windsor Castle (Millar, *Pictures in the Royal Collection*, p.40, no.798, fig.8, pls.66–68).

35 London, National Portrait Gallery (5515). The portrait's uneasy composition can be explained as the canvas was cut at the bottom and the right hand side (David Mannings, *Sir Joshua Reynolds: A Complete Catalogue of his Paintings*, New Haven and London 2000, 2 vols., p.185, no.599, fig.1423).

36 Pew Fine Arts Center, Grove City College, Pennsylvania (Mannings, *Sir Joshua Reynolds*, p.160, no.481, fig.1428).

37 Perhaps the painting now at Holkham or one of the copies made from it (Mannings, *Sir Joshua Reynolds*, pp.202–3, no.674, fig.1380).

38 Thomas Warton, Professor of Poetry at Oxford, now at Trinity College, Oxford (146; Mannings, *Sir Joshua Reynolds*, p.463, no.1838, fig.1441).

39 Exhibited at the Royal Academy in 1776 (236) and shown in Reynolds' studio until the artist's posthumous sale in 1796. Private collection on loan to the National Gallery of Ireland, Dublin (Mannings, *Sir Joshua Reynolds*, p.357, no.1363, pl.101, fig.1191).

40 Yale University Art Gallery, New Haven (Mannings, *Sir Joshua Reynolds*, p.432, no.1696, fig.1452).

41 Probably the portrait at Chatsworth (527) that remained unfinished. This is the only record that suggests it was cut down from a three-quarter length (Mannings, *Sir Joshua Reynolds*, p.124, no.328, fig.1342).

42 Presumably the portrait of John Murray, 4th Earl of Dunmore which remained in the artist's studio until after the artist's death. There is no other evidence to suggest that the drapery was unfinished in 1785 (Mannings, *Sir Joshua Reynolds*, p.347, no.1316, pl.61, fig.834).

43 Perhaps the portrait of Frederick William Ernest, Count of Schaumburg-Lippe painted between 1764 and 1767 that is now in the Royal Collection (Mannings, *Sir Joshua Reynolds*, p.308, no.1132, pl.57, fig.820; Millar, *Pictures in the Royal Collection*, p.105, no.1027, pl.92).

44 The portrait, now destroyed, was painted in 1779 but remained in the artist's studio until after Reynolds' death (Mannings, *Sir Joshua Reynolds*, p.235, no.809, pl.1304).

45 The portraits of Georgiana, Duchess of Devonshire and John Spencer, brother and sister, were exhibited together in 1776 but the bill of £315 for the two portraits was only settled on 8 December 1783 and both canvases appear to have remained in the artist's studio for some time (Mannings, *Sir Joshua Reynolds*, pp.124, 426–27, nos. 327, 1675, pls.76, 77, figs.1166, 1128). Both portraits were at Althorp until the portrait of the Duchess was sold. It is now in the Huntington Art Collections, San Marino (25.20; Robyn Asleson and Shelley M. Bennett, *British Paintings at the Huntington*, New Haven and London 2001, pp.336–41 repr. col.).

46 The portrait was originally painted in 1763. The correspondent in the *Morning Herald* (Wednesday, 30 March 1785) explains why it had returned to Reynolds' studio: 'The portraits of Lord *Bute*, and his confidential secretary Charles *Jenkinson* in conference, which were painted for his Majesty by Sir Joshua Reynolds, about twenty-five years since, have lately been transferred from *Royal possession* to Lord Mountstewart. Sir *Joshua* has this amiable *principal* and *agent* now in his study, to furbish up, by means of the *cosmetics* of his *palette*, that they may be fit to be seen.' Presumably the flesh tones had faded and Reynolds had been asked to revitalize the sitters' complexions. Richardson and the account in the newspaper misinterpreted the event recorded in the portrait: it shows Bute handing over the premiership to his secretary, Jenkinson, in readiness for his successor (Mannings, *Sir Joshua Reynolds*, p.518, no.1722, fig.741). The circumstances of the gift are given by W. T. Whitley, *Artists and their Friends in England 1700-1799*, 2 vols., London and Boston 1928, vol.1, pp.253-54.

47 Probably the *Cimon and Iphigenia* in the Royal Collection that was not exhibited until 1789 (Mannings, *Sir Joshua Reynolds*, p.518, no.2045, pl.128, fig.1603; Millar, *Pictures in the Royal Collection*, pp.106–7, no.1030, pl.103).

48 Perhaps Dorman about whom nothing is recorded except that he exhibited a miniature 'Diana and her nymphs' at the Society of Artists in 1768 (274). At the time he was living at the Feathers, Clare Market, Lincoln's Inn Fields. The two miniatures seen by Richardson appear to be copies after Reynolds, one of his portrait of Lady Albemarle of 1760 and a detail, perhaps not a slavish copy, of Sir Banastre Tarleton of 1782 (both National Gallery: 1259 and 5985; Mannings, *Sir Joshua Reynolds*, p.287, 439–40, nos.1035, 1733, pls.29, 116, figs.427, 1400).

49 The portrait of Reynolds is in the National Gallery of Art, Washington DC (1942.8.21) and that of Benjamin West in the National Portrait Gallery, London (349). They come from a group of fifteen portraits of artists and engravers commissioned by Joseph Boydell from Gilbert Stuart in the summer of 1782 which was completed in 1786 (Carrie Rebora Barratt and Ellen G. Miles, *Gilbert Stuart*, exhibition catalogue, Metropolitan Museum of Art, New York and the National Portrait Gallery, Washington DC 2004–6, pp.48–62).

50 The painting (Tate: N00733), together with his *Death of Lord Chatham* and *Watson and the Shark*, had been exhibited at 28 Haymarket to great acclaim in May 1784 and *The Death of Peirson* was installed in Cheapside by 6 August in the frame commissioned from Robert Adam. Two finished designs and one sketch incorporating portraits by Gilbert Stuart of the painter, copyist and engraver, are preserved in the Sir John Soane's Museum. The oval portrait in the centre was of Copley (National Portrait Gallery, London: 2143), the roundel in the top left corner was of Josiah Boydell, John Boydell's nephew and partner, and the corresponding portrait on the right, who Richardson misidentified as Miller, showed James Heath, the engraver of the painting, a print that was only published in 1796. The portraits of Boydell and Heath are now in Rhode Island School of Design Museum of Art, Providence and the Wadsworth Atheneum, Hartford, Connecticut respectively. Boydell also commissioned frames for the portraits of other artists and engravers that he had commissioned from Gilbert Stuart and another drawing in the Soane Museum suggests an arrangement for the hang at Cheapside (Eileen Harris, 'Robert Adam's Ornaments for Alderman Boydell's Picture Frames', *Furniture History Society*, vol.26, 1990, pp.93–96; Emily B. Neff, *John Singleton Copley in England*, exhibition catalogue, National Gallery of Art, Washington DC and Museum of Fine Arts, Houston 1995–96, pp.67–70 repr.).

51 Richard Earlom produced a stipple engraving with etching, presumably using this drawing, that was published by Boydell on 1 September 1785 (J.E. Wessely, *Richard Earlom, Verzeichniss seiner Radirungen und Schabkunstblätter*, Hamburg 1886, no. 6). Reynolds paintings of the Virtues – Boydell published individual prints of them in 1781 and 1782 – are in a private collection (Mannings, *Sir Joshua Reynolds*, pp.548–51, nos.2113–21, figs.1662–68).

52 These copies are omitted from von Erffa and Staley but each was published as a print by Boydell. The *Hannibal* of 1770 (see von Erffa and Staley, *The Paintings of Benjamin West*, New Haven and London, 1986, pp.170–71, no.17 repr.), in the Royal Collection, was engraved in mezzotint by Valentine Green and published on 1 November 1773; *The Death of Wolfe* of 1770 (see von Erffa and Staley, *op.cit.*, pp.170–71, no.17 repr.), now in the National Gallery of Canada, was engraved by William Wollett and published on 1 January 1776; the *Regulus* of 1769 (see von Erffa and Staley, *op. cit.*, 1986, pp.48, 49, 168, no.10 repr. col), in the Royal Collection, was engraved in mezzotint by Green and published on 14 November 1771; *Mark Antony*, exhibited in 1775 (see von Erffa and Staley, *op. cit.*, 1986, pp.177–78, no.28 repr.), now lost, was engraved in mezzotint by Green and published on 17 September 1781. Several of the original paintings had been seen by Richardson at Buckingham House in 1775 (JRUL, Eng MSS 1124, fol.94).

53 Unrecorded, perhaps the picture, now lost, engraved in mezzotint as *Virtue and Innocence* by Valentine Green and published on 21 December 1781 (von Erffa and Staley, *The Paintings of Benjamin West*, pp.405, no.425 repr.).

54 West is not known to have painted a Transfiguration but the painting Richardson saw may have been the *Resurrection* now in the Philadelphia Museum of Art before it was reworked (von Erffa and Staley, *The Paintings of Benjamin West*, pp.366–67, no.365 repr.).

55 The canvas, now in Tate, London (N00132), had presumably returned from St George's Chapel, Windsor – it had been seen in West's room at Windsor by Samuel Shoemaker in October 1784 – for the 1785 Royal Academy exhibition (von Erffa and Staley, *The Paintings of Benjamin West*, pp.352–53, no.344 repr.).

56 Now in the Bob Jones University Museum and Gallery, Greenville, South Carolina (von Erffa and Staley, *The Paintings of Benjamin West*, 1986, pp.374–76, no.380 repr.).

57 The canvas, now destroyed, that was painted in 1780–81 for St George's Chapel, Windsor and was subsequently at St Etheldreda's, Fulham (von Erffa and Staley, *The Paintings of Benjamin West*, pp.345–46, no.334 repr.).

58 The painting remained in West's studio until his death and eventually entered the Philadelphia Museum of Art (1899–1106). It was exhibited at the Royal Academy in 1775 (334) and was subsequently retouched (von Erffa and Staley, *The Paintings of Benjamin West*, pp.313–14, no.278 repr.).

59 Like the previous canvas *Daniel Interpreting to Belshazzar the Writing on the Wall* was painted in 1775, exhibited Royal Academy 1776 (317), and remained in the artist's studio until his death. It is now in Berkshire Museum, Pittsfield, Massachusetts (von Erffa and Staley, *The Paintings of Benjamin West*, pp.84, 319–20, no.288 repr. col.).

60 The portrait had been commissioned immediately after the death of Prince Octavius on 3 May 1783 and the 'trifling alterations' noted by Richardson had not been previously recorded. The canvas remains in the Royal Collection at Windsor (von Erffa and Staley, *The Paintings of Benjamin West*, pp.480–81, no.575 repr.; Millar, *Pictures in the Royal Collection*, p.130, pl.116).

61 There are two recorded versions of the subject, perhaps both dating from 1772, one in the Yale Center for British Art, New Haven (B1977.14.113) and the other in the Art Complex Museum, Duxbury, Massachusetts. Both paintings remained in the artist's studio until his death (von Erffa and Staley, *The Paintings of Benjamin West*, pp.82, 278–79, nos.220, 221 repr.).

62 The portrait of *c*.1776, now in Baltimore Museum of Art (1981.73), remained in the artist's studio until West's death (von Erffa and Staley, *The Paintings of Benjamin West*, pp.vi, 451–52, no.526 repr. col.).

63 Unidentified. A study of an Indian warrior taking leave of his wife of *c*.1760 may give some indication of the appearance of the canvas (von Erffa and Staley, *The Paintings of Benjamin West*, pp.420–21, no.452 repr.).

64 Unidentified.

65 The Corporation of London approached both West and Copley to produce the huge painting of *The Siege of Gibraltar*, and Copley secured the commission in 1783. The finished painting is now in the Guildhall Art Gallery, London and a smaller replica of the composition is in Tate (N00787). The painting seen by Richardson may have been the study West prepared for the Corporation that is not otherwise known.

66 Perhaps the *Fidelia and Speranza* of 1776; the early provenance of the canvas is unrecorded (Putnam Foundation Collection, Timken Art Museum, San Diego).

67 The landscape was exhibited at the Royal Academy 1785 (31) and it is still in the Royal Collection (von Erffa and Staley, *The Paintings of Benjamin West*, pp.429–31, no.473 repr.; Millar, *Pictures in the Royal Collection*, pp.135–36, no.1168, pl.118).

68 The painting was intended for St George's, Windsor but does not appear to have been delivered. The character 'smother'd in woollen drapery' is perhaps the figure in profile in the lower right of the composition (von Erffa and Staley, *The Paintings of Benjamin West*, pp.378–79, no.385 repr.). The canvas is now in the Bob Jones University Museum and Gallery, Greenville, South Carolina.

69 Richardson had been disappointed by the pictures that she had seen at Buckingham House in 1775: 'having heard him complimented with the name of the American Raphael, my expectations were much rais'd for I had never seen any of his works; but must own myself greatly disappointed. – his colouring is glaring, his composition in general too crouded & I think he never enough particularizes the principal Figure except in the Death of General Wolf ' (Eng MSS 1124, fols.93–94). The pictures she saw and described in detail were the *Death of Wolfe*, his *Regulus's return to Carthage* and his *Hannibal brought by his father Hamilar to the altar of Jupiter* (see note 52 above).

70 Probably the full-face study of *Serena Reading* now in a private collection (Alex Kidson, *George Romney (1734–1802)*, exhibition catalogue, Walker Art Gallery, Liverpool and National Portrait Gallery, London 2002, p.166, fig.50).

71 The portrait is probably the canvas showing Serena in profile now in the Harris Museum and Art Gallery, Preston (Kidson, *George Romney*, pp.165–66, cat.no. 97 repr. col.). There is an off chance that the writer missed the literary allusion and that she is describing the reclining figure of *Serena in the Boat of Apathy* (Christie's 17 June 1966, lot 84, see Kidson, *George Romney*, p.166, fig.49).

72 Romney had presumably repainted the dog at Charles Greville's request before the portrait was sent to his uncle, Sir William Hamilton, in Naples. The canvas is now in a private collection (Ian Jenkins and Kim Sloan, *Vases and Volcanoes: Sir William Hamilton and his Collection*, exhibition catalogue, British Museum, London 1996, pp.267–69 repr. col.).

73 Mary Isabella, Duchess to the 4th Duke of Rutland. Perhaps the original was destroyed in the fire at Belvoir Castle in 1816 and the full length that appeared in the Butcher sale, Christie's 16 March 1844, lot 107, was only a copy. From Richardson's description it can be assumed that the portrait was related to the half length of 1780 painted for the sitter's mother, the Dowager Duchess of Beaufort (Humphry Ward and William Roberts, *Romney: catalogue raisonné*, 2 vols., privately printed, London and New York 1904, vol.2, p.138).

74 Romney painted Wortley Montagu's portrait in March/April 1775 and made a replica of it before selling the original to the Earl of Warwick. The replica, recorded by Richardson, remained in Romney's studio until it was sold to John Milnes in 1788. It is now in the collection of the Sheffield Museum and Galleries Trust (Kidson, *George Romney*, pp.101–2).

75 Richard Cumberland (1732–1811), the portrait is now in the National Portrait Gallery, London. As Kidson says (*George Romney*, pp.91–92, cat.no.37 repr. col.) the dating of the work is problematic and it was only sent as a gift to the sitter's son in September 1787.

76 A head and shoulders portrait dating from 1783–84 now in the National Gallery of Art, Washington DC (1970.17.133; Hayes, *British Paintings of the Sixteenth through Nineteenth Centuries*, pp.239–240; Jenkins and Sloan, *Vases and Volcanoes*, pp.118–19, no.8 repr. col.; Ward and Roberts, *Romney*, vol.2, pp.69–70).

77 This pair of full-length portraits of John Christian (d.1829) and his second wife Isabella, the daughter and heir of Henry Curwen, were commissioned to mark their wedding on 5 October 1782. £100 was paid at the outset of the commission on 5 September 1782 and the balance of £200 was paid on 10 September 1785. They were then sent off to Workington Hall, Cumbria with two portraits of Serena (perhaps those mentioned by Richardson) on 7 August 1788 (Ward and Roberts, *Romney*, vol.2, p.29). The ownership of the portraits is split: the portrait of Mr Christian is in a private collection in Essex and the portrait of his wife was recorded in *c*.1995 in a private collection in Johannesburg.

78 The portrait of Emma Hamilton as St Cecilia (Swinton Castle Estates). The portrait was purchased by Montague Burgoyne for £73.5s in October/November 1785 (Ward and Roberts, *Romney*, vol.2, p.185).

79 According to Ward and Roberts Romney painted three full-length portraits of Lord Thurlow (Ward and Roberts, *Romney*, vol.2, p.157). Sittings began in November 1780 and continued until 10 January 1784. One of the canvases formerly in the collections of the Duke of Sutherland was engraved in 1800 by W. Dickinson; the portrait of 1782, formerly in the collection of Lord Kenyon, is now in the House of Lords (David Cross, *A Striking Likeness: The Life of George Romney*, Aldershot 2000, pl. XV col.) but the third, last recorded at Bonhams Knightsbridge 26 October 2011, lot 246 repr. col. (Jennifer C. Watson, *George Romney in Canada*, exhibition catalogue, Kitchener-Waterloo Art Gallery 1985, no.30, pl. V repr.), is no longer considered autograph.

80 Caroline Yorke (b.1765) was the daughter of Hon. Charles Yorke (d.1770). She sat to Romney in 1783 and the portrait, now in a private collection, was paid for in 1787.

81 George, 4th Duke of Marlborough (1738–1817). The portrait is a pendant with one of his wife and both were delivered on 30 July 1787 (Ward and Roberts, *Romney*, vol.2, p.100; Cross, *A Striking Likeness*, p.91, pl.19). Both canvases are still at Blenheim.

82 Admiral Sir Joshua Rowley (*c*.1730–90). Ward and Roberts (*Romney*, vol.2, p.136) records three versions of this portrait. The prime version appears to be that which was commissioned by Rowley's steward, Mr Lewis, and two half payments of £10. 10s were made on 5 August 1784 and 2 June 1792. One of the other versions is now in the National Maritime Museum, Greenwich (BHC2985).

83 The portrait, painted in 1780–81, remained with the artist until his death. It is now in the Wallace Collection, London (P37). See Ward and Roberts, *Romney*, vol.2, pp.132–33.

84 Mrs Thomas Thornhill, née Eleanor Lynne (1761–97). Presumably the portrait painted to commemorate the sitter's marriage in 1779. The canvas is illustrated in Sedelmeyer 1895, no.94. See Ward and Roberts, *Romney*, vol.2, p.156.

85 Edmund Burke (1730–97). Perhaps the replica painted for Oliver Farrer which was paid for July 1786 (Ward and Roberts, *Romney*, vol.2, p.22).

86 Barbara Gunning, later Mrs Alexander Ross (d. 1844), a daughter of Sir Robert Gunning, who sat for her portrait in the early 1780s. Payment for the portrait and one of her sister was made in August 1786 (Ward and Roberts, *Romney*, vol.2, p.68; Watson, *George Romney in Canada*, pp.60–61, fig.14).

87 A head and shoulders portrait of Greville was sent with three other portraits by Romney to his uncle in Naples. The portrait is last recorded at Sotheby's on 28 November 1973, lot 54 repr. col. (Ward and Roberts, *Romney*, vol.2, pp.65–66; Jenkins and Sloan, *Vases and Volcanoes*, pp.16, 174–75, fig.4).

88 The portrait of Emma Hamilton in a straw hat was sold to Charles Greville and is now in the Huntington Art Collections (Asleson and Bennett, *British Paintings at the Huntington*, pp.424–27 repr. col.).

89 The canvas in Tate collection (N00100) lent to the National Portrait Gallery, London dates from 1779–80 (Jules David Prown, *John Singleton Copley* vol. I *In America 1738–1774* vol. II *In England 1774–1815*, Cambridge, Massachusetts 1966, vol.2, pp.275–91). The print by Bartolozzi was eagerly awaited in 1785 and after much delay it was finally published in 1791 (Prown, *op. cit.*, 1966, vol.2, pp.289–90).

90 The version seen in Copley's studio is now in the Museum of Fine Arts, Boston (89.481) and dates from 1778 (Prown, *John Singleton Copley*, vol.2, pp.270–74). Both this canvas and the *Death of Chatham* had been exhibited in Haymarket the previous year (see note 50 above).

91 The group portrait (National Gallery of Art, Washington DC) was painted in 1776–77 soon after the artist's return from Italy in October 1775. It was painted to celebrate Copley's reunion with his wife Susanna and their children. His father-in-law, Richard Clarke, joined the family later in 1775 (Prown, *John*

Singleton Copley, vol.2, pp.262–63, fig.344; Ellen G. Miles, *American Paintings of the Eighteenth Century: National Gallery of Art, Washington*, New York and Oxford 1995, pp.46–54). By 'in miniature', a term Richardson also uses for the Izard group portrait, the author must have meant finely painted.

92 Presumably the portrait of Henry Laurens (National Portrait Gallery, Washington DC) painted in 1782 (Prown, *John Singleton Copley*, vol.2, p.293, fig.416).

93 Sir William Lyttleton, 7th Bart (1724–1808), created Baron Westcote in the Irish Peerage in 1766 and Baron Lyttleton in the peerage of Great Britain in 1794. The group portrait, formerly at Hagley Hall, Worcestershire, was destroyed by fire in 1925 and a number of preparatory drawings are recorded. Prown dates the portrait 1785–88 (Prown, *John Singleton Copley*, vol.2, p.320, pl.478–82).

94 Richardson must have misheard the name of the sitter. She presumably refers to the portrait of Henry Pelham, Copley's half-brother, of 1765 (Museum of Fine Arts, Boston: 1978.297) that had been sent from America to show at the Society of Artists exhibition in 1766 and 1768. The canvas appears to have remained in England in the care of Captain R. G. Bruce

who had transported the portrait to London. It was returned to Copley after he settled in London in 1775 and, presumably, the artist gave it to the sitter soon after he arrived in London to lodge with the Copleys in the following year. The small animal in the portrait, which Richardson described as a dormouse, is a flying squirrel, a native of the eastern seaboard and a popular pet that appears in a number of Copley's early portraits (Prown, *John Singleton Copley*, vol.1, fig.163, vol.2, p.265, note 15; Carrie Rebora et al., *John Singleton Copley in America*, exhibition catalogue, Museum of Fine Arts, Boston, The Metropolitan Museum of Art, New York, Museum of Fine Arts, Houston and Milwaukee Art Museum 1995–96, pp.215–19, no.25 repr. col.).

95 Probably Richardson mistook the name, and the portrait is of Mr and Mrs Ralph Izard, now in the Museum of Fine Arts, Boston (03.1033). It was painted in Italy in the spring of 1775 and remained in Copley's studio until the 1790s (Prown, *John Singleton Copley*, vol.2, p.352, fig.342; Maurie D. McInnis and Angela Mack, *In Pursuit of Refinement: Charlestonians Abroad 1740–1860*, exhibition catalogue, Gibbes Art Gallery, Charleston 1998, pp.116–19, no.12 repr. col.). For the term 'in miniature' see note 91 above.

THE FORGOTTEN 'ATHENIAN'
Drawings by Willey Reveley

Frank Salmon

Fig. 84   ?Willey Reveley, *'The Temple of the Sun and Moon [Venus and Rome] as seen from the Amphitheatre [Colosseum]',* Rome, c.1784-85, watercolour and graphite, 48.9 x 37.5 cm, Yale Center for British Art, Paul Mellon Collection

THE FORGOTTEN 'ATHENIAN'
Drawings by Willey Reveley

Frank Salmon

*T*he Yale Center for British Art possesses a collection of some thirty watercolours made by a British architect during a Mediterranean tour in the mid-1780s that formed part of an album acquired by Paul Mellon in 1960. These drawings had originally entered the market at a Christie's sale held in May 1801, following their creator's sudden death on 6 July 1799 'after a few hours' illness, in the prime of life, at his house in Oxford Street', a stone's throw from the present-day Paul Mellon Centre's Bloomsbury base in London.[1] The Christie's catalogue foregrounds the drawings in particular on its title page amongst the designs, books and other effects of the late architect, describing them as the works of

> that distinguished Artist and Civil Engineer, The Athenian Reveley, Dec[eased], consisting of His Well-Known Topographical views and Drawings of the celebrated Remains of Antiquity, which were accurately measured and delineated by him during a Journey through Italy, Egypt, and Greece, in the Years 1785 and 1786; the Whole accompanied with numerous Remarks in M:S: by himself, which render them highly Curious and Valuable to the Lover of the Arts and Classic Antiquity.[2]

Even allowing for the auctioneer's hyperbole, we learn from this that at the time of his death Willey Reveley was widely reputed a notable artist and 'Civil Engineer', that he was well known for his first-hand experience of classical antiquities, about which he had made numerous (and curious) remarks, and that he was the second late eighteenth-century British figure to have acquired the sobriquet 'Athenian'.

Unlike the far better known James 'Athenian' Stuart, however, the Athenian Reveley's name has left little trace during the two centuries of antiquarianism and architectural history that have followed his untimely demise in his fortieth year. Indeed, the few graphic works by Reveley listed as surviving – in the latest edition of Howard Colvin's *Biographical Dictionary of British Architects 1600–1840* – do not even include the drawings now at Yale, only two of which appear previously to have been published.[3]

It must be admitted straight away that Reveley's watercolours are not of the outstanding quality of those by his contemporaries who specialised in the medium. In the Mellon Centre's Brinsley Ford Archive there is a note by Sir Brinsley himself on Reveley's drawing of the Temple of Ceres [actually of Athena] at Paestum (now in the Victoria and Albert Museum) stating that: 'It looked very prosaic when hung next to the Dramatic Ruins of Paestum by J.R. Cozens'.[4] Reveley's claims on posterity rest less on his abilities as draughtsman and *vedutista* than they do on his singular personality and outlook on architecture and topography. Our knowledge of these characteristics is due in large part to the survival of his barely studied 'Manuscript material for [a] Dictionary of Architecture, and of a journey through Italy, Greece, Egypt etc.', a 331-folio vellum-bound volume now at the Royal Institute of British Architects.[5] This eccentric work, mostly written in neat but with numerous pastings in, is only partly an attempt at a comprehensive dictionary. More particularly it represents an attempt by Reveley to expound personal opinions he had gained during his European and Mediterranean travels. Thus the only entry under the letter 'J' is a neat copied description of the 'Journey' he made in 1785 and early 1786 from Rome to southern Italy and around the Mediterranean 'with the Rt Hon. Sir Richard Worsley Bart. as his architect & draftsman'.[6] Worsley, a member of the Society of Dilettanti since 1778, was seeking solace in antiquarian pursuits after a disastrous divorce suit of 1783. He, too, maintained a journal and also compiled a catalogue of 200 drawings connected to his itinerary, both now at the Lincolnshire Archives.[7] From these four sources, then (referred to in this essay as Reveley's 'Journey' and 'Dictionary', and Worsley's 'Journal' and 'Catalogue'), we can build up the contexts within which the drawings now at Yale were made. There is not space here to publish them all, so reproduced in this essay are only those that were made in Rome (where Reveley and Worsley met), or that can be certainly identified as belonging to the early part of their expedition, that is up to July 1785, when Reveley's Journey breaks off after the pair reached Rhodes. The greater part of Reveley's observations in Athens and Greece more generally has to be inferred from comments made elsewhere in the Dictionary, from his work in editing the third volume of James Stuart's and Nicholas Revett's *Antiquities of Athens* (published in 1794), and from Worsley's Journal and Catalogue. This material, along with Reveley's observations of things seen in Egypt and Turkey, will be left to a subsequent article.

Willey Reveley's cruelly curtailed life has left relatively few details for the modern-day architectural historian, but previous accounts that have been given contain some loose ends that are worth picking up.[8] Born in Yorkshire on 14 March 1760, he became a pupil of William Chambers in London in 1777 and a student of the Royal Academy Schools from the same year. From July 1781 to December 1782 he was an Assistant Clerk of Works at his master's Somerset House, then under construction. Chambers, who had himself studied in Italy in the early 1750s, was insistent upon the necessity of travel as the means by which British architectural students should complete their educations, and this doubtless explains why, by 1784, Reveley was to be found living at Rome. There he met Thomas Maynard Hesilrige of Hoxne Hall, Suffolk, who in turn recommended him as draughtsman to Worsley.[9] The two men set off from Rome on their expedition in February 1785, Worsley not returning until April 1787, by which time he had continued northwards from Turkey, reaching as far as St Petersburg. Reveley, however, had quarrelled with his patron – it appears early in 1786, since he was back in Italy by May of that year (the date given on the reverse of his drawing of the Temple of Ceres at Paestum). By the autumn of 1786 he was again resident in Rome.[10]

In the Eternal City in the Spring of 1788, and now resident in Piazza Mignanelli adjacent to Piazza di Spagna, Reveley became involved in one of the more sensational incidents to befall any travelling British architectural student. As Elizabeth Cooper wrote to her common-law husband, the amateur artist and collector George Cumberland, on 23 April of that year:

> There is one peece of news which I can not help telling you. Revly [h]as been found in bed with Miss James by the Father and thay whare both oblighd to run naked to his Lodgings at 11 o Clock at Night. Revly had not so much as a Shirt on for the Father had torn it quite of and poor Miss nothing but her Shift. They whare marrid the next Night by an Inglish Clirgeman hear and there is a

Subscription amongst the Ladys to by her some cloths for the Father will not give her anything and he [h]as not a shilling in the w[orld]. What will become of them god knows but it is such a long story that I can not tell you half of it.[11]

The young woman with whom Willey had been caught *in flagrante delicto* was Maria James who, after his premature death, would marry John Gisborne, move back to Italy and become intimate with Mary and Percy Bysshe Shelley, inspiring the latter to write his poetic 'Letter to Maria Gisborne' in 1820. It is to Mary Shelley, as well as to a memoir of 1832 written by Maria herself, that we owe an account of both her early life and of her years married to Reveley.[12] She had been first abandoned with her mother then effectively kidnapped by her derelict merchant father by whom, Mary Shelley reported, she was 'left to run wild as she might, and at a very early stage had gone through the romance of life'. John James had brought Maria to Rome in 1785, aged 15, where she studied painting under Angelica Kauffman prior to her liaison with Reveley. Mary Shelley does not report the exact circumstances of the shot-gun marriage, suggesting instead that James 'refused to consent to the match, only, as it would seem, as an excuse for giving his daughter no fortune'. The absence of a dowry, coupled to the fact that Reveley's father outlived him, left the couple (and the two children very soon born to them) seriously impecunious. Maria estimated that they lived in London on about £140 per annum and, as late as 1796, Reveley complained to the Committee overseeing construction of his design for All Saints' Church in Southampton that 'the delay ... in paying my bill is cruel & underserved ... & having more than £1000 due to me from various persons I have not five pounds in the house'.[13]

Reveley's relatively short career as an architect does not appear to have been a great success. The church in Southampton was probably his most important building, and he is also credited with the design of two minor country houses and gate lodges at Parham and Stourhead.[14] However, he lost major commissions for the County Infirmary at Canterbury (where he quite reasonably objected to the Building Committee's proposal to turn over his designs to a local builder for execution) as well as the new Pump Room at Bath, and the Christie's sale catalogue of his effects includes design drawings for numerous other unfulfilled projects. As has been seen above, the sale catalogue does not refer to Reveley as an architect but rather as an 'Artist' and 'Civil Engineer'. The latter title perhaps derived from the plans he had submitted to Parliament in April 1796 for wet docks on the River

Thames.[15] The former – together with the epithet 'The Athenian Reveley' –
doubtless comes from the authority on Greek antiquity he enjoyed among London
cognoscenti, acquired as a result of his European drawings and as the editor for the
third volume of *The Antiquities of Athens*, a role for which he was chosen by James
Stuart's widow after the death of William Newton, editor of the second
volume. Reveley's own obituary, appearing just five years later in *The Gentleman's
Magazine*, stated that he had 'rather an awkward way of letting loose his real
opinions; and had habituated himself to a sarcastic mode of delivering them ...
not calculated to render himself popular [and influencing] many, who were
disposed to employ him, to seek architects of more pliant and accommodating
dispositions.'[16] The directness of Reveley's speech perhaps related (if not to his
Yorkshire upbringing) then to the radical politics that he and Maria shared. As
Mary Shelley reported, Reveley

> joined the liberal side, and entered with enthusiasm into the hopes and
> expectations of political freedom, which then filled every heart to bursting.
> The consequence of these principles was to lead to his acquaintance with many
> of their popular advocates, and among them with [William] Godwin and
> [Thomas] Holcroft.[17]

Reveley also met Jeremy Bentham whilst travelling and, indeed, assisted him in
realising the Panopticon in 1791–92.[18] It might be noted, however, that Reveley's
liberal outspokenness was not coupled to any cynical exploitation of the established
or the wealthy classes, for the obituary in *The Gentleman's Magazine* also reported
that he was 'a man of strict integrity in all his dealings, and the little eccentricities
of his character had no tendency to weaken the main supporters of it.'

Professional disappointments and financial insecurity lay, however, in the
unforeseen future for Willey Reveley when, aged 24, he was brought to the
attention of Sir Richard Worsley in Rome. At the start of his own travel Journal
Worsley noted, on 11 February 1785: 'Before my departure from Rome on my
intended tour through Greece & Egypt I engaged Mr Reveley an English artist then
at Rome to accompany me, to make drawings of architecture, & the most
interesting Ruins.'[19] Of the respective accounts kept by the two men, Reveley's
Journey is the more anecdotal, frequently making references (mostly negative) to
personal circumstances such as travelling or sleeping conditions, or food. It appears

to have been transcribed much as originally written – but we should bear in mind that Reveley was probably keeping separately the detailed architectural notes on which he later depended when compiling his Dictionary. Worsley's Journal is more focused on recording antiquities and natural phenonema. Frequent references to and quotations from classical texts, not to mention the consistently neat hand, suggests that Worsley's account was not just transcribed but significantly elaborated at a later date. Indeed, Worsley's description of Lecce opens on 7 March 1785 by stating that 'I was detained until the nineteenth by Mr Reveleys being seized with an ague.'[20] Since Worsley cannot, on 7 March, have anticipated the twelve-day delay he was about to endure as a result of Reveley's indisposition, we can only conclude that the Journal, as we have it, was written up in retrospect.

Worsley's reference to Reveley's illness is one of the relatively few instances where he made specific mention of his travelling companion – and Reveley rarely mentions his patron either. Thus we get little sense of the relationship between the two men and little insight into the grounds for the breach between them that occurred, probably in Constantinople early in 1786. According to a letter in the Mellon Centre's Brinsley Ford archive by the late Lindsay Boynton,

> Reveley wrote in detail to Hesilrege concerning the terms he had made with Worsley. These letters were later forwarded to the Earl of Bradford as Worsley's trustee, and extracts made. The extracts survive, but they were intended to show Worsley's movements only, and omit all details about the arrangements and quarrel.[21]

The unspecified details of the argument are germane to the problematic issue of the provenance of the drawings now at Yale, because their history is equally mysterious. What is known for certain is that Paul Mellon purchased them (in 1960) from the New Haven dealer C.A. Stonehill, who in turn had acquired them from Maggs in London, where they had been in 1959.[22] They were in an album of 71 drawings entitled 'Views in the Levant', and recent study of this album's contents by Jonathan Yarker has established that it contained material specifically connected with Worsley's monumental publication of his collection, the two-volume *Museum Worsleyanum*, completed between 1794 and 1800.[23] Most of the Reveley drawings can be correlated with descriptions found among the 200 images listed in Worsley's 'Catalogue containing an accurate Description of the original Drawings / taken on the spot / in the Travels of the Right Honorable Sir Richard Worsley Baronet ...'.[24] However, as was stated at the start of this essay, many of the drawings at Yale also correlate with the descriptions of 116 drawings that were in Reveley's estate at the time of his death in 1799, where they are listed as 'Valuable and highly curious Views of the most celebrated Monuments of Antiquity [which] were made on the Spots by the late Mr. Reveley during his Journey through Italy, Aegypt, and Greece, in the years 1785 and 1786'.[25] Moreover, Reveley's obituary in *The Gentleman's Magazine* explicitly stated that, having parted from Worsley 'on some difference', Reveley had 'retained his own drawings, which he afterwards exhibited to his particular friends.' The Athenian must, indeed, have had many particular friends, for the writer added that his collection of drawings was 'universally known to all the lovers of art, and admirers of classic Antiquity'.[26]

There is only one conclusion that can be drawn as to why the images now at Yale have a Worsley provenance, which is that Sir Richard must have bought them back at the 1801 Christie's sale of Reveley's effects. This suggestion cannot be confirmed absolutely, but three points may be made in support of it. First, it is known that at the turn of the nineteenth century Worsley was trying to regain works of art he had collected whilst British Resident in Venice from 1793–97, lost when a ship transporting them to England was seized by a French privateer and the goods sold in Spain. News of this loss reached Worsley in early 1801, just at the time of the sale of Reveley's effects.[27] Second, Worsley's Catalogue of drawings is clearly no more contemporary with his mid-1780s travels than is his Journal in its present form. It is copied out neatly and contains both retrospective comments as well as some descriptions that correspond almost verbatim with the text of the Journal. Finally, whilst both Reveley's 116 drawings and Worsley's 200 appear broadly arranged according to their mutual travel itinerary, the sequence in Worsley's Catalogue sometimes precisely follows that of the lots in the Reveley sale. For example Lot 42 in the Reveley sale contained drawings 55 and 56 (showing respectively the door of the Temple of Bacchus on Naxos and the Church of the Panagia on Paros, figs. 95 and 96 here) and these became numbers 81 and 82 in Worsley's Catalogue.

As may be seen, then, the numbering of the drawings in the respective Worsley and Reveley lists is not the same and, to make matters still more complicated, a third set of numbers unrelated to either appear on the top left corners of some of the drawings at Yale.[28] Whilst we can be sure from the Christie's sale catalogue that Reveley had made at least 116 drawings during his travels with Worsley, the latter's Catalogue never mentions Reveley; but it does contain references to works involving the authorship of others. Number 29, for example, was a 'View of Mount Etna in Sicily taken at sea about ten miles distant March 30th 1785 … finished with many others at Rome in the latter end of the year 1787 by Il Signor Del drago [presumably the *vedutista* Antonio del Drago], when the late eruption of Mount Etna was added copied from a drawing made with accuracy on the spot'.[29] Other drawings were identified as by a Venetian artist living at Cairo, a Turk at Mecca, a Greek artist at Constantinople and two Russians (an engineer and an officer).[30] Most interesting of all, however, was the inclusion by Worsley of no fewer than 20 (or possibly 21) drawings that he apparently owned made by William Pars in 1765, when travelling as draughtsman to the Society of Dilettanti's Ionian expedition led by Dr Richard Chandler.[31]

Worsley, as has been mentioned, had become a member of the Society of Dilettanti in 1778, joining at a time when serious antiquarian enquiry among the membership seems to have gained the upper hand over more social activities. Certainly he made several references to *Ionian Antiquities* in his Catalogue of drawings. Indeed, on the very first page he included a quote from the fourth page of the preface to the first volume of that publication (1769) on the value even of fragments of Greek sculpture in giving evidence of ideas of proportion and symmetry 'at that happy period of Taste'. On the same, opening page of his Catalogue, Worsley also quoted from the eighth page of James Stuart's introduction to the first volume of *The Antiquities of Athens*: 'I have taken none of those Liberties with which painters are apt to indulge themselves, from a desire of rendering their representations of places more agreeably to the Eye & better pictures.' He then quoted from Stuart's and Revett's 1748 'Proposals' for the *Antiquities*, as given in footnote on page five of the preface to their first volume: 'the best verbal descriptions cannot be supposed to convey so adequate an Idea of the Magnificence and Elegance of Buildings, the fine form, expression, or proportion of Sculptures; the beauty and variety of a Country, or the exact scene of any celebrated action as may be formed from drawings made on the spot with diligence and fidelity by the hand of an artist.' Finally he added his own comment that 'the Figures in the several drawings are designed to give an Idea of the size without recurring to the Measures'. It is clear, then, that when preparing in Rome for his expedition to the eastern Mediterranean, Worsley was seeking a draughtsman who could be depended upon primarily for topographical accuracy. He was not concerned to make detailed measurements (as the Dilettanti's Ionian trip had been, in recruiting Revett alongside Pars), and he was not particularly concerned that the artist should be good at representing the human form (since figures were to be included principally for scale). Evidently, of the students available for hire in Rome in late 1784, Willey Reveley fitted this bill.

As has been seen, Reveley was recommended to Worsley by Thomas Maynard Hesilrige, but it is quite probable that Worsley required – and obtained – some proof of Reveley's artistic abilities prior to their departure together from Rome in February 1785. Worsley's Catalogue of travel drawings begins, in fact, with six views of Venice and one of Padua. There then follow eight views of Rome and two at Tivoli before one reaches the Arch of Trajan at Benevento, the first drawing definitely made by Reveley as he and Worsley headed south through Italy together, now to be found in the British Museum.[32] Of the eight views showing Rome, three descriptions correspond with drawings that are now at Yale.[33] These are numbers 9, 10 and 13 in the Catalogue: 'The Temple of the Sun and Moon as seen from the Amphitheatre'; 'The ancient Gate leading to Tibur, now Porta St. Lorenzo'; and 'View of the Ruins of the Temple of Minerva Medica, the Church of Santa Maria Maggiore, and the Villa Negroni' (figs. 84, 85 and 86). The authorship of these images cannot be attributed to Reveley with certainty for, whilst they embody some of the character of his draughtsmanship (for example in the handling of masonry and in the palette of figs. 84 and 85), the spikey foliage detailing and quite sophisticated *staffage* appear to be by another hand. Figure 84 also has gum applied to the surface, a technique that is not found in other drawings by Reveley (although it is possible that he could have deployed it more easily in watercolours finished in a studio in Rome than when travelling in the field). Figure 86, meanwhile, is in grey and brown wash only with ink detailing, and a grid of faint pencil lines suggests it was 'squared up' for engraving, again unlike any of Reveley's other surviving drawings.[34] As has been seen above, however, in the case of his view of Mount Etna, described by Worsley as 'finished with many others at Rome in the latter end of the year 1787 by Il Signor Del drago', Reveley was presumably not averse to collaborating with other artists and may, indeed, have done so in these instances in order to strengthen his case for Worsley's employment.

With regard to 'The ancient Gate leading to Tibur, now Porta St. Lorenzo' (fig. 85) there are no accompanying comments from either Worsley or Reveley to add

Fig. 85 ?Willey Reveley, '*The ancient Gate leading to Tibur [Tivoli], now Porta St. Lorenzo*', *Rome*, c.1784-85, watercolour over graphite on laid paper, 32.5 x 50.2cm, Yale Center for British Art, Paul Mellon Collection

to the pleasing view of the Gate from just outside the Aurelian Wall.[35] Figure 84, however, shows the surviving east apse of what is today recognised as the Temple of Venus of Rome, which was described by Reveley in the section on 'Temples' of his Dictionary:

> Temples of the Sun & Moon near the Arch of Titus at Rome: That towards the east is supposed to be the temple of the Sun & that looking westward to be that of the Moon. Palladio says that these two temples were built by T. Tatius, King of the Romans. Part of these temples now remains, the two great niches being entire & the flank walls 5 or 6 ft high. He confesses that the fronts & all the inside ornaments except those of the great nich are his own composition his

Fig. 86 ?Willey Reveley: *'View of the Ruins of the Temple of Minerva Medica, the Church of Santa Maria Maggiore, and the Villa Negroni', Rome,* c.1784-85, pen and brown ink with grey and brown wash, squared in graphite, 29 x 47 cm, Yale Center for British Art, Paul Mellon Collection

only guide being the foundations. There are square & semicircular niches alternating in the flanks of the eastern temple withinside & compartments in the head of the great nich called losenges thus [Reveley provides a sketch] all of which I saw but could not get into the other temple.[36]

It is interesting to note that in the 1780s (or 1790s, when Reveley's Dictionary was presumably compiled), Palladio's record of Roman temples as given in *I quattro libri dell'architettura* of 1570 continued to represent the point of departure for British architects, notwithstanding more recent advances in archaeological and topographical understanding in Rome. This may serve, in fact, as a useful reminder that the quasi-scientific approach to the naming and contextualising of ruins by men such as Stuart, Revett and Chandler (and also Robert Wood, author of *The Ruins of Palmyra* of 1753 and *The Ruins of Balbec* of 1757) only represented one end of the spectrum of later eighteenth-century British attitudes to antiquities. The other end, as seen in the Roman studies of Robert Adam and his circle, was fragmentary, eclectic and Picturesque. Reveley's image of the Temple of Venus and Rome is relatively faithful in its topography, much as Worsley would doubtless have wished given his expressed concern to avoid the 'liberties' taken by painters. The view is framed by one ground-level arch of the Colosseum; the unexcavated podium of the Temple is depicted as a rolling terrain of scrub and small trees; the Romanesque bell tower of S. Francesca Romana rises above the lozenge-coffered east niche. By contrast, a view made from almost exactly the same point by Charles-Louis Clérisseau for Adam (now in the Clerk of Penicuik collection) entirely removes the medieval bell tower and conventual buildings.[37] Reveley's only possible tampering, by comparison, appears to have been the removal of the unsightly retaining wall that, in Clérisseau's view, ran across the east end of the site of the Temple's podium, and it is possible that this could have been overgrown in the thirty years that elapsed between the two views having been made.

A fourth Roman view in the collection at Yale (fig. 87) is of the same type as figs. 84 and 85 – including the use of gum as in the former – and may thus represent another instance of collaboration by Reveley with a local artist. It does not, however, correspond however with any of the images described in Worsley's Catalogue, appearing to show a view taken in a south-easterly direction near the Porta Maggiore, looking along the inside of the Aurelian Wall. The inner side of the Gate itself, in its large rectangular form, appears centre left, then to the right of that the ruins of the so-called Temple of Venus and Cupid, followed by the church of the S. Croce in Gerusalemme, with its twelfth-century bell tower (the clock face in the penultimate storey) and its 1743 west façade replete with roof-line statuary. The largish house in the right foreground would seem to be the Villa Conti, to judge from Giambattista Nolli's famous plan of Rome of 1747 which corresponds quite well with this view. However, the wall that can be seen between the Porta Maggiore and the Church is harder to interpret. Possibly it could be intended to represent the Aqueduct – of Claudius, according to Nolli – that ran south-west from the Gate, or the wall of the Villa Conti and Garden of S. Croce that he shows. What is clearer is that, at the right extreme of the drawing, the

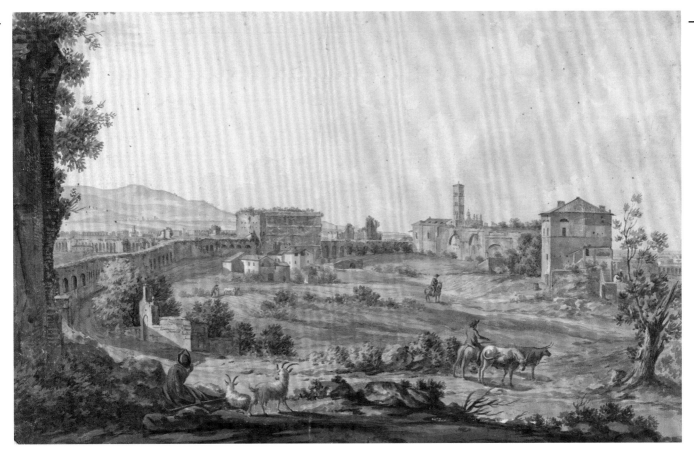

Fig. 87 ?Willey Reveley, *The Aurelian Wall, Porta Maggiore, the Temple of Venus and Cupid and the Church of S. Croce in Gerusalemme, Rome, c.1784-85*, watercolour, 31.6 x 48.7 cm, Yale Center for British Art, Paul Mellon Collection

Aurelian Wall continues in the Anfiteatro Castrense area, and that the hills seen in the distance on the left are the Tiburtine.[38]

On 12 February 1785 Worsley and Reveley left Rome to begin their expedition, following the old Via Appia south through Albano, Velletri and Terracina, and entering the Kingdom of Naples at Fundi. Their route then brought them south to Capua and Caserta, where they made an extensive study of the new royal palace designed by Luigi Vanvitelli. From there they took a diversion to the east in order to visit Benevento and study the Arch of Trajan. Then, having bypassed Naples, they proceeded south along the east side of Vesuvius to Salerno and from thence via Eboli to Paestum, where they arrived at four in the afternoon of 20 February.

Fig. 88 Willey Reveley,
'A Perspective View of the three
ancient Temples at Posidonia or
Paestum', 21-24 February 1785,
watercolour with pen and grey
ink over graphite on laid paper,
36.5 x 51.9 cm, Yale Center for
British Art, Paul Mellon
Collection

This was a signal moment in the life of Reveley – his first encounter with the ancient Greek architecture from which he would later gain his sobriquet 'The Athenian'. Moreover, as so few of his drawings made in Athens or the Greek Archipelago itself survive, his drawings of Paestum represent for us the architectural qualities that he admired in ruined Greek buildings more generally.[39]

The collection of drawings at Yale includes two made at Paestum. The first records all three temples, looking from south to north (fig. 88). In the right foreground is the west end of the Temple of Hera I, known in the eighteenth century as the 'Basilica'. A short distance beyond that stands the largest or 'Great'

Fig. 89 Willey Reveley, 'North
East View of the same Temple
[Neptune/Hera II] at Paestum
traced in a Camera obscura
February 21 1785', watercolour
over ink on board, 28.1 x 47.2 cm,
Yale Center for British Art,
Paul Mellon Collection

temple, that of Hera II – generally thought to have been dedicated to Neptune
(Poseidon) in Reveley's period. Then, in the distance one sees the outline of the
small Temple of Athena, thought to have been that of Ceres. The second Yale
drawing shows the Temple of Neptune from the north-east (fig. 89).[40] These two
views seem to correspond with numbers 19 and 21 in Worsley's Catalogue, which
in turn appear to have been numbers 4 and 9 in Reveley's sale catalogue.[41] (The
latter is described as 'taken in a camera obscura' – one of only two mentions
Reveley made of his use of this device, perhaps suggestive of its infrequency.) The
sale included a further seven views of Paestum (nine in total), while Worsley's
Catalogue shows that he owned five views overall.[42]

By 1785, when Reveley reached Paestum, the three temples were hardly as
unknown to the European architectural fraternity as they had been just thirty years

before. Visits to the site had started to become more frequent, and in England Thomas Major's *Ruins of Paestum*, based on surveys made by Italian, French and British draughtsmen, had been published in 1768. It is noteworthy, however, that Reveley – trained in the office of the arch-opponent of the rising tide of interest in Greek architecture, William Chambers – never mentions Major's account of the temples in his Journey or elsewhere in his Dictionary.[43] Instead, the book that formed the backdrop to his responses to Paestum was Padre Paolo Antonio Paoli's *Rovine della Città di Pesto detta ancora Posidonia*, published in Rome in 1784 but based on surveys made in the 1750s under the supervision of Count Felice Gazzola. Whilst Reveley may have known Paoli's book before reaching Paestum with Worsley in 1785, it was not until 1786, 'having taken it with me to Pesto on my second journey there,' that he entered into the closest of dialogues with that work.[44] Reveley made entries in his Dictionary under the letter 'P' for both 'Paestum' and, most oddly, 'Padre Paolo' (who appears between 'Pyramid' and the Monument of 'Philopappus'!).[45] He also referred to Paoli in his Journey, so that we cannot be sure from his own papers which of his observations on Paestum date from the 1785 visit as opposed to that made in 1786 (or from later still). Worsley's Journal, however, in a rare explicit mention of his travelling companion's opinions, states:

> Mr Reveley speaking of the Temples observes that the Temple of Neptune has its architrave complete but not the least appearance of drops [guttae] or a fillet, such as accompany the Doric order. Therefore he concludes that there never were any such ornaments although the order is Doric[.] He adds there is not a single block of the frieze or cornice on the ground. The Temple of Juno he says is by much the most considerable, its columns being thirty feet high ... The Temple of Diana he compares to that of Neptune but says he found it in a more perfect state.[46]

By the Temple of 'Neptune' Worsley was in fact referring to the Basilica, for it is of that notorious building, of course, that Reveley's own comments record: 'There being no ornament on the small part of the frieze remaining ... nor any fragment on the ground I am at a loss to guess whether it had Triglyphs or not,' and the plain entablature can be seen clearly at the right extremity of fig. 88.[47] Moreover, Worsley's Temple of 'Juno' (an inadvertently correct, if Romanised, identification of the Temple of Hera II) must be that of Neptune, which has the largest columns of the three at just over 29 feet. (Reveley's imprecision with the measurement can be excused as he doubtless had little surveying equipment to hand, although fig.

89 shows that a ladder perhaps twenty feet long had been procured.) Worsley also reverses the relationship between the small Temple (which he calls of 'Diana') and that of Neptune because it is the latter that was in a 'more perfect state'.[48] All this confusion notwithstanding, Sir Richard's comment on Reveley's early observations at Paestum show the architect's concern with issues of detailing in Doric architecture, such as whether the order could have been designed without triglyfs and whether triglyfs or guttae were cut out of the same stone as the frieze and architrave, or let in. Reveley's concern with precise observation of detail is further born out by the numerous errors in Paoli's visual record of the buildings that he seizes on in the Dictionary, and he even used little sketches of capitals and mouldings to illustrate his corrections.

There was, however, a larger purpose to Reveley's close and minute observations of the Paestum temples – which was nothing less than an attempt to understand the nature of early Greek Doric design, an understanding that would later play a part in an extraordinary public attack that he was to make on his former master, Chambers. By the 1780s the issue of whether the city of Paestum had been founded by the Etruscans or as a Greek colony was under heated discussion, the particular architectural dimension of this debate being the question of whether or not the Basilica was a Greek temple at all. To Paoli it was an 'Atrio Etrusco', as Reveley noted,[49] but he had read the histories of the city offered by Diodorus Siculus, Strabo and Pliny and was dismissive in his Journey of Paoli's conclusions:

> The principal information concerning Paestum as far as I have been able to understand Padre Paola's book which is written in the most elegant and abstruse Italian language is, that we know hardly any history at all concerning it. He does not prove a single fact that he asserts about its foundation by the Etruscans, his chief argument being the similitude of the architecture of the temples to Etruscan works which is preposterous as they are evidently of greek architecture & certainly built long after the foundation of the city.[50]

Later, under the 'Paestum' entry in his Dictionary, Reveley returned to this point, saying that the temples were in any case not 'erected at the foundation of the city ... nor are they all of the same age evidently.'[51]

Having subsequently travelled widely in Greece and the Archipelago, the issue raised by Paestum for Reveley was not one of the temples' Greek identity but rather one of their chronology. This marks him out in the eighteenth century as an early authority on the history of Greek architecture. He did not need to find comparative aesthetic reasons outside of architecture before accepting that these temples were designed by Greeks (as did Johann-Wilhelm Goethe when he visited Paestum in 1787), nor did he subscribe to an idealistic notion of Greek design incompatible with its rapid progress to Periclean excellence that led so many of his contemporaries, including Paoli, into historical error. In his Journey Reveley opined:

> Padre Paolo ... says if Architecture such as we call Doric had its rise in Greece why do we not see some examples of that heavy ancient style before the art was refined to the proportion of the fine greek doric (Diss. 3rd. 51) Note that there are two examples one near mount Laurium in attica & the other at Corinth. WR.[52]

The Temple at Corinth later formed the basis of chapter 7 in the third volume of Stuart's and Revett's *Antiquities of Athens* (edited by Reveley), where it is described as 'built before architecture had received the improvements it afterwards did in the time of Pericles'.[53] Worsley's Journal records that he and Reveley visited it in May 1785. Both the plan and elevation of the surviving columns and entablature (also without triglyfs) that features as plate II in the *Antiquities* and the details of the order at large (plate III) were drawn by Reveley, so he knew the ruin very well.[54] He took both this mid-sixth-century BC temple and the probably contemporary Basilica at Paestum to be representative of the early working out of the Doric formula. The mid-fifth-century BC Temple of Neptune, by contrast, which 'has the principal and most striking marks of Greek architecture', he rightly understood in relation to the refinements of the nearly coeval Parthenon. Three pages in his Dictionary were devoted to puzzling over similarities between the two monuments (for example the column diameter to height ratios) and differences (such as the unusual arrangement of fourteen columns in the flank at Paestum). Although Reveley appreciated that the Temple of Neptune had originally been covered with stucco to imitate marble, his final observation was that 'this building is now of a beautiful orange tint,' a point he succeeded in capturing well in fig. 89.[55]

It was Reveley's understanding of the origins and progress of Greek architecture that led him, when editing the third volume of *The Antiquities of Athens* in the early 1790s, to a polemical attack on his erstwhile master, Chambers. Sir William had, in 1791, produced the third edition of his *Treatise on the Decorative Part of* *Civil Architecture* (first published 1759), to the preface of which he added those condemnations of the growing trend of Greek Revivalism that had long been in his mind. In order to counter this modern practice, Chambers felt the need to criticise ancient Greek architecture and defend what he saw as the refinements introduced by the Romans and followed in the Renaissance. Never having seen a Greek building himself, Chambers was dependent for his understanding of Greek architecture on books – and especially on what Reveley referred to in his preface as the 'imperfect specimens of Le Roi' (Julien-David Le Roy's *Ruines des plus beaux monuments de la Grèce* of 1758).[56] For Reveley, who had travelled so extensively in Greece and the Archipelago and who had studied Greek buildings so intently, Chambers' attack was insupportable. He countered his former mentor's arguments on many points, in one instance using his experience of Paestum to good effect. As part of a list of supposed defects in Greek design, Chambers had focussed on 'their temples with a range of columns running in the center to support the roof; contrary to every rule, either of beauty or convenience.'[57] Reveley provided a footnote:

> Of this I believe there is but one instance in all the antiquities now remaining, which is a temple at Pesto. This edifice, by the proportions of its order appears to be of the highest antiquity. ... It can be no proof of general ignorance in the Greeks, that one temple of this kind has been built in one of their distant colonies; ... As we have no accounts in any authors of this species of temple, this most likely is the only one ever built, though Sir William finds it convenient to represent this as one only of a number of the same description.[58]

As has been suggested earlier, Reveley had probably been encouraged to travel in the Mediterranean by Chambers, who advocated the importance of direct experience of architecture from the time he drafted Royal Academy lectures in 1770 until he incorporated that advice in the third edition of his *Treatise*. Reveley could scarcely believe how completely Chambers had departed from his own principle in attempting to justify a visceral but unqualified dislike of Greek architecture and, whilst we may see his counter-arguments as another instance of the injudicious plain-speaking for which he was renowned, there is no doubt that he had the facts on his side.

Reveley's first encounter with Greek architecture at Paestum was not, however, accompanied by warm feelings towards the place itself, which he discovered 'abounds with snakes, vipers, knats & other venomous animals', or towards its hardly more civilised inhabitants, who 'will bully & might murder any person if they chose it, for it is out of the way of all justice or enquiry.'[59] Neither were he and Worsley blessed with good weather whilst there, for they were detained until 25 February and Reveley recorded that 'so much rain fell during our stay that the River Sele overflowed its banks, which rendered it impassable in the ferry boat for four of the five days we stayed there.'[60] None the less, they managed to return to Salerno and Avellino in order to cross to the east coast of Italy. The journey over the Apennines took them via Ariano (Irpino) and Bovino, running the gauntlet of banditti in the mountainous woods along the way. At Castellucio they had their first view of the distant Adriatic, and from there they proceeded to Cerignola and then to the coast at Barletta. The most notable object in this town was the colossal antique bronze statue standing against an outer bay of the Duomo, much as it does today. Reveley's small drawing of this sculpture (fig. 90), made on 2 March, is remarkably uncouth, but it is evident from his Journey account that this was its intended effect:

> In the market place is the bronze statue of Herakleus according to Swinburn but by others thought to be that of Constantine which I rather believe, as it holds a cross elevated in his right hand; in his left holds a globe. It is 17 feet 3 inches high and of the most execrable sculpture. I drew it although the cold was excessive & it snowed during the time, as well as I could, & endeavoured to give an idea of the barberous style of it. It was found in the sand near Barletta in the year 1491.[61]

From Barletta he and Worsley proceeded along the Adriatic coast to Bari and then to Brindisi, where they arrived on 6 March. The monument that captured their attention there was the pair of Roman columns near the harbour, on the top of which fires were lit to produce a bifurcatory line as a navigational guide to ships' captains. Reveley's drawing (fig. 91) not only records the columns but, uniquely among those now at Yale, presents a descriptive tablet and scale bar at its foot, as though the work were intended for engraving. Below this Reveley has written 'Taken on the spot March 7 1785' and signed it. The inscription and the text on the

Fig. 90 Willey Reveley, '*Sketch of a Colossal Statue in Bronze of the Emperor Constantine measuring seventeen feet three inches in height ... in the Publick Place at Barletta a city of Apulea*', 2 March 1785, watercolour, 21.3 x 14.9 cm, Yale Center for British Art, Paul Mellon Collection

tablet feature almost verbatim in Worsley's Catalogue, where the drawing was number 26, although Worsley did not of course mention Reveley's signature. In his Journey, Reveley described the columns in the following terms:

Two columns were erected here by Augustus Caesar, on which lights were placed to shew the entrance of the harbour. One of them still remains entire, it is of the corinthian order raised upon a pedestal & finished with a circular architrave which held the light: the capital is composed of a single row of leaves, & over it in the center of each face is a Triton & a Syren alternately & at each angle two Syrens which support the abacus[.] The whole is of cipolino marble

Fig. 91 Willey Reveley, '*The Columns of Augustus at Brundisium [Brindisi]. Lights were anciently placed on these columns to shew the Communication between the Harbours. Taken on the spot March 7 1785*', pen and black ink and watercolour, 41.6 x 27 cm, Yale Center for British Art, Paul Mellon Collection

the shaft plain & but little diminished & the base attic; at 22 feet 6 ins distant is the pedestal & the base of the other column the upper part having been thrown down by an earthquake in 1456, which destroyed the greater part of the city. The columns stand on a line so that on entering the harbour you look between them. ... Here I had a severe fit of my fever, but the next morning I went out & drew the columns; I guess them to be about 70 feet high in all.[62]

In addition to fig. 91, Reveley made a detailed study of the remarkably designed 'Capital of the column of Augustus at Brundusium drawn on the spot from the Ground', giving the dimensions of the pedestal and the distance between the pair of columns on the reverse. This survives in the volume of Reveley drawings now in Sir John Soane's Museum.[63] It is not clear, however, that his verbal description of the capital figures is entirely correct, since the pairs of figures under each corner protrusion of the abaci possess muscular male torsos (these can still be seen in the original, although now further weathered) and are more likely to be sea beasts than sirens.

Over the next few days Reveley and Worsley continued southwards, visiting Lecce and Otranto, where Reveley found that the castle 'so celebrated in Mr Walpole's novel is now a pitiful fort neither large nor strong.' This did not stop him from drawing it twice, and one version survives in the British Museum.[64] At Otranto Worsley's intention to head directly for Athens was thwarted, for he found that they were not 'able to procure a passage at this season of the year from there to Greece.'[65] Instead, on 26 March he and Reveley boarded the *San Antonio di Padua* bound south-west for Malta, initially following the southern coast of Calabria towards Sicily. The weather was bad and Reveley spent three days seasick – but he managed to put a positive spin on this, as he considered that taking no food for 72 hours had purged him finally of the fever that had dogged him since the start of the month. Spending most the time below deck also provided an unexpected *coup de théâtre* when, on 29 March, 'I came up & on a sudden saw an object so striking it had the more effect on me.'[66] This was a sublime view of Mount Etna at about 15 miles distance, covered with snow. Reveley drew the volcano then – and again on 1 April, when the *San Antonio* was in the Gulf of Catania. Both of these drawings were in the posthumous Reveley sale and were subsequently owned by Worsley, but neither are to be found at Yale.[67] Over the five days that the ship spent near the Sicilian coast, Reveley recorded making several more drawings, for which there

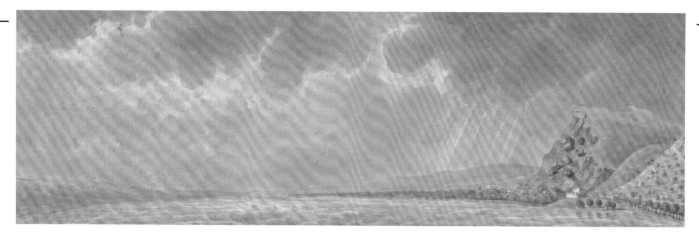

are some candidates among those now at Yale. Only one can be identified with certainty, however. This is number 27 in Worsley's Catalogue, a 'View of a Mountain near Reggio in Calabria, which was broken in the manner expressed in the drawing by the Earthquake of the fifth of February 1783, together with a part of the Straits of Messina, drawn on the spot March 29 1785' (fig. 92).[68]

The derelict state of the city of Reggio and the parlous condition of its inhabitants just two years after this major earthquake made for a sorry departure point from Italy for Worsley and Reveley as they headed south across the Mediterranean, nor could there have been more of a contrast with the tremendously impressive harbour of Malta, at which they arrived on 4 April. Quarantine restrictions prevented them from exploring on foot, but on 6 April Reveley recorded that 'Sir Rd Worsley was allowed as a particular favour to see the harbour accompanied by the Governor in his boat.'[69] Reveley made three drawings of the port, which later became numbers 19–21 in the posthumous sale of his effects and numbers 33–35 in Worsley's Catalogue. One of these is to be found at Yale (fig. 93), evidently Worsley's number 35: a 'View of the Quays, Warehouses, Health Office and the entrance of the port at Malta, taken April 10 1785'. The geography of the port of Malta is complex, but the site here is the Grand Harbour along the south side of Valetta, modern-day Quarry Wharf, looking north-east towards the open sea beyond the lighthouse at the point of Fort Ricasoli.[70] The warehouses shown by Reveley still survive, although the quays he shows now have other buildings on

Fig. 92 Willey Reveley, *'View of a Mountain near Reggio in Calabria, which was broken in the manner expressed in the drawing by the Earthquake of the fifth of February 1783, together with a part of the Straights of Messina, drawn on the spot March 29 1785'*, watercolour, 18.7 x 58.9 cm, Yale Center for British Art, Paul Mellon Collection

Fig. 93 Willey Reveley, '*View of the Quays, Warehouses, Health Office and the entrance of the port at Malta, taken April 10 1785*', watercolour with pen and grey ink on laid paper, 26.7 x 45.4 cm, Yale Center for British Art, Paul Mellon Collection

them. The gateway surmounted by a cross that one sees above, in the Lower Barracca Gardens, was replaced in 1810 by a neo-Greek portico dedicated to the first *de facto* British Governor, Sir Alexander John Ball, Bt. Reveley considered the harbour 'one of the finest in the world', noting on the west side (Valetta) – as fig. 93 shows – 'the sides of the Rock are cut down so as to form one line with the wall on the top of it. An amazing number of cannon point into the harbour; below the city is a fine quay with the health office & divisions for people in quarantine, & fine ware houses all, as well as the city, built of stone.'[71]

On 14 April, Worsley and Reveley departed from Malta on a ship called the *St. Trifon* heading for Crete, where they were to spend ten days before finally sailing for Attica.[72] A brief trip ashore at Sunium on 7 May enabled Reveley to study the

Temple of Poseidon and to update Le Roy's 1750s account of what remained standing. Then they sailed on to Piraeus, arriving late in the afternoon of 9 May. Worsley's impatience to reach Athens can be gauged from the fact that he immediately set out to walk the five miles or so to the city, leaving Reveley to follow on horseback the next morning. Unfortunately there is a month's omission in Reveley's Journey from the time of his arrival in Athens (where he was immediately impressed by the completeness of the Theseion [Hephaesteion]) until 11 June and, as has been seen, hardly any of the drawings he made in Athens can be identified.[73] As far as the men's itinerary is concerned, however, Worsley's Journal supplies the deficiency. On 16 May they set off on an expedition to the west of Athens and the Peloponnese, which took them by boat to Salamina and Eleusis, then to Megara, Corinth, Argos, Sparta, Epidauros and, by boat again, to Aegina.[74] Their first visit to Eleusis thus took place on 17 May – although Reveley only recorded a short second trip they made there together from Athens on 27 June. During the latter he drew the colossal caryatid figure which, in 1785, was semi-submerged in the ground near the fragmentary ruins of the Sanctuary of Demeter (fig. 94). Of the site and statue Reveley wrote:

> There are fragments of doric capitals lying about but not large enough to belong to the famous temple. There are also some ionic capitals of elegant design but badly worked. The fragment of the Statue of Ceres which is only the head & shoulders is now standing on the spot [crossed through, with 'near the bottom of the hill' written in the margin], the face is beat off; her hair is tied with a ribband behind & on her head is a circular Vessel like a basket elegantly carved with wheat ears & other ornaments.[75]

Reveley made further notes about Eleusis in the 'Temples' section of his Dictionary, where he mentioned that the 'statue of Ceres was above 15 feet high'.[76] Worsley, meanwhile, referred in his Catalogue to the drawing as a 'View of the Colossal statue of Proserpina at Eleusis, drawn June 1785', noting that ears of corn were attributes of that goddess as well as of Ceres and paraphrasing Le Roy in saying that 'the drapery is of good taste, & in the manner of that of the Caryatids of the Pandroseum'.[77] During their first visit to the site, in May, however, Worsley had had a good deal more to say, as can be seen from his Journal, where he described the figure as

Fig. 94   Willey Reveley, '*View of the Colossal statue of Proserpina [a Priestess of the Sanctuary of Demeter] at Eleusis, drawn June [27] 1785*', pen and ink and watercolour, 29.2 x 20.6 cm, Yale Center for British Art, Paul Mellon Collection

of the most beautiful white marble and of such fine sculpture that it has been attributed to Praxiteles, who had carved a statue of that Goddess [Ceres] in a Temple that was dedicated to her at Athens. There is only a part of the statue appearing at present, the remainder of it being buried in the earth, but from what appears in view, it must probably have been fourteen or fifteen feet high. The face of the figure has been disfigured, by time and the turks, who spare the faces of none of the antique statues or busts that fall in their way, which makes it now very difficult in Greece to find any statue or bust with any of the features of the face intire. The head dress is beautiful but singular, like a basket round which are clusters of wheat ears and bundles with flowers of poppy, the attributes of the goddess, who is said to have first taught the Greeks to sew corn at Eleusis.[78]

Worsley also mentioned that 'the Venetians attempted to remove this statue, and found it too large to take away'. Sixteen years after his visit, however, it was indeed excavated and removed by E.D. Clarke, who presented it to the Fitzwilliam Museum in Cambridge where it can be seen today. Its pair, better preserved because unexcavated until the late nineteenth century, remains in the museum at Eleusis. The two caryatids, of pentelic marble, are now thought to represent priestesses and to have flanked the doorway to the inner courtyard of the Sanctuary of Demeter. Dated to about 50 BC, they were carved when Greece was a Roman province. The attribution to Praxiteles and comparisons with the caryatids of the Erechtheion may thus be seen as a deliberately historicising gesture on the part of the Roman colonisers, as well as a recognition of the continuing importance of the Eleusian fertility and afterlife rituals.

Reveley's and Worsley's Peleponnese trip occupied the second half of May 1785 and they were back at Athens on 6 June. Shortly afterwards, however, they formed a second expeditionary party for a journey eastwards from the city. For this they were joined by their French landlord at Athens, Mr Gaspery, his wife and the English Consul Mr Macree.[79] Reveley and Macree climbed Mount Hymettus on 12 June and the party continued on to Mount Pentelicus and the Plain of Marathon.[80] As has been seen, Worsley and Reveley made one further visit to Eleusis, when fig. 94 was drawn, and then prepared to journey on to Asia Minor. 'Saturday July the first, having finished the necessary drawings, I left Athens with the greatest regret', wrote Worsley, and Reveley was in almost total accord, departing from Athens 'with infinite regret.'[81]

The early part of July saw Worsley and Reveley sailing between the Cyclades Islands, visiting Mykonos, Delos, Naxos and Paros.[82] At the last two of these Reveley made drawings which are the latest related to his Journey to survive in the collection at Yale (figs. 95 and 96). The first, drawn on 9 July, shows the famous isolated standing doorway of the 'Temple of Bacchus' on Naxos, described thus in Worsley's Catalogue:

> View of the Door Case, or Gateway of the Temple of Bacchus upon a small Island or rock adjoining to the town of Naxos drawn in July 1785. Upon a small rocky Island not far from the Town, part of a Gate of white Marble is still standing among a heap of Ruins of the same stone intermixed with pieces of Granite. These according to the opinion of the Inhabitants of Naxos are the

Fig. 95   Willey Reveley, 'View of
the Door Case, or Gateway of the
Temple of Bacchus upon a small
Island or rock adjoining to the
town of Naxos drawn [on 9] July
1785', pen and ink and
watercolour, 34.6 x 21.9 cm,
Yale Center for British Art,
Paul Mellon Collection

remains of the Palace of Bacchus, but more probably of a Temple dedicated to
that God.[83]

The following day, 10 July, Worsley and Reveley sailed to Paros. Reveley's Journey
only mentions that he saw a wall made from various fragments on a white marble

Fig. 96 Willey Reveley, '*The Church of the Panagia, virgin, or Catapoliani [Ekatontapiliani] at the Gate of Paros drawn [on 10] July 1785*', pen and ink and watercolour, 24.8 x 35.6 cm, Yale Center for British Art, Paul Mellon Collection

Doric temple on Paros, so for a description of fig. 96 we have to turn to Worsley:

> The Church of the Panagia, virgin, or Catapoliani at the Gate of Paros drawn in July 1785. The church of Katapoliani dedicated to the Virgin which stands just without the City Gate, is the largest & handsomest in the Archipelago, and the only one with bells. It is enclosed in a Christum or Court, the inside arched, & supported by Antique columns of different Dimentions, which have been taken out of the Ruins of the ancient City of Paros, now called likewise Parechia. Some of the columns are very beautiful; & probably belonged to the Temple of Ceres, the remains of which are still visible at the Castle.[84]

Located in Parikia, the Church of the Panagia Ekatontapiliani (Our Lady of the Hundred Doors) remains today both an important site of pilgrimage and example of Byzantine architecture in Greece. It stands on the site of a fourth-century church, said to have been built by order of Saint Helena, mother of Constantine the Great, when she was delayed at Paros on her way to the Holy Land in a quest to retrieve the True Cross. The façade has been altered since Reveley's day, but he well captured the complicated design of the belfries.

After two days on Paros, Worsley and Reveley returned to Mykonos. There they waited for a week, hoping for the wind to change so that they could sail north-east for Smyrna. The wind continued to come from the north, however, so they changed plans and sailed south-east instead, bound for Egypt, and arriving at Rhodes on 21 July. Here Reveley's Journey abruptly breaks off – although, as has been mentioned, he was to continue in Worsley's company for at least another six months, visiting northern Egypt, the west coast of Turkey, the Dardanelles and Constantinople.

Little can Paul Mellon have known, when purchasing the 'Views from the Levant' album in New Haven in 1960, that he was obtaining what were effectively illustrations to so extraordinarily well documented an expedition as that made by Sir Richard Worsley and his feisty architect-draughtsman Willey Reveley in southern Italy and the Mediterranean in 1785–86. Through their respective memoranda a fascinating insight can be gained to late eighteenth-century British antiquarianism and social observation in the pursuit of the Grand Tour. The journey, and the collections he started to form through it, projected Worsley to his status as a leading dilettante of the end of the century. Meanwhile Reveley was transformed from being merely one of the many later eighteenth-century architectural students who broadened their educations in Rome to being the second of only two Britons to acquire – and to merit – the sobriquet 'Athenian'. His attempts, beginning notably at Paestum in February 1785, to penetrate beyond idealised notions to a truer understanding of the reality and progress of ancient Greek architecture by a combination of close observation and historical research, foreshadow the great discoveries of the early years of the nineteenth century by his successors, such as entasis and the inward inclination of columns.[85] These, not to mention the almost total dominance of Greek Revivalism in British public architecture, Willey would have lived to see had he reached the age of 70, as he might reasonably have expected to do. Instead, some catastrophic bodily event took him off at his Oxford Street residence aged only 39, right on the eve of the new century, and he quickly slipped into an obscurity from which this essay has attempted, at least in part, to reclaim him.

I am very grateful to the Earl of Yarborough for permission to quote from the papers on his ancestor, Sir Richard Worsley, Bt., now on deposit at the Lincolnshire Archives. In having prepared this essay I owe a particular debt to Jonathan Yarker, who kindly re-examined for me the drawings that form its subject during a recent study visit to the Yale Center for British Art. At the Center itself I must thank Scott Wilcox for his expert advice, and Melissa Fournier and Maria Singer for their assistance. At the Lincolnshire Archives I thank Rob Waddington and James Stevenson for their help. I am also grateful to Sue Palmer at Sir John Soane's Museum and to Ian Jenkins and Kim Sloan at the British Museum. Clare Hornsby kindly gave me her advice on Roman topography, as did Christos Tsirogiannis on a Greek inscription on one Reveley drawing. William (Hank) Johnson kindly shared with me notes he had taken on Reveley's 'Dictionary'. To Guilland Sutherland and other former colleagues of mine at the Paul Mellon Centre for Studies in British Art and Yale University Press, I owe a debt of gratitude for all their assistance – and forbearance.

1   Samuel Redgrave, *A Dictionary of Artists of the English School*, revised ed., London 1878, p.353.

2   A copy of the sale catalogue is bound into Reveley's 'Manuscript of material for [a] Dictionary of Architecture' in the British Architectural Library (Royal Institute of British Architects [hereafter RIBA]) ReW/1. It appears to have belonged to 'Mr Gandon, No. 94 Jermyn Street' (probably not the architect James Gandon, who was domiciled in Great Portland Street 1798–99 but back in Ireland in 1801). Another copy, documenting purchases made by John Soane, is now in Soane's Museum.

3   Howard Colvin, *A Biographical Dictionary of British Architects 1600–1840*, New Haven and London 2008, p.857, listing drawings now at the Victoria and Albert Museum (of which there are in fact 5), a volume comprising 60 tracings and sketches of Greek and Roman ornament from the Pio-Clementino Museum and other miscellaneous items at Sir John Soane's Museum (Volume 31), which was lot 95 on day one of the Christie's sale of Reveley's effects, and an album of early (that is 1776) architectural designs sold at Sotheby's in November 1979 and again at Christie's in December 1982. In addition to the drawings at Yale missed by Colvin, there are four at the British Museum. The Yale drawing of the Temple of Venus and Rome in Rome (YCBA B1977.14.19455) was reproduced in Frank Salmon, 'The Impact of the Archaeology of Rome on British Architects and their Work c.1750–1840', in Clare Hornsby (ed.), *The Impact of Italy: The Grand Tour and Beyond*, London 2000, p.225, fig. 2; and in Frank Salmon, *Building on Ruins: The Rediscovery of Rome and English Architecture*, Aldershot 2000, p.44, fig. 26. For the second previously published drawing see note 34 below.

4   Paul Mellon Centre, London: RBF/1/686. The Reveley drawing is V&A D446-1887. The Cozens is in Oldham Art Gallery.

5   This 'Dictionary' appears to have been the very last lot in the Christie's sale of Reveley's effects and to comprise the 'numerous Remarks in M:S: by himself' mentioned by the catalogue. It was presented to the RIBA by Thomas Leverton Donaldson in 1851. There are some variations in the handwriting at the following places: fols. 289r–293v; 297r–298v; 301r–307v.

6   RIBA, ReW/1, fol. 165r (the 'Journey' occupies fols. 165r to 188v of the 'Dictionary' and is transcribed on the same paper as the rest of the 'Dictionary').

7   Lincolnshire Archives [hereafter LA], Worsley Mss. 23 and 24 (the Journal, in two volumes) and 38 (the Catalogue of images). Ms. 38 is not paginated, so references to it will be made by using the drawing number (from 1 to 200).

8 The principal sources are Colvin, *Biographical Dictionary*, pp.856–57, and (for Reveley's Italian years) Frank Salmon in John Ingamells, *A Dictionary of British and Irish Travellers in Italy 1701–1800*, New Haven and London 1997, pp.807–8. The portrait of Reveley that Colvin mentions as in the possession of a C.E. Kenney (who became 'late' between the 1978 and 1995 editions) has sadly not been traced.

9 LA, Bradford Mss. 2/4/49: '9 Ap: 1806 ... Conference with Mr Maynard of Hoxne Hall respecting the places of Sir R Worsley's Residence in the year 1785 when he informed me that he and Sir Richard were at Rome together in 1784, and that he had recommended to Sir Richard, Mr. Reveley, an Artist, to accompany him to Greece. Mr Reveley did so; and he was with Sir Richard at Constantinople when Sir Robert Ainslie was our Ambassador there. ... Mr Reveley's Father lives in Lambs Conduit Street; and his Brother is an Attorney in that part of the Town. Mr Reveley's widow may be living.'

10 Paul Mellon Centre, London, Brinsley Ford Archive, RBF/1/686 file: Journal of Peter Cowling, October 24, 1786, Rome: 'In the Afternoon walk'd with Mr Reveley to the Villa of Prince Borghese.'

11 British Library, Add. Ms. 36495, fol, 343 (full stops have been added to the quote). Reveley and Miss James must have been known characters among the English expatriate community at Rome. Reveley certainly knew the great impresario James Byres (see RIBA, ReW/1, fols. 278v and 302v), Elizabeth Cooper's landlord during George Cumberland's absence. In a letter written earlier the same month (fol. 320), Mrs Cooper had also mentioned Sir Richard Worsley. The marriage of Willey and Maria took place on 17 April 1788, according to John James' will (cited by Howard Colvin, in his file of papers on Reveley now at the RIBA).

12 These accounts are both reproduced in Frederick L. Jones (ed.), *Maria Gisborne & Edward E. Williams – Shelley's Friends: Their Journals and Letters*, Norman, Oklahoma 1951, pp.3–5.

13 See Terry Friedman, 'Willey Reveley's All Saints', Southampton', *The Georgian Group Journal*, vol.12 2002, p.89. At this time the Reveleys were living in Lisson Street, Edgware Road, but they must frequently have moved house for in 1790 they had been at 75 Great Titchfield Street, Portland Place (*ibid.*, p.77) and in September 1794 at Southampton-row, Edgware-road (James Stuart and Nicholas Revett, ed. Willey Reveley, *The Antiquities of Athens: Volume the Third*, London: John Nichols, 1794, p.xviii).

14 Richard Colt Hoare, who corresponded with Reveley when in Italy from 1788 to 1791, recorded having built ten lodges at Stourhead and Reveley sent designs for more than one of these in December 1797 (see Kenneth Woodbridge, *Landscape and Antiquity: Aspects of English Culture at Stourhead 1718–1838*, Oxford 1970, pp.131 and 153).

15 Reveley was one of eight people to submit schemes. His three proposals were the most ambitious, involving huge diversion works for the Thames between Woolwich and Wapping. The Committee considered him an 'architect and engineer' (a fellow competitor was Samuel Wyatt, described just as an 'architect') and Reveley's ideas were said to be 'novel, grand and captivating' – but not practicable (see Joseph Broodbank, *History of the Port of London*, 2 vols., London 1921, vol.1 pp.85 and 87. See also *The Monthly Magazine*, vol. 7 Part I, July 1799, p.147, for the statement that Reveley's ideas for the port were 'nearly ready for publication' (at the time of his death). Lindsay Boynton reported seeing Reveley drawings for the port on exhibition at the Guildhall in 1975 (Paul Mellon Centre, London: RBF/1/686).

16 *The Gentleman's Magazine*, vol. 69 Part II, July 1799, p.627. See also Redgrave, *Dictionary* (1878), p.353: 'he was eccentric, expressed his opinions sarcastically, and did not succeed to the measure of his abilities.'

17 Jones, *Maria Gisborne*, p.4. Godwin, himself widowed since the death of Mary Wollstonecraft in 1797, proposed marriage to Maria within a month of Willey's death.

18 J. Bowring (ed.), *The Works of Jeremy Bentham*, vol. 10, 1843, pp.251–52. Bentham described Reveley as having 'an admirable pair of hands' but evidently appreciated Maria still more highly.

19 LA, Worsley Ms. 23, fol. 2. The following day Worsley reported leaving Rome with 'Mr Reveley an English architect' (*ibid.*, fol. 3).

20 LA, Worsley Ms. 23, fol. 33.

21 Paul Mellon Centre, London, RBF/1/686 file: letter from Lindsay Boynton to Brinsley Ford, 21 October 1975. Worsley's sister had married the Hon. John Bridgeman (named Simpson from 1785), and their daughter Henrietta was his heir. Since Henrietta was a minor when Worsley died in 1805, her paternal uncle Orlando Bridgeman, later 1st Earl of Bradford, acted as trustee.

22 YCBA File information, courtesy of Scott Wilcox.

23 Jonathan Yarker has pointed out that the 'Views in the Levant' album contained, in addition to the Reveley drawings, the highly finished drawing by Luigi Schiavenetti of Nathaniel Marchant's carved headstone intaglio of the 'Death of General Wolfe' (YCBA B1977.14.19417) which appears at the end of the second volume of the *Museum Worsleyanum*, as well as an unattributed watercolour of the cottage by the sea on the Isle of Wight to which Worsley retired in 1797 (B1977.14.19393). Plate 95 in the *Museum* shows the caryatid figure ('Ceres') from Eleusis that Worsley first saw with Reveley, but the plate is not based on Reveley's drawing (fig. 94 here).

24 LA, Worsley Ms. 38. In fact the Catalogue only contains 198 drawings, the numbers 145 and 149 being omitted, and by no means were all of the drawings 'taken on the spot' in the 1780s (or, therefore, by Reveley).

25 These drawings comprised the last set of lots of the Christie's sale, and it is noted that 'they are more fully described in a M.S. Catalogue, to which Reference may be made, according to the Numbers added to each Lot.' This 'M.S. Catalogue' has not been identified.

26 *Gentleman's Magazine*, July 1799, p. 627.

27 For a recent account of the fate of Worsley's paintings see Jonathan Yarker, 'The Last Resident: Richard Worsley, Lucien Bonaparte and his Collection of Venetian Paintings', *The Burlington Magazine*, January 2012, pp.37–43. Worsley's Journal itself (LA, Worsley Ms. 23) has a note inside the flyleaf saying that it was purchased from a sale at Malaga in 1806 – so that Worsley had it with him in Venice and it was returned to his estate after his death in 1805.

28 For example the two Paestum drawings at Yale (figs. 88 and 89 here) are clearly numbered 13 and 14 top left, whereas in the Reveley sale catalogue Paestum views fall between numbers 3 and 11 (lots 2–10) and in Worsley's catalogue between numbers 19 and 23.

29 One might infer from this that, back in Rome in 1787, Worsley commissioned Antonio del Drago to complete drawings from his own sketches (Worsley was a competent draughtsman himself) in order to replace those Reveley had retained or, since Reveley was also in Rome in 1787–88, that Reveley allowed del Drago to work on his drawings. In the Reveley sale catalogue, numbers 17 and 18 were indeed two views of 'Mount Etna, drawn at sea', the latter 'drawn at 15 miles distance'.

30 LA, Worsley Ms. 38, nos. 93–94 and 115–116 (the Venetian artist), 123–124 (the Turk), 178 (the Greek artist), 184–186 (the Russians). Moreover, Lady Berwick reported from Venice in 1795 that Worsley (British Resident there 1793–96) 'has a very valuable collection of drawings taken on the spot in Sicily & Greece' (Paul Mellon Centre, London: RBF/1/686).

31 For a recent article on Pars and the Ionian expedition see Ann Gunn, 'Paul Sandby, William Pars and the Society of Dilettanti', *The Burlington Magazine*, April 2010, pp.219–27. Worsley is not mentioned there, but in the Yale collection are what appear to be Pars's initial 1765 views of Sunium (YCBA B1977.14.19424), which is an early version of British Museum Mm,11.8, and of the Sacred Cave of Archidamus (B1977.14.19437), an early version of British Museum Mm, 11.6 (their corresponding Sandby aquatints are also present at Yale). Finally there is a Pars view of the Temple of Jupiter Panhellenius on Aegina (B1977.14.19425), which has no worked up equivalent in the British Museum. These three drawings were numbers 39, 73 and 76 in Worsley's Catalogue.

32 British Museum, Department of Prints and Drawings, 1894.0516.17 (purchased by the Museum from Robert Jackson). This view, showing the east side of the Arch, was number 1 in the Christie's sale catalogue of Reveley's effects and became number 18 in Worsley's own Catalogue.

33 The only items at the Christie's sale of Reveley's effects that might correspond with these views, however, were lot 10 on Day 1 (which contained 'Fourteen of Roman Antiquities and Views in Italy' but these were 'Outlines' only, not watercolours), and Lot 11, which was the 'Pantheon at Rome, and 2 others in Colours'.

34 This drawing was reproduced in Andrew Wilton, *The Art of Alexander and John Robert Cozens*, New Haven, Yale Center for British Art, 1980, plate 2 (catalogue 141, where it is dated to *c*.1740 and said to be by an anonymous artist).

35 There is a very similar view of 1885 by Ettore Roesler Franz from an almost identical vantage point in the Museo di Roma [in Trastevere], Inventario: MR 119.

36 RIBA, ReW/1, fol. 311.

37 For the comparative illustrations and a discussion see the two works by Frank Salmon cited in note 3 above.

38 I am very grateful to Clare Hornsby for her assistance in placing this location. Of the other remaining views of Rome recorded in Worsley's Catalogue, Number 11 is a 'View of the Claudian Aqueduct and the Reservoir over Porta Nevia'. Porta Nevia was a Gate in the Servian Wall of Rome just at the south-west corner of the Baths of Caracalla (and thus near the western end of the Aqua Claudia), mentioned by Varro and Festus but not surviving in the eighteenth century. Number 12 was a drawing 'taken from a window of the saloon in the Villa Negroni taking in the Temple of Minerva Medica, the Aqua Claudia and Frascati' on 30 May 1787 according to Worsley, who was evidently residing at the Villa Negroni after returning to Rome from his expedition (Ingamells, *Dictionary*, p.1019, cites Worsley's letter of 20 September 1787 thanking the Accademia di San Luca for his election as Honorary Member as addressed 'Dalla Villa Negroni').

39 Reveley's sale catalogue lists 23 drawings made in Athens, only one of which can be identified with certainty: an oblique view of the Doric portico in the Agora (number 38: 'An exact S.W. View of the Agora or Temple of Augustus', which survives as V&A 116-1877 (illustrated in Sigrid de Jong, 'Rediscovering Architecture: Paestum in Eighteenth-Century Architectural Experience and Theory', PhD diss., University of Leiden 2010, p.107, fig.1.20). Dated June 1785 on the mount, this drawing was evidently number 65 in Worsley's Catalogue, but its subsequent sale history has taken it elsewhere than Yale. The Yale collection does, however, contain two other drawings that may represent structures in Athens: YCBA B1977.14.19410 and B1977.14.19406. Reveley's sale catalogue lists, in a single lot, numbers 32 and 33, 'View of a Ruin at Athens, agreed by Stuart, Revet, and Chandler, to be the Gymnasium of Ptolemy; also a Ruin with Inscription, supposed to belong to the preceding.' These images and descriptions appear to correspond with numbers 63 and 68 in Worsley's Catalogue.

40 The north-east corner of the cornice and pediment is seen to be broken off in fig. 89, whereas the south-west corner can be seen entire in fig. 88. Also, in fig. 89 one can see a few pen strokes at the left which indicate the position, to the south, of the Basilica [Temple of Hera I] which Reveley decided to omit.

41 LA, Worsley Ms. 38, no. 19: 'A Perspective View of the Three ancient Temples at Posidonia or Paestum'; and no. 21: 'North East view of the same [Great] Temple at Paestum traced in a Camera obscura February 21 1785.' The Reveley sale catalogue number 9 was 'N.E. view of the same [Central or largest Temple] taken in a camera-obscura.' Number 4, however, the general view, mentions that 'N.B. The Tree is added, but the Rest of the Drawing is accurate.' It is not clear that fig. 88 includes the added tree.

42 In addition to the two drawings at Yale, two more Reveley drawings of Paestum survive at the Victoria and Albert Museum: V&A, D.446-1887 and D.140-1888 (both illustrated in de Jong, 'Rediscovering Architecture', p.106, fig.1.19). The former shows the Temple of [Athena] from the north-west (far less of the west pediment survived than the east into the eighteenth century). Reveley's catalogue mentions two views of that temple (numbers 5 and 6), but they were said to be from the south-east and south-west respectively. Worsley's Catalogue (number 22) was a 'South West View of an ancient Temple at Paestum, supposed to have been dedicated to Diana, drawn on the Spot Feb 21 1785.' The second V&A drawing, dated May 1786 on the back and thus made during Reveley's second visit to Paestum, shows the north side of the Temple of Neptune [Hera II]. It corresponds with number 8 in his catalogue: 'View of the North Side of the Central or largest Temple at Pesto. The tree is added.' Here the tree is very prominent at the right edge of the drawing (see note 41 above). Worsley did not have this view.

43 This is notwithstanding the fact that Chambers owned a copy of Major's book (and also Stuart's *Antiquities* and the first edition of Julien-David Le Roy's *Les ruines des plus beaux monuments de la Grèce* of 1758 (see David Watkin (ed.), *Sale Catalogues of Libraries of Eminent Persons, Volume 4: Architects*, London 1972, p.125).

44 RIBA, ReW/1, fol. 244v.

45 RIBA, ReW/1, fol, 229r.

46 LA, Worsley Ms. 23, fols. 22–23.

47 RIBA, ReW/1, fol, 247r.

48 Reveley noted that there was a temple of Diana near Paestum, mentioned by Diodorus Siculus (RIBA, ReW, fol. 171r).

49 RIBA, ReW/1, fol. 247r.

50 RIBA, ReW/1, fol. 171r.

51 RIBA, ReW/1, fol. 244r.

52 RIBA, ReW/1, fol. 171v.

53 Stuart and Revett, ed. Reveley, *Antiquities*, vol.3, p.41.

54 Worsley's Catalogue (number 77) lists a 'View of a Doric Temple at Corinth built before the Time of Pericles' but, as there was no drawing of Corinth in the Christie's sale of Reveley's effects, this may have been drawn by someone else.

55 RIBA, ReW/1, fols. 245v–246v. On fol. 245r Reveley found it harder to appraise the small Temple of Ceres, in part because of its ruinous condition but also because of features that he struggled to reconcile with his understanding of Greek architecture: 'It is difficult to say when this temple was erected. The proportion of 6 to 13 cols: is Greek, as is also the general appearance of the cols: but not entirely. The disposition of the triglyphs is roman, & the pitch of the pediment approaches more to Roman than Greek.'

56 Stuart and Revett, ed. Reveley, *Antiquities*, vol.3, p.xi.

57 Stuart and Revett, ed. Reveley, *Antiquities*, vol.3, p.xiii.

58 Stuart and Revett, ed. Reveley, *Antiquities*, vol.3, p.xiii. Covering the same point in the Dictionary (RIBA, ReW/1, fol. 247r), Reveley observed that Le Roy had erroneously identified the Temple of Jupiter Panhellenius on Aegina as similarly having an uneven number of columns 'in the front' (see Robin Middleton and David Britt, *Julien-David Le Roy: The Ruins of the most Beautiful Monuments of Greece*, Los Angeles 2004, p.232, n.12.

59 RIBA, ReW/1, fol 171v.

60 RIBA, ReW/1, fol. 172r.

61 RIBA, ReW/1, fol. 173v. In his Catalogue, Worsley compared the statue's 'crown of laurel … or perhaps of oak' to that of the figure of Constantine at the Capitol in Rome, and also opined that 'the cross in the Emperors hand is modern' (LA, Worsley Ms. 38, number 24). Reveley's reference is to Henry Swinburne, *Travels in the Two Sicilies 1777–80* (first edition London: J. Davis for P. Elmsly, 1783–85; second edition 1790).

62 RIBA, ReW/1, fol. 175v. Worsley's Catalogue contains a closely similar description, but adds that the right column had

collapsed during the earthquake of 1456 and had been subsequently sold to the people of Lecce (LA, Worsley Ms. 38, number 26). This information is repeated in Worsley's Journal (LA, Worsley Ms. 23, fols. 32–33). Worsley also mentions a modern inscription on the base of one column which might, potentially, relate to the inscription tablet on fig. 91.

63 Sir John Soane's Museum, Volume 31, no. 59.

64 RIBA, ReW/1, fol. 177r; British Museum, Department of Prints and Drawings 1927.0712.8. Lot 13 in the 1801 Christie's sale of Reveley's effects included 'Two W. Views of the Castle of Otranto', but Worsley's Catalogue does not include the Castle at all. The version in the British Museum must be a third one, because its provenance suggests that Worsley presented it to Horace Walpole, through the agency of Elizabeth Lady Craven, with whom he was at Constantinople in April–May 1786. Walpole discussed the drawing, Reveley's authorship and Lady Craven's presentation of it, in a letter of 17 January 1788 (and, in engraved form, it appeared in editions of *The Castle of Otranto* from 1791). See Ingamells, *Dictionary*, p.251.

65 LA, Worsley Ms. 23, fol. 37.

66 RIBA, ReW/1, fol. 177r.

67 The drawings were reversed chronologically as numbers 17 and 18 in the Reveley sale catalogue but are put back into order as 29 and 30 in Worsley's Catalogue. See note 29 above for discussion of the possible subsequent history of number 29.

68 Conceivably this is the drawing described by Reveley as 'a view of the castle & coasts of Calabria & Sicily looking towards the Streight of Messina' (possibly number 16 in his posthumous sale catalogue: 'S. View of the Streight of Messina.'). It is odd, however, that he should not mention – as does Worsley – a feature as distinctive as the spectacularly fractured mountain. Reveley also described making 'two views of Reggio one as we were in front of it & the other while at anchor' (RIBA, ReW/1, fol. 177v). One of these must have been number 28 in Worsley's Catalogue: 'East view of the city of Reggio drawn from the ship March 30 1785.' Reveley's own sale catalogue has, as number 14, a 'S.W. View of the City of Reggio in Calabria Ultra, drawn from the sea March 30th 1785.' YCBA B1977.14.19447 is a candidate for one of these views of Reggio, which Reveley described as 'a city of considerable length close to the sea on a gentle slope backed by bare mountains forming a beautiful object. Only one of

its seven churches is now standing and that has a clumsy tower shook awry' (*ibid.*, fol. 177v). That description applies more obviously, however, to a Reveley drawing of Reggio now in the British Museum (Department of Prints and Drawings, 1878.0713.1277, purchased in 1878 from J. Hogarth & Sons). On 2 April Reveley drew Syracuse whilst becalmed off the shore, 'but being very far off it was but just perceivable' (*ibid.*, fol. 178r). The Syracuse view could be YCBA B1977.14.19398.

69   RIBA, ReW/1, fol. 179v.

70   The other two views were more panoramic: number 33 took in the Castle St Angelo, the three cities of Vittoriosa, Burmola and Senglea as well as well as the Custom House and quays of Valetta; number 34 took in the point of Castle St Elmo but also Fort Ricasoli, the northern part of Vittoriosa and Castle St Angelo.

71   RIBA, ReW/1, fol. 178v. The Castle St Angelo, on the opposite side of the city, was also 'built on a rock cut down', with four rows of batteries pointing to the harbour mouth. Reveley provided a long translation describing the harbour by a French officer.

72   YCBA, B1977.14.19402 appears to correspond with Worsley's Journal description of a Turkish cemetery just outside Canea on Crete (LA, Worsley Ms. 23, fol. 54). Reveley also described the cemetery (including the 'turband' headstones that feature on the drawing), but he does not say that he drew it (RIBA, ReW/1, fol. 180r). Moreover, the single drawing of Crete listed in both Reveley's sale catalogue (number 22) and Worsley's Catalogue (LA, Worsley Ms. 38, number 36) was a view in the port at Canea.

73   RIBA, ReW/1, fol. 184v is left blank. For details on Reveley's Athenian drawings see note 39 above.

74   LA, Worsley Ms. 23, fol. 138.

75   RIBA, ReW/1, fol. 187r. Figure 94 was number 55 in the posthumous sale of Reveley's effects.

76   These notes occur in two sections: RIBA, ReW/1, fol. 265r and fols. 266r–v.

77   LA, Worsley Ms. 38, number 74. See Middleton and Britt, *Le Roy*, p.428.

78   LA, Worsley Ms. 23, fols. 141–142. For Worsley's inclusion of this statue in the *Museum Worsleyanum*, see note 23 above.

79   LA, Worsley Ms. 23, fol. 206. Reveley recalled that the 'family' additionally included Gaspery's brother-in-law, Mrs Gaspery's sister Mlle. Miette, and a Dr de Villoison (RIBA, ReW/1, fol. 186v). The attractive Mlle. Miette evidently caught Reveley's eye, for his pencil profile portrait of her was 'drawn at Athens June 1785' (Sir John Soane's Museum, Volume 31, no. 44).

80   YCBA, B1977.14.19416 is very possibly the drawing made at Marathon listed as number 72 in Worsley's catalogue (LA, Worsley Ms. 38): 'South west view of the Plain of Marathon/ drawn June the 15 1785.'

81   LA, Worsley Ms. 23, fol. 224; RIBA, ReW/1, fol. 187r.

82   YCBA B1977.14.19399 possibly shows 'Magdalena, one of the common Greek women of the Isle of Miconi in the dress of the country drawn July 18th 1785' (LA, Worsley Ms. 38, number 80). However, that portrait is said to show the figure 'front & back', so the drawing might rather be number 119, 'A drawing of a Maddalena, one of the people that go about the streets of Cairo singing the praises of Mahomet, drawn from life August the 5th 1785.'

83   LA, Worsley Ms. 38, number 81. The description relates closely to that in Worsley's Journal (LA, Worsley Ms. 23, fol. 238). Reveley's Journey merely records that, at six in the morning on 9 July, 'we saw the door architrave of the temple of Bacchus of white marble which stands up although there are no vestiges of the other parts of the temple' (RIBA, ReW/1, fol. 188r). As has been seen, the drawing was number 55 in Reveley's sale catalogue, part of the same lot (42) as the Church of the Panagin on Paros.

84   LA, Worsley Ms. 38, number 82. The wording from the Catalogue here is almost verbatim that of Worsley's Journal (LA, Worsley Ms. 23, fol. 241) and, as has been seen, the drawing was number 56 in Reveley's sale catalogue, part of the same lot (42) as the Temple of Bacchus on Naxos.

85   See Frank Salmon, 'C.R. Cockerell and the Discovery of Entasis in the Columns of the Parthenon', in Frank Salmon (ed.), *The Persistence of the Classical: Essays on Architecture Presented to David Watkin*, London 2008, pp.106–23. Entasis and the inward inclination of columns were both announced in print for the first time in the supplementary, fifth volume of *The Antiquities of Athens* in 1830, although their actual discoveries date to the second decade of the nineteenth century.

Late Romney, A Re-appraisal

Alex Kidson

Fig. 97   Benjamin Smith after George Romney, *Tempest Act I Scene I*, published 27 September 1797, stipple engraving, 44 x 59 cm

Late Romney, A Re-appraisal

Alex Kidson

In April 1790 George Romney finally delivered his huge painting of the first scenes of *The Tempest* to the Boydell Shakespeare Gallery (fig.97). It was a portentous moment for him. Ever since the announcement of the Gallery over three years earlier, it had been known that he was one of its chief instigators, and his failure so far to deliver a single contribution had been remarked upon in the press.[1] Furthermore, this would be the first time in eighteen years that Romney had exhibited a picture in public: the occasion when he would reverse at a stroke his policy of seclusion – or more exactly, would make it apparent that he was not against exhibiting in principle so much as against exhibiting at the Royal Academy. From his position as England's leading non-Academician painter, Romney was about to issue a public challenge to the whole edifice of preconception and aesthetic prescription that was entailed in the Royal Academy's ever-growing cultural hegemony and prestige.

Nor was the moment of private significance to Romney alone. The British art world itself was at a moment of tectonic shift. Romney's three chief rivals in the field of portrait painting over the past decade had passed him, or were in the process of passing him, their mantle. In 1787 Gilbert Stuart had fled London for Dublin in order to escape his creditors. Thomas Gainsborough had died the following year. And on 11 February 1790 Sir Joshua Reynolds had resigned as President of the Royal Academy. Although this turned out to be a temporary state of affairs – he was re-instated the following month – people knew that he was going blind and that his career was coming to an end. The Academicians were casting around anxiously for someone to fill Sir Joshua's place; and at their exhibition of 1790, only a matter of days after Romney's huge canvas went on show, their new champion, Thomas Lawrence, created a carefully prepared sensation with his full-length portraits of the queen and the actress Eliza Farren.

What happened next has become one of the axioms of British art history. Largely on the strength of his performance at the 1790 Royal Academy, Lawrence was chosen at the age of 22 to succeed Reynolds as Painter in Ordinary to George III, and went on to create a style that would define a new generation. Romney, his career supposedly ruined by the criticism heaped upon his masterpiece, descended into anonymity. 'In all but a few of his works' according to Sir Ellis Waterhouse, there was 'a falling off in quality', and by 1798, when he retired, 'he was more or less imbecile'.[2] Following in Waterhouse's footsteps, other writers have claimed that Romney 'died insane',[3] and in one recent formulation, his 'mental collapse' as early as 1790 was one of the chief factors in Lawrence's rise.[4] More realistic (although no doubt itself not free from bias) was the assessment of John Romney, expressed in a draft letter of June 1806 to his father's old friend and now biographer William Hayley, that at the end of the 1780s Romney 'was at the acme of his powers, ample fortune and transcendent fame were in his grasp'.[5] Visiting Revolutionary Paris in the summer of 1790, to be met and escorted around the Luxembourg palace by Jacques-Louis David, Romney as the one leading English painter free from the taint of royalist association would have felt entitled to share the sense that 'bliss was it in that dawn to be alive'.

One of the most familiar explanations for the collapse of Romney's aspirations in the 1790s is that the *Tempest* painting was universally panned.[6] On closer inspection, this is far from obviously the case. Most of the known newspaper criticism of the picture published in the year after it was put on exhibition at the Boydell Shakespeare Gallery was strongly in its favour. For example, an early notice by a critic calling himself 'Piranezi' in the *Morning Chronicle* reported:

> Mr Romney claims the first notice. His painting from the Tempest has all the grandeur of the Antients. The composition and figures are in the best style of the Old Masters; the colouring is of the Venetian school: – Splendid, chaste, harmonious. It looks like a picture of other times, and reminds us of those immortal works which have had the sanction of ages, and gave an exalted and permanent situation in the Temple of Fame.[7]

Another critic commented of the picture:

> *Materiem Superabat Opus* – And with Shakspere, as in the Palace of the Sun, what praise can go further? Than this, which says the subject grand and varied as it is, is more than equalled by the grandeur with which it is treated.[8]

The *Public Advertiser* declared the representation of the *Tempest* 'splendid',[9] while in January 1791 the *Diary or Woodfall's Journal* observed that it appeared to 'delight every impartial judge of the fine arts. We are ready to acknowledge that it has much transcended our expectations.'[10] The operative word in this last comment was 'impartial'. The previous month a critic for *The Times*, professing himself 'uninfluenced but by a simple love of the fine arts', had noted that while Romney had violated the unity of the scene, and 'two parts of the play are brought together which should have been represented in different pictures', nevertheless the head of Prospero was 'grand', and the face of Miranda 'enchanting', the naked back of [Antonio] 'ever affords an example of superior design and colour'; 'the hurry on board the ship is conceived and executed with all the spirit of the poet ... Ariel is the floating, incorporeal lovely form of Shakespeare; while the fiery confusion on the upper part of the picture is managed in a style that marks the pencil of genius. It is on the whole a most impressive, grand and finely executed work.' As for the 'violent severity of criticism with which it has been treated', this was entirely ascribable to professional jealousy:

> If, therefore, a professor of this delightful art should burst forth with a novelty of excellence, the exhibition of the work that displays it will call the professional pack to their game, where it will be attacked by bold condemnation and sneering interrogatory, by censure of its merits and praise of its faults, till there is not a square inch of the canvas but is stained by the various blame of professional criticism ... Mr Romney is not a Member of the Royal Academy; and that he should paint a better picture than could be produced by any one of that body, will be voted by them, not to be an act of presumption, but of absolute blasphemy against that sacred College of the British Arts. – It becomes, therefore the duty of their corporate criticism to revenge the insult upon the criminal painting.[11]

The notion that Romney's picture was victim of a whispering campaign on the part of Royal Academicians puts a new complexion on the artist's reputation during the 1790s and afterwards. Joseph Farington's observation in his diary in July 1794 that the publisher Robert Bowyer was afraid to employ Romney on his projected illustrated edition of Hume's *History of England* 'on acct. of the unpopularity of his Tempest picture'[12] – a comment which has weighed with posterity perhaps more than other – suddenly acquires the flavour not of reportage but gloating. Romney's own plea to Hayley, six months earlier, to keep secret his plans for new series of pictures on Shakespearean and Miltonic themes, because 'if my name was mentioned, I should hear nothing but abuse, and that I cannot bear ... my nerves are too weak for supporting anything in public',[13] appears less the paranoid delusions of an 'insane' artist than a realistic admission that the Academicians' campaign had succeeded. These remarks were published in Hayley's biography of Romney of 1809, which, with its agenda of emphasising Romney's neurotic, 'child of nature' characteristics at the expense of his professionalism, had no compunction in pandering to the Academic consensus on the *Tempest* painting. Hayley, no doubt concerned for his own posthumous reputation as an arbiter of taste, flagrantly suppressed the degree to which the painting had been shaped by his own advice, and pretended that the artist had made repeated efforts to correct the 'radical error' of combining separate scenes in the same picture [14] (when it is clear from the succession of his studies that Romney deliberately evolved the composition that way). For Hayley, it was enough to observe that Romney himself 'was happily conscious, that it was the production of no ordinary painter', and to recall that on Rev. Mordaunt Cracherode, that 'nice, and rather fastidious, Connoisseur', the work made a powerful effect: 'an evident and acknowledged triumph over the prejudices of a refined taste, that had long idolized the designs of the great Italian school, and expected but little from English art'.[15] Hayley's defensiveness perpetuated the Academic orthodoxy that had been cemented by the poor showing of the picture at the Boydell sale in 1805 (when it fetched 50 guineas), by the debacle of Romney's studio sale at Christie's in 1807, and by recent dismissive articles on him by Henry Fuseli and Edward Edwards.[16] When in 1812 the pendulum began to swing and a freshly positive attitude to Romney began to make itself felt in the contributions of Thomas Phillips and Walter H. Watts to John Britton's *Fine Arts of the English School*, the *Tempest* painting was beyond reclamation. Phillips – who had entered on his artistic career in London at the very moment that the picture had gone on exhibition – invoked pure and abstract connoisseurship to rehabilitate Romney, concluding his article with the prediction that 'the lover of art who knows how to appreciate truly what is most valuable in painting, will hold [his name] in increasing estimation, the more frequently and impartially he examines his productions'.[17] In 1811 Watts, a parliamentary journalist and part-time miniaturist who had studied with Romney as a boy, recalled in a letter to the artist's son that when he had first entered Romney's painting room 'the impression made upon my mind was such as I have never since experienced from viewing the pictures of any artist whatsoever', and acknowledged 'his claim to *the highest* professional reputation which, either the jealousy of Mr Romney's contemporaries, or some other circumstance to me inexplicable, has certainly rendered the world at large hitherto tardy to acknowledge'.[18]

* * *

The painting selected by Watts as the subject of his mini-essay for Britton was another Shakespearean subject, *Titania, Puck and the Changeling* from *A Midsummer Night's Dream* (fig. 98), a work painted in the wake of the exhibition of the *Tempest* picture. In some ways, the *Titania* displayed deep-seated continuities with the earlier painting, notably in its bold use of colour to create atmosphere, and in its insistence on re-interpreting the source rather than simply illustrating a moment of the play that could be witnessed on stage. As Watts put it, Romney was frequently 'less solicitous to adhere, with scrupulous fidelity, to his author, than to produce a work which should comprehend all the beauties of his own art', and *Titania, Puck and the Changeling* was 'the result of a profound consideration of the whole play ... a select assemblage of those images which, in the artist's judgment, could be combined by his art to the happiest effect'.[19] But in other respects the work diverged sharply in character from the *Tempest* painting. It stood as a demonstration of the lessons he had learnt from completing the earlier picture and as a blueprint for the new directions he wanted his paintings of the imagination to take in the new decade (directions that Romney hinted at in a set of notes for a Discourse on Painting written out in a sketchbook of that period).[20] In the first place it was intimate, with only three figures, not the kind of huge, crowded Academic machine demanded by theory. It was unfinished, or more

Fig. 98 George Romney,
Titania, Puck and the Changeling,
from Shakespeare's 'A
Midsummer Night's Dream',
1791–93, oil on canvas, 104 x 135 cm,
National Gallery of Ireland

precisely, taken to just the level of finish that the artist wanted, not that which was prescribed by the rules. And most importantly of all, rather than being a single all-encompassing statement, it was one of a group of inter-related treatments of the material, exploratory in nature rather than summative. At the same time that Romney began *Titania, Puck and the Changeling*, in the summer of 1791 with his beloved Emma as a model, he was making studies for a larger scene depicting the queen of the fairies in her bower, conceived as a more academic female nude (the *Titania Reposing with her Indian Votaries* now at Stratford). Over the next eighteen months the dialectic between these two canvases yielded no fewer than five further paintings inspired by the fairy world of Shakespeare's play: each different in character, but all suffused with a magical poetry and a remarkable modernity. This corpus of paintings alone would justify the view that for Romney the 1790s witnessed not free fall but a flowering of creative maturity.[21]

Fig. 99   George Romney,
The Indian Woman, 1792-93,
oil on canvas, 118.5 x 148.5 cm,
Private Collection, London

Part of the recalcitrance of these works for Romney's contemporaries resided in their lack of public exposure; but this changed in 1797 when one of them, *The Indian Woman* (fig. 99), was bought for 300 guineas – a remarkable sum for a painting of moderate size and no pretensions to high finish – by William Beckford, who hung it in the entrance hall at Fonthill. The musky atmosphere of the work was well calculated to appeal to the author of *Vathek,* and there is clear evidence that Romney regarded it as the pride of his *Midsummer Night's Dream* litter. In his mention of its recent completion, in a letter of April 1793 to his brother in India, there is an unmistakeable sense of false modesty and pride;[22] and eleven months later in a letter to his son, Romney mentioned it as one of four recent historical works that had done him 'Greater Credit than any I have painted before ... they are in a great stile. I have had all the critics and they are surprised I do not pursue History' [i.e. exclusively].[23] The pictures concerned, besides *The Indian Woman,* were *Milton and his Daughters, Susan, when the Seas were Roaring* from John Gay, and *Ophelia*, and in the light of Romney's statement it seems fair to identify this quartet as the best available index of his development as a painter of the imagination in the first half of the 1790s. Regrettably – if somehow inevitably – two of the four have been lost for the past two centuries, and can now be only very superficially visualised. One, the *Susan*, must have represented his definitive treatment of a theme – the abandoned woman on the storm-tossed seashore with the corpse of her drowned lover – that he had been exploring all his life, and numerous pen and ink sketches for various earlier adumbrations of the idea survive; either the 1794 painting or a previous version of it was the subject of one of Anna Seward's most fulsome paeans in Romney's praise. For the second lost work, *Ophelia*, no preliminary drawings are known at all, and impressions of it can be formed only from the descriptions of John Flaxman (in Hayley's biography) and Thomas Phillips. According to Flaxman 'the most pathetic perhaps of all his works', it showed Ophelia 'with the flowers she had gathered in her hand, sitting on the branch of a tree, which was breaking under her, while the melancholy distraction visible in her lovely countenance accounts for her insensibility to danger'[24] (it is also known that the background contained 'Ruined Buildings and Romantic Scenery');[25] whilst for Phillips the picture was alone sufficient proof of the assertion that 'Romney thrills and gratifies the heart with truth and force of expression, in action and countenance, wrought' – as compared to the paintings of Reynolds – 'with more simplicity, but less art'.[26]

In the remaining painting of the four, *Milton and his Daughters* (fig. 100), Romney as in the *Titania* pictures had consciously crystallised aspects of his developing anti-academic aesthetic, but the more public context of the painting's gestation had encouraged a more subtly subversive approach to this. The work was painted to be engraved as the frontispiece of Hayley's new biography of the poet John Milton for the Boydells, and this was a project with a multi-faceted cultural profile (all the more fraught as contemporary events in France gave a new slant to Milton's historic republicanism). In the context of his colleagues' expectations – for Hayley, the Boydells and their partner George Nicol all had their own views about the pictorial treatment – Romney had a struggle on his hands to be true to his own vision of the work. Hayley, whose views about the treatment of Milton's daughters Romney resisted, later dismissed the picture – using just the language of aesthetic orthodoxy

Fig. 100 George Romney,
Milton and his Daughters,
1792-93, oil on canvas,
206 x 206 cm,
Private Collection, UK

that Romney was attempting to get away from – as 'a kind of painting that seems to hold a middle rank between portrait and history'.[27] Unkind in its reminder of the cheap contemporary criticism of Romney that his historical pictures were bound to be infected by his long commitment to society portraiture, this assessment superficially conveys something of the work's domestic character, but it does not get to the heart of the picture's subversive originality. As a painting whose ostensible purpose was to be engraved for a book illustration, the *Milton* confounded expectation by its grand scale; in painting such a large work Romney was insisting on its creative independence from the project which had given birth to it. He proceeded to underline this by painting a pendant, *Newton and the Prism*, as part of a cycle of works about the lives of British cultural heroes (further canvases in this series, devoted to Bacon and Wren, were never begun). On the other hand, viewed simply as a large-scale history painting, the *Milton* defied convention in its unheroic, positively downbeat air, in its preference for a small handful of figures (and even those studied in isolation, rather than being effectively 'combined' in the understood academic sense) and in its consciously awkward design, with the three figures falling away from a blank central space. Ironically it was probably the work's political overtones, the very aspect of it that Hayley and the Boydells were anxious to disguise, that appealed to the keen Whig patron Samuel Whitbread, who bought it in April 1796. According to John Romney, Whitbread took none other than Charles James Fox with him to Romney's studio to look at the picture, and it was with his approbation that the purchase was made.[28]

The *Milton*, together with *The Indian Woman* and two fancy portraits of Lady Hamilton as a Magdalen and Calypso which were purchased by the Prince of Wales, constituted the chief visible evidence of Romney's appeal to prestigious patrons of High Art during the 1790s and for the remainder of his life. In 1807, however, they were joined by the *Titania, Puck and the Changeling* (fig. 98), which was purchased at Romney's posthumous sale by Sir John Leicester, owner of the nation's most celebrated collection of English pictures. The description of this work in the sale catalogue as 'a surprising Picture of Poetical Sportive Invention, treated with Corregiesque taste and magic effect, one of the happiest efforts of the Artist!' sounds all too like marketing hype, but its juxtaposition of Romney's name with Correggio's is of particular interest, for there are signs that this was not a flight of fancy on the part of the Christie's cataloguer so much as an association propagated by Romney's immediate circle, and deriving ultimately from the artist himself. John Flaxman in his sketch of Romney's professional character for Hayley observed that 'several of his pictures breathe a kindred spirit with the Sigismonda of Corregio';[29] while both Hayley and John Romney in their biographies of the artist described individual pictures as Correggiesque in such a way as to leave little doubt they were recording Romney's own view of them. The first of these pictures was *The Infant Shakespeare Nursed by Tragedy and Comedy* (fig. 101), which, in Hayley's words, had 'charms of expression not inferior to the finest Greek gems; each figure

Fig.101 George Romney,
*The Infant Shakespeare Nursed by
Tragedy and Comedy*, 1791,
oil on canvas, 120.5 x 164 cm,
Private Collection, West Sussex

is perfect in its character ... Romney in this performance has rivalled the tenderness of pencil, and the graceful sweetness of expression, that he greatly admired in his favourite Corregio'.[30] The second Correggiesque work was Romney's intended sequel to the *Tempest* picture, in which Ferdinand, who has struggled to shore after the shipwreck, encounters Prospero and Miranda on the beach by Prospero's magic cell. This canvas, which was included in his posthumous sale and has since disappeared, and whose composition is known only from an

Fig. 102   George Romney, *Ferdinand Led by Music in the Air*, *c.*1786, pen with black ink, black and grey watercolour wash over graphite on laid paper, 34 x 36 cm, Fitzwilliam Museum, Cambridge

earlier drawing showing the composition in reverse (fig. 102), seems from the price it fetched to have been something of a trifle; yet it was described at fond length as 'a large picture in the *Correggiesque* style' by John Romney. He related it to his father's study of Correggio and Parmigianino in Parma on his trip to Italy in the mid-1770s; yet even though Romney may have retained affection for the Parmese school from that moment onward, it seems most likely that he consciously sought to paint in a new 'Correggiesque' manner after 1790. Both these pictures were begun just after that date, while Romney's one known oil copy after Correggio – also included in the posthumous sale – was a study from the Parmese artist's *Mystic Marriage of St Catherine* in the Louvre, a work it seems very likely that Romney made on his visit to Paris in the summer of 1790 rather than at an earlier stage of his career.[31]

Given Romney's public image as a successful, but isolated, society portraitist, few people can have been conscious of the extent to which his works of the imagination obeyed the instinct in every artist to imitate and draw strength from the works of others. Besides Correggio, Romney had long studied Titian, Raphael, and works of classical sculpture especially keenly (as late as 1794 taking delivery of large numbers of casts sent to him from Rome by Flaxman, a strong sign of his enlarged ambitions as a history painter). Amongst his contemporaries in London, the most influential, over a long period, had been Henry Fuseli. Romney had got to know the latter's work in Rome and throughout the late 1770s and 1780s he seems to have kept a watching brief on it, at times borrowing his designs from Fuseli's quite overtly. From 1790, however, Romney appears to have viewed Fuseli's work in a different light. Whether or not his new interest in the characters of Titania and Puck, which first emerged at the level of sketches and studies in the late 1780s, was born from an awareness that Fuseli had already begun making pictures from *A Midsummer Night's Dream,* his paintings of the early 1790s diverged as sharply from the complex and overloaded pictures that Fuseli produced for the Boydells as it would be possible to imagine. They constituted a parting of the ways from Fuseli. Equally, there are signs that Romney persuaded the Boydells to commission a Milton biography from Hayley in 1791 because he now saw Fuseli's involvement in Johnson's edition of Milton's poems as a threat, not a prop, to his own ideas regarding Milton illustration. The finished *Milton and his Daughters,* in its studied simplicity and instant legibility, was duly worlds away from the learned and psychologically dense world of Fuseli's art. However, when Fuseli opened his Milton Gallery at the end of the 1790s, it would have been possible for viewers to have detected (of all things) a debt to Romney in the Swiss artist's relatively low-key depictions of incidents in Milton's life.

∗ ∗ ∗

Romney's ability to devote more energy to 'historical' paintings after 1790 – and his improved completion rate represents perhaps the most striking contrast with the pattern of his work over the previous twenty years – might imply a concomitant slackening in his commitment to society portraiture. It is true that the number of his sitters tailed off to some extent after 1790, and it is also true that for years past, Romney had adopted a cynical approach to the production-line of portraiture, seldom eschewing the routine unless something in his sitter's personality – most notably in the case of Emma Hart – stirred him to creative adventure. Yet, selectively, his engagement with portraiture remained intact; a steady stream of new clients still beat their way to his door, and there are signs in certain portraits of the 1790s that he was continuing to evolve new styles and concerns, as he had done throughout his career. Although he chose to stand apart from his colleagues socially, he had always been conscious of their work, and some of his late portraits

Fig. 103 George Romney,
Lady Mary Stopford, 1793,
oil on canvas, 76 x 63.5 cm,
Private Collection

strongly suggest his awareness of the younger generation, even while he probably viewed them as in some sense as his own offspring. It would have been surprising, for example, if he had not considered the language of Lawrence's early portraiture to have derived from his own work: key aspects of it, such as the bright, rather cold palette, the manneristic elongation of the figures, or the liking for abrupt, panoramic landscape backdrops, could all be seen to have had their origins in Romney's portraits of the 1780s, which the teenaged Lawrence is known to have admired. Given the frustration and jealousy Romney must have felt towards his young rival in the early 1790s (as late as 1792, Lawrence showed at the Royal Academy his huge *Prospero Raising the Storm*, an obvious political tilt at Romney that misfired) the notion of Romney taking from Lawrence might appear inconceivable. Yet in a work such as the *Lady Mary Stopford* (fig. 103), the uncharacteristic fussiness of the paint handling, the slightly silvery tonality, and the edgy, exaggerated scale of the figure in the landscape all read as a conscious nod in Lawrence's direction. It must be significant that the sitter was one of Romney's very few clients from court circles, and he may have been indulging in a reflection, possibly ironic, on court taste.

Equally elusive is the notion of Romney responding to the work of Henry Raeburn. Again in the late 1780s fundamental elements of Romney's style had rubbed off on the younger artist when he visited the studios of London artists on his way back from Italy to Edinburgh (clearly detectible, although seldom recognised, in such works as *Lieutenant-Col. George Lyon*, *Lady Forbes* or his first full-length, *Mrs Mary Downey*). In 1792, Raeburn sent for exhibition in London his latest important work, a double portrait of Sir John Clerk and his wife. Intended for the Royal Academy, it arrived too late, and was hung instead in the Boydell Shakespeare Gallery, a change of plan that Romney must have been aware of and it is tempting to think may even have been involved in. Raeburn's poetic depiction of the two figures caught in a very specific half-light was a radical crystallization of trends already becoming visible in Romney's portraiture of the previous decade, and it is difficult to believe that while *Sir John and Lady Clerk* was on exhibition in London it passed unnoticed by the older artist. For an increasing boldness in depicting his sitters in poetic, hazy and above all crepuscular light was one of the two distinctive new trends in Romney's portraiture of the 1790s. Perhaps the most strikingly Raeburnesque of Romney's late works is the full-length portrait, dating from 1795, of Master Winchcombe Henry Hartley (fig. 104); the figure is both bathed in light that steals over the ridge of a hillside, and caught on the turn, in arrested movement, in the same way that Raeburn's figure of Sir John Clerk is.

The second development in Romney's late portraiture was his interest, right at the end of his career, in painting groups. In the thirty years before 1795, Romney is known to have painted only a tiny handful of portraits containing more than three figures, and they caused him increasing difficulty; in his last three years of artistic activity he painted six more. This belated enthusiasm may have been kindled by his work on what he called 'the Great picture': the well-known full-length (now at Yale) of himself with the Hayleys, father and son, and John Flaxman, in what may have been intended as a *paragone* between painting and sculpture,[32] and was certainly a deeply considered and personal celebration of an old friendship newly rekindled

Fig. 104   George Romney, *Master Winchcombe Henry Hartley*, 1795, oil on canvas, 231.5 x 140 cm, Detroit Athletic Club

Fig. 105   George Romney, *John Flaxman Modeling the Bust of William Hayley*, 1795-96, oil on canvas, 226.1 x 144.8 cm, Yale Center for British Art, Paul Mellon Collection

Fig. 106   George Romney,
The Bosanquet Family, 1795,
oil on canvas, 239 x 205 cm,
Private Collection, UK

(fig. 105). But the 'Great picture' was preceded chronologically by *The Bosanquet Family*, a large portrait of the beautiful wife of a banker and their five young children (fig. 106), whose alluring and contrasted figures may well have been even

Fig. 107 George Romney,
The Scott Family, c.1796-97,
oil on canvas, 104 x 127 cm,
Lawrence Steigrad Fine Arts,
New York

more seductive muses than his friends. To judge from his remark to Hayley about
the completed picture, 'I think it has unity and sentiment',[33] Romney was
specifically concerned with the creation of an overall, unifying mood whilst at the
same time maximising the element of variation between the six individuals
portrayed: a complex, theoretical task that the laboured working out of the design
suggests that he approached with more perspiration than inspiration. The same
might be said of one of his very last works, *The Scott Family* (fig. 107),[34] in which
there is an unmistakeably modern, 'photographic' feeling of the four figures frozen
in mid-movement, caught on the wing; but at the same time the sense of an almost
Baroque essay in contrasts, in the effects of *chiar'oscuro*, the range of the sitters'

expressions, and the almost abstract play of shapes. Such pictures, for all their solecisms, reveal Romney taking his portraiture to a fresh level of ambition and invention. They stand as the opening of a new phase in his career, not in any sense a winding down.

At the end of 1795 many of the most salient themes of Romney's recent work were brought together in a single grand statement. This was *The Egremont Family* (fig. 108), a commission from Lord Egremont for a portrait of his long-term partner, Elizabeth Ilive, and four of their young children. The commission was engineered by Lord Egremont's Sussex neighbour, William Hayley, and unusually, it was carried out not in Romney's London studio but in Sussex, where, at Petworth House, Romney was treated as a friend and encouraged in his designs in just the way that later J.M.W. Turner would be. The resulting work could scarcely be termed a formal portrait at all, for it was a bold and deeply subjective vision of his hostess and her children as Shakespeare's Titania and her fairies: a reprise on a grander scale of one of his most poetic recent *Midsummer Night's Dream* paintings, *Titania's Attendants Chasing Bats*. Miss Ilive herself is shown recumbent, arm outstretched and head tilted in one of the most extraordinary poses in eighteenth-century British portraiture, while her children, grouped with what appears total disdain for conventional pictorial values, are completely absorbed in their fictitious pursuits. The scene is bathed in such a deep twilight that the figures – at least they are clothed – sink almost into darkness; the distant last rays of the sun are what hold the centre ground of the composition. Clearly such an image could only have been the product of a remarkable empathy between artist and patron; but, when given the opportunity of working in an unusually congenial environment, Romney has not faltered. He has seized the chance to produce the summative work of his career, one in which his most evolved personal instincts as an artist have been articulated.

* * *

It would be idle to pretend, of course, that *The Egremont Family* registers as an unequivocal masterpiece, just as it would be difficult to claim that any of the works of Romney's last years carries greater authority than anything he had painted before. Equally it is true that in his later years Romney was often depressed, sometimes to the point where (as with Joseph Wright of Derby) he was unable to

Fig. 108   George Romney, *The Egremont Family*, 1795-96, oil on canvas, 169 x 228.5 cm, Private Collection, West Sussex

paint; he suffered several minor strokes and endured other physical tribulations that ultimately affected his ability to control his paintbrush and even caused him to ruin pictures he had begun. But at the same time there is an undeniable sense that in these last years he enlarged his horizons and arrived at a maturity and self-reliance that took his work not only onto a new plane, but also to a conceptual level that few if any of his contemporaries had reached. Romney in 1792 was right to see himself and not Lawrence, the young lad who had created a splash with a few showy portraits, as the true heir of Reynolds. His application to become Painter to the King in that year – later reported to Farington by Nathaniel Marchant – was not the action of a crank, but the recognition that after thirty years in London his time had finally arrived; this was the implication of his promise that if appointed, he would begin exhibiting at the Royal Academy.[35]

No doubt it is impossible to conceive Romney and the Royal Academy setting their differences aside; and no doubt too Romney's political image as a Radical – never more than a fair-weather affectation, but easily turned against him – contributed to his increasing isolation. Even so, it is not entirely an exercise in futility to suspend reality and wonder what the terrain of British art would have looked like if after 1790 Romney had achieved the recognition he craved in the eyes of his contemporaries, and found the conditions in which to paint all the masterpieces with which his imagination teemed. Would Lawrence have established the same stranglehold on the language of portraiture, or the mindset of leading patrons? Would Turner's achievement in the realm of the literary landscape have seemed in retrospect so remarkable? Would Pre-Raphaelitism have happened? The answer to each of these questions, one might well conclude, is no.

1 *Morning Post*, 1 September 1789: 'Romney the painter was one of the most active advisers of the Boydell Shakespeare and promised to do such things! It is curious, however, that he has not yet contributed one picture'.

2 Sir Ellis Waterhouse, *The Dictionary of British 18th Century Painters*, Woodbridge 1981, p.318.

3 David Bindman, 'Romney, George' in David Bindman, ed., *The Thames and Hudson Encyclopaedia of British Art*, London 1985, p.207.

4 Lucy Peltz, 'Arrival on the Scene: The 1790s' in A.C. Albinson, P. Funnell and L. Peltz, eds., *Thomas Lawrence, Regency Power and Brilliance*, exh. cat., National Portrait Gallery London and Yale Center for British Art, New Haven (2010–11), p.88.

5 Draft letter, John Romney to William Hayley, dated 23 June 1806, Romney mss, Fitzwilliam Museum Cambridge.

6 The present writer has been guilty of perpetuating this view; e.g. *George Romney 1734–1802*, exh. cat., Walker Art Gallery Liverpool, National Portrait Gallery London and Huntington Art Collections, San Marino, Calif. (2002), p.36: 'the unambiguous failure of the work'. I am grateful to Dr Suzanne May for re-focusing my attention on the *Tempest* criticism, and for wider discussion of writing about Romney, a revisionist view of which is presented in her '*Sublime and Infernal Reveries': George Romney and the Creation of an eighteenth-century History Painter*, 2 vols., PhD diss., Liverpool John Moores University (2007).

7 Witt Library Press Cuttings Volume, an album of press cuttings concerning the visual arts, 1737–1811, formerly held in the Witt Library, Courtauld Institute of Art, now lost: undated cutting headed *For the Morning Chronicle. The Gallery of Shakspeare.*

8 *Ibid.*, undated cutting headed *Romney's Tempest.*

9 Burney Collection of 18th Century Newspapers, *Public Advertiser*, 10 December 1790.

10 Burney Collection of 18th Century Newspapers, *Diary or Woodfall's Journal*, 31 January 1791.

11 *The Times*, 21 December 1790.

12 K. Garlick, A. Macintyre and K. Cave, eds., *The Diary of Joseph Farington*, 16 vols., New Haven and London 1978–84, vol.2, p.215 (entry of 17 July 1794).

13 William Hayley, *The Life of George Romney Esq.*, Chichester 1809, p.212.

14 Hayley, *Life of George Romney*, p.141.

15 Hayley, *Life of George Romney*, pp.141, 142.

16 Henry Fuseli, ed., *A Dictionary of Painters from the Revival of the Art to the Present Period* by the Rev. M. Pilkington A.M., London 1805, pp.466–67; Edward Edwards, *Anecdotes of Painters who have Resided or Been Born in England*, London 1808, pp.276–79.

17 Thomas Phillips, 'A Brief Biographical Memoir of George Romney, Historical and Portrait Painter' in John Britton, ed., *The Fine Arts of The English School*, Chiswick 1812, part 1, p.28.

18 W.H. Watts to Rev. John Romney, letter, 10 September 1811, Pierpont Morgan Library, New York, Department of Literary and Historical Manuscripts.

19 W. H. Watts, 'Titania, Puck, The Changeling, etc ... painted by George Romney Esq.' in Britton, *The Fine Arts of The English School*, part 2, p.7.

20 Folger Shakespeare Library, sketchbook Art Vol. c61, pp. 72–74. The notes appear most conveniently in Yvonne Romney Dixon, *'Designs from Fancy': George Romney's Shakespearean Drawings*, exh. cat., Folger Shakespeare Library, Washington DC (1998), pp.232–33.

21 These seven paintings, the relationship between them, and their preparatory sketches are discussed in greater detail by the present writer in Lowell Libson, ed., *George Romney's 'Titania and her Attendants'*, London 2011, pp.11–19.

22 Letter, Romney to James Romney, 8 April 1793, Romney mss, National Art Library L.1957/942/1.1.

23 Letter, Romney to John Romney, 15 [or 18] March 1794, Romney mss, National Art Library L.1948/4031/3.

24 John Flaxman, 'Sketch of Romney's Professional Character', in Hayley, *Life of George Romney*, p.309.

25 Christie's sale catalogue, 27 April 1807, lot 115.

26 Phillips, 'A Brief Biographical Memoir of George Romney', p.27.

27 Hayley, *Life of George Romney*, p.186.

28 John Romney, *Memoirs of the Life and Works of George Romney*, London 1830, p.229.

29 Flaxman, *loc. cit.* in Hayley, *Life of George Romney*, p.309.

30 Hayley, *Life of George Romney*, p.304.

31 A similar work in the posthumous sale, *Jupiter and Antiope*, can be directly related through drawings dateable to 1790, to Titian's painting of that title in the Louvre.

32 For this interpretation, see Todd Magreta, 'George Romney's Late Group Portraits at Abbot Hall and Yale', *British Art Journal*, vol.8, no.1 (Autumn 2007), pp.58–66.

33 Hayley, *Life of George Romney*, p.233.

34 I am grateful to Brian Allen for bringing this undocumented and unpublished work to my attention.

35 Garlick, Macintyre and Cave, *Diary of Joseph Farington*, vol.3, p.910 (entry of 29 October 1797).

BRITAIN AT PEACE AND WAR
J.M.W. Turner's Four 'State of the Nation' Surveys, 1793–1836

Eric Shanes

And also because Brian Allen has resided in Windsor, Berkshire for many years

Fig. 109 J.M.W. Turner, *Britain at Peace* (known as *'Imaginary Landscape with Windsor Castle'*), here dated to 1793, pencil and watercolour with some gouache, 46.1 x 73.9 cm, Tate, London

BRITAIN AT PEACE AND WAR
J.M.W. Turner's Four 'State of the Nation' Surveys, 1793–1836

Eric Shanes

On many occasions throughout his life J.M.W. Turner (1775–1851) openly avowed his allegiance to the Theory of Poetic Painting, that nexus of ideas concerning the equation of poetry with the visual arts. At the heart of the theory was the requirement that artists should tackle subjects that enjoy the widest relevance to humanity. It was because History painting did precisely this that Sir Joshua Reynolds deemed it a more elevated genre than, say, portraiture or landscape painting, which he regarded as dealing merely with particularities; and it is equally why, on four occasions, Turner addressed the broadest of subjects available to a patriotic Englishman, namely the state of his nation. The first of these surveys was created in 1793, when he was just seventeen years of age; the last of them in 1836, when he was sixty-one. In each of the four we see a range of people who denote the spectrum of social class in British society, either through overt depiction or by some more covert signifiers of that span, or by a mixture of the two.

By 1793 Turner had already begun to grasp that by investing landscape painting with the human reach that could be encountered in History painting he could instil his preferred genre with a seriousness of moral purpose that would inevitably elevate its cultural standing and, in the process, raise his own artistic status. The development of such an aspiration reflects the fact that by that date he had already been a student in the Royal Academy Schools for more than three years and had thus come into very close contact with the ideas of Reynolds. Turner heard the great pedagogue speak publicly for the very last time in December 1790, and he had read the Discourses in their published form both before and after that date. Moreover, during the summer of

1791 he had actually worked in Reynolds's house in Leicester Fields for some weeks.[1] And then there was his professional advancement within the Royal Academy: since 1790 he had been regularly showing watercolours in its annual exhibitions and by 1793 one of his drawings had finally made it to the top floor of Somerset House, where the most prestigious exhibits went on display.[2] From his growing awareness of his powers, and from the increasingly favourable response to his works, emerged a desire to tackle challenging subjects and create images that enjoyed the widest possible relevance to humanity. In this respect, nothing could have been more ambitious than a work dating from 1793 that reflected upon the state of Britain, particularly since the nation had been at war for almost three months by the time the 1793 Royal Academy Exhibition opened its doors to the public on 29 April of that year.[3]

The very large watercolour (fig.109) in which Turner effected this first state-of-the-nation survey is known today as 'Imaginary Landscape with Windsor Castle', although that title did not emanate from the artist and it fails to do justice to the image, as we shall see.[4] It depicts a Windsor Castle far removed from its normal setting in Berkshire. Instead, it is placed upon an incline that rises towards what looks very like a section of the Avon Gorge near Bristol. The work has always been dated to 1797 or later, although it shares all the stylistic characteristics of drawings made during the 1792–94 period.[5] For example, the spindly man in the foreground (fig.110) is extremely similar in draughtsmanship, style and handling to the gardener in the forefront of *The Founder's Tower, Magdalen College* (Salting Bequest, British Museum), as well as to the men on the right of *Rochester* (figs.111, 112), both of which watercolours indubitably date from 1793. Similarly, in draughtsmanship, style and handling the adjacent pack mule closely resembles the animals in a view of St Mary's Church from Oriel Lane, Oxford of 1792 (Turner Bequest, Tate Britain), the creatures in a depiction of Tom Tower, Christ Church, Oxford of 1792–93 (Turner Bequest, Tate Britain), a horse in a representation of the interior of Eltham Palace of 1793 (Yale Center for British Art, New Haven), and animals that appear in many other works of the latter year. No less tellingly, the drawing of Windsor Castle (see figs.109 and 113) demonstrates the looseness in the depiction of architecture that is still occasionally encountered by 1793 but not by much later; for a comparison, see the 1793 drawing of Rochester (fig.112) where the free way of drawing the distant city is identical. The plants, foliage, grasses, boats and body of water in the 'Imaginary Landscape with Windsor Castle' equally accord in

Fig. 110   J.M.W. Turner, *Britain at Peace* (detail)

Fig. 111   J.M.W. Turner, *Rochester* (detail)

Fig. 112   J.M.W. Turner, *Rochester*, *c.*1793, pencil and watercolour on paper, 21.6 x 27.9 cm, Sterling and Francine Clark Art Institute, Williamstown, Massachusetts, USA

draughtsmanship, style and handling with similar forms and objects encountered in other watercolours of 1792–94. Moreover, the fact that part of the Avon Gorge has been brought into the image further supports its dating to 1793; that valley was still very much in Turner's mind at the time, as is made clear from his exhibiting two views of it at the Royal Academy that year (one of them being the watercolour displayed on the top floor of Somerset House). After that date he never again created a finished view of the Avon Gorge.

Clearly the 'Imaginary Landscape with Windsor Castle' is an artificial construct that brings together two or more landscape entities which are located far apart in reality. Such a synthesis had been recommended by Sir Joshua Reynolds in his fourth Discourse, wherein he asserted that landscape painters are overly beholden to the 'accidents of nature'.[6] By this he meant that such artists, if they were to remain true to their experiences, must be ruled by the apparent arbitrariness shared by every shifting phenomenon within the natural world – its unpredictable weather, its changing light and its seasonal transformations. Equally, they are forced to respect the fairly arbitrary way in which those effects are encountered, and by the seeming arbitrariness and confusion, at least for landscape painters, in which the world itself is laid out. Yet Reynolds had allowed that there was a way of transcending such changeability, randomness and disorder. This was through ideal synthesis, the approach adopted by the French-born painter of idealised classical landscapes and Italian vistas, Claude le Lorrain (1700–1782). As far as is known, Claude seems almost always to have limited himself to drawing in front of nature, with his large and medium-sized oil paintings being developed back in his studio from the resulting small studies, as well as from memory and imagination. During this process he would combine what he deemed to be the finest parts of many scenes in order to effect a synthesis that would transcend the arbitrary. For Reynolds, the approach followed by Claude represented the only valid way of creating landscape paintings and quite evidently Turner employed exactly the same synthesising procedure when putting together the 'Imaginary Landscape with Windsor Castle'. To a greater or lesser degree, it was an approach he would follow throughout the rest of his life, at least in those many works he put on public display or sold privately.

The title this watercolour has been given, 'Imaginary Landscape with Windsor Castle', fails to invest it with any coherent meaning. It suggests that Turner has brought together all its subsidiary components at random. Yet if we take note of what all those elements signify in their own right, then it does become possible to understand what the image means in overall terms. Additionally, because we possess evidence that Turner expressed himself associatively,[7] it seems logical to investigate whether he did so here as well. Certainly we should not be surprised if, upon close examination, the 'Imaginary Landscape with Windsor Castle' does turn out to be an associative image, for the annual exhibitions of the Royal Academy were crammed with works containing associative meanings. Turner would have remained very much an outsider had he failed to express himself associatively, at least on occasion.

Fig. 113 J.M.W. Turner,
Britain at Peace (detail)

The vital clues that we are looking at an associative depiction in 'Imaginary Landscape with Windsor Castle' reside precisely in its components: a royal castle, a brightly lit church spire, a collection of habitations, a large and very prominent industrial building, an adjacent river, some cultivated land, and so on. Put together, with the social order symbolically headed by Windsor Castle, everything falls into place to form a systematically ordered allegory of peace and harmonious social relations.

By 1793, Windsor Castle had long served as the principal royal residence in England, with King George III especially making it his home. That is why for most people it was synonymous with the monarchy, and quite evidently why Turner placed it centrally in his watercolour. Highlighted in front of that impressive symbol of regal power is a spire, which betokens the Church of England and is thus symbolic of the spiritual realm. This vertical structure necessarily implies the presence of a city, town or village. Such a conurbation could well begin with the buildings situated on the brow of the hill in front of the spire, and continue over that crest to surround the church itself. Much nearer to hand, a large mill and its ancillary buildings collectively signify industry (fig.113).[8] There can be no doubt that we are looking at an industrial mill here. By the time of Turner's watercolour, Richard Arkwright's three cotton mills of 1771-83 in Cromford, Derbyshire had set the architectural pattern for mills and factories throughout Britain,[9] and Turner's mill is of an analogous design. The fact that Turner's building is placed near a river that could have supplied it with power further encourages this reading.

The quay in front of the mill points to the most efficient way of taking industrial goods to market in a pre-railway Britain that possessed few surfaced roads, and in which canals and rivers instead served as major industrial and commercial arteries. Obviously the moored vessels represent such river transportation. Beyond the boats are cultivated fields, with smoke issuing from a building that might well be a farmhouse. The smoke indicates that peaceful life is being enjoyed there. To right and left of the fields, and across the entire foreground, are stretches of wilderness, out of which all the areas of civilisation and tamed nature have been wrested. In the foreground a road and a pack-mule (see fig.110) serve as additional reminders of commerce. The sky is very peaceful, with no storm-clouds that might associatively denote stress and conflict anywhere to be seen.

Turner's image therefore contains representative examples of most of the leading aspects of British life. Only one important sector of society is unrepresented, the military, which could easily have been signified by the introduction of a few soldiers and/or sailors into the landscape. Their absence makes it evident that this is a peaceful scene and that, taken as a whole, we are witnessing a systematic analysis of British society immediately prior to the outbreak of war early in 1793. To effect this symbolic depiction of peace and socio-economic order, Turner necessarily resorted to a synthesizing approach, for there was no other way of bringing together all the associative pointers he required. What the image most certainly is *not* is topographically cavalier, for clearly topographical accuracy played no part in its conception. Instead, Turner wanted to remind his fellow countrymen of what had been lost when Britain went to war with France. He was looking back nostalgically at a nation at peace and, by implication, hoping that peace would soon return. And that is why it is appropriate to rename the watercolour *Britain at Peace*, for such a title bestows a far more accurate description of its contents than the inadequate, wholly inauthentic and misleading name under which it labours at present.

Given the scale and complexity of the image, Turner probably worked on it over a period of several months. Indeed, it was surely his most ambitious work to date. That he put so much effort into it was only fitting, given its thematic ambitiousness. It is not known why he failed to display it, for its size and detailing strongly suggest that it was made with exhibition in mind. Perhaps the realisation that such a wistful view of Britain at peace might be interpreted as anti-patriotic when the nation was at war prevented the artist from exhibiting it. He may also have felt that some more subtle form of reference to matters of such wide-ranging national significance could be found, and this would indeed prove to be the case before too long. Alternatively, he may have concluded that the associationism of the image overrode the demands of geography just a little too much. And Windsor Castle looks odd for yet another reason. Positioned as it is beneath the summits of nearby hills, such a low placing in reality would have made it militarily extremely vulnerable. That weakness would surely have been heavily criticised if any army officer trained in military topography (as most were) had ever seen the work in public. Far from incongruously placing Windsor Castle 'among mountain scenery derived from Turner's Welsh tours' and displaying 'a whimsical humour totally uncharacteristic of the artist' that is 'hardly to be paralleled elsewhere in his output',[10] the *Britain at Peace* of 1793 should be seen as Turner's first generalised landscape in the grand manner, albeit only in watercolour; his first associative landscape of any consequence; his first extended allegory; and, by its allusions to his country's recent past and possible future, his first large-scale historical composition. As such, it undoubtedly forms one of the key works in his *oeuvre*.

About sixteen years later Turner made his next state-of-the-nation image. This was *Plowing up Turnips near Slough* (fig.114) which, despite its title,[11] is quite evidently another depiction of that symbol of the British monarchy, Windsor Castle. It formed the ninth work listed in the catalogue of the exhibition that the artist mounted between 24 April and 3 June 1809 in the gallery he had created some five years earlier out of an 'outbuilding' immediately to the rear of the house he had been partially or wholly renting at 64 Harley Street, Marylebone since November 1799. In this canvas Turner represented the view looking southwards across the Thames valley from near the village of Slough soon after dawn. In terms of its meaning, the oil painting was

Fig. 114   J.M.W. Turner, *Plowing up Turnips near Slough*, exhibited 1809, oil on canvas, 101.9 x 130.2 cm, Tate, London

undoubtedly the most complex and challenging work in the 1809 exhibition. It has been asserted that it makes an 'especially patriotic' statement about the significance of agriculture in wartime,[12] with the King – represented by Windsor Castle – at the apex of the nation and the farm labourers at its base. However, this interpretation is based upon a superficial reading of the image. When we look more carefully at its details and put them within their wider context, we can see that the picture proffers a subtle political warning instead.

A clue to that meaning may reside in the incorporation of the name of Slough in the title of this work rather than Windsor Castle or Eton, the latter being even nearer than Slough to the pictorial viewpoint employed. Turner may have titled it thus because he wished to suggest that the people depicted have reason to be despondent, and an immediate way of achieving that end was to link their surroundings with the Slough of Despond in John Bunyan's *The Pilgrim's Progress* of 1678.[13] Given Turner's pronounced associationism, such a thesis is completely tenable, for a great many English agricultural workers did have cause to be despondent by 1809, not least of all in relation to the humble turnip.

At the time the root vegetable was widely disliked for the social stigma attached to eating it; it was more usually fed to cattle, even though it was not a nutritious animal food and its taste often found its way into cow's milk, to the detriment of the latter. Turnips had an additional significance: they typified rural dispossession, for their cultivation was only viable within a system of land enclosure. Prior to the largescale spread of that system during the eighteenth century, most agricultural workers in England were not reduced to eating such a lowly foodstuff; instead, they had usually survived on what they could raise on small plots of common land. But by 1809 land enclosure had long determined that agricultural labourers were forced to accept subsistence wages or be forced off the land. When harvests were poor, wages would fall or vanish entirely, and then the eating of turnips by rural workers and their families could easily become an unpalatable necessity. Poor harvests had occurred in 1808 and in many previous years. Moreover, by specifying the 'plowing up' of turnips in his picture title, Turner was further reminding us that turnips were most efficiently grown as part of a crop-rotation system that depended upon land enclosure. Crop-rotation may have greatly increased the productivity of British agriculture by 1809 but many of the people forced to implement it paid a high price for that improved efficiency.

Figs. 115, 116   J.M.W. Turner,
Plowing up Turnips near Slough
(detail)

The 'plowing up' is the necessary preparation for the planting of a new crop, and the plough is visible immediately beyond the women pulling up turnips to the right of centre (fig.115). It is being drawn by four horses rather than the usual pair because the muddiness of the soil has necessitated extra effort.[14] In the centre a wooden seed drill is being assembled so that the seeding can take place (fig.116). This device had been invented in China in ancient times and used in mainland Europe from the sixteenth century onwards but it only reached England in 1701 when Jethro Tull had greatly refined its design. Unfortunately his idea was technologically ahead of its time, for eighteenth-century seed drills were rarely strong enough to cope with the demands made upon them by working heavy soil. Because of the need for strength, seed drills would only become fully practicable when advances in metallurgy and mechanical engineering took place later in the nineteenth century.

Essentially a seed drill bores holes in the soil at regular intervals and then plants its seeds down the tubes employed for drilling. The use of such a machine ensures the regular spacing of the seeds and their alignment in rows. This both maximises the potential of nutrients in the soil and makes weeding far easier. The drilling of seeds replaced the broadcasting or scattering of seeds by hand, which produces a much more random, wasteful and uneven planting, and makes weeding far more difficult. And therein partially lies the rub in Turner's picture, for at the centre the artist has juxtaposed a farmworker holding a seedlip or basket from which to scatter seeds by hand, and two men assembling a seed-drill.[15] Quite clearly, this encounter between the old and the new has so unnerved the man who is screwing the seed drill together that unwittingly he has made one of its arms face upwards instead of downwards. Doubtless the drill will be reassembled when he realises his mistake, with the seeding to follow. But even then there is no guarantee that the weather will encourage the new crop to flourish. Should it not do so, the labourers and their families might well be forced to subsist upon turnips for some time to come.

On the left two women sit upon the heavy roller that will be used to break up the large clods of earth left by the ploughing. One of the women breastfeeds her infant, reminding us that the milk of turnip-fed cows could never taste as sweet as mother's milk. On the right a cow sniffs at some turnips, obviously to induce associations of the turnips fed to cattle. Next to the cow a tankard hangs from the handle of a wheelbarrow, clearly to allude to the tankard variety of turnip. Near the tankard are a bottle and a bag. Although it has been claimed that the bottle was intended to remind us of the frequent resort to alcohol by the rurally dispossessed,[16] in combination with the bag it surely represents no more than someone's breakfast or lunch. Probably the bottle contains small beer, another reason for the presence of the tankard. Slightly further to the left an overseer records on a roll of paper the numbers of turnips being collected by the women bending in front of him. His prominence might well have been intended to remind us of the new economic order brought about by land enclosure and by the rise of factory farming.

In the distance, Windsor Castle indirectly reminds us of improvements in farming methods too, for the monarch whose principal home it was had long been associated with good farming practice, especially in Windsor Great Park on the far side of the residence. Although King George III had often been ridiculed as 'Farmer George' by the radical press and satirical print-makers for his promotion of efficient farming, far more people in Britain thought positively of the sovereign for his agricultural aspirations than not. Turner might well have been one of them. Yet the fact remains that, by means of its subject and the associations it generates,

Fig. 117 J.M.W. Turner, *Plowing up Turnips near Slough* (detail)

Plowing up Turnips near Slough addresses the harsh reality of survival for the rural poor, not least because, when all else failed, the turnip provided them with virtually their only source of sustenance. Had Turner not wanted to generate such an association he could easily have depicted a different rotational crop being gathered and then ploughed up, such as wheat, oats or barley.[17]

Pictorially, the composition of the figures in the image is unusually disorganised and that disarray was surely intentional, for had Turner wished to impose visual order he could easily have done so. But in that comparative chaos lies our principal clue to his ultimate intention: he wanted to contrast the disordered, impoverished and uncertain life of the peasantry with the ordered, luxurious and seemingly secure life of the monarchy that ruled over it, as signified by Windsor Castle towering up majestically in the distance. And in order to advance that meaning even further, Turner has placed a raging fire beneath the castle. Although the clouds of smoke produced by this conflagration have always previously been thought to constitute an early morning river mist,[18] that is simply not the case. Close examination (fig.117) reveals that the clouds are billowing with a vigour and a profusion that are never to be found in the gentle swirlings of a river mist. Moreover, at its source the smoke is red-tinged, with the colouring gradually diminishing in intensity to the right, so there can be no doubt that it is issuing from a fire. By placing such an inferno beneath the castle that particularly stood for the British monarchy, Turner was clearly reminding us of what had happened fairly recently to the French monarchy when it turned its back on the poor. In these terms, *Plowing up Turnips near Slough* was not simply about farming and the confrontations that could be generated between traditional and modern ways of doing things; far more importantly, it addressed the huge political, social and economic gulf that existed at the very heart of British society in 1809. It is entirely unsurprising that Turner made such a statement, for nobody in Britain who possessed even the slightest modicum of human sympathy could have felt wholly indifferent to the plight of the rural poor, let alone happy with what they were forced to swallow far too frequently.

Ten years later Turner exhibited his third state-of-the-nation image. This was the oil painting entitled *England: Richmond Hill on the Prince Regent's birthday* (fig.118) which was displayed as exhibit 206 within the Great Room of Somerset House as part of the 1819 Royal Academy Exhibition. There its title was accompanied in the catalogue by the following lines drawn from the 'Summer' section of James Thomson's poem *The Seasons*:

Which way, Amanda, shall we bend our course?
The choice perplexes. Wherefore should we chuse?
All is the same with thee. Say, shall we wind
Along the streams? or walk the smiling mead?
Or court the forest glades? or wander wild
Among the waving harvests? or ascend,
While radiant Summer opens all its pride,
Thy hill, delightful Shene?

In Turner's day these verses were inscribed on a board affixed to a tree standing at the summit of Richmond Hill. Additionally, and as the painter was well aware, that hill was associated not only with James Thomson but equally with Sir Joshua Reynolds, who had built a house there. Turner had known the view from Richmond Hill since his boyhood, and had made many watercolour depictions of it before creating this painting.

Fig. 118   J.M.W. Turner, *England: Richmond Hill on the Prince Regent's Birthday*, exhibited 1819, oil on canvas, 180 x 334.6 cm, Tate London

The Prince Regent's official birthday was 23 April, which was also St George's Day. In addition to being the name-day of the English national saint, it was also William Shakespeare's birthday and – if Turner is to be believed – his own birthday too.[19] However, the actual birthday of the Prince Regent fell on 12 August and, as Jean Golt has demonstrated, *England: Richmond Hill on the Prince Regent's birthday* celebrated that date, for it depicts a garden party given on Tuesday 12 August 1817 in private grounds on Richmond Hill by the Dowager Countess of Cardigan in honour of the heir to the throne.[20] Turner could not have been present at that celebration, for he had sailed for the Continent two days earlier. But he must have known about it, as preparations for the event had involved a great many people for several weeks beforehand both in Richmond and just across the river in Twickenham (where he possessed a second home, Sandycombe Lodge, that he had

Fig. 119   J.M.W. Turner, *England: Richmond Hill on the Prince Regent's Birthday* (detail)

designed and built himself). Moreover, the newspapers reported the party in great detail. Turner could therefore have easily learned of it in advance, or following his return from abroad. By 1817–19 Turner had created Greek, Carthaginian and Roman scenes: he would certainly have encountered no problems in reconstructing much more recent occurrences on one of his own doorsteps.

The Prince Regent attended the 1817 party on Richmond Hill, as did other members of the Royal Family and the Lord Mayor of London. Although none of these dignitaries is visible, the Lord Mayor's barge is discernible on the Thames (fig.119). Turner's own house is indicated far above the discarded drum in the right-foreground, for the top of a cypress tree just intersects with the horizon at the exact point at which Sandycombe Lodge is located. In the centre some people seem to be gossiping about a woman dressed in white who stares out at us. Turner may have intended her to allude to the estranged wife of the Prince Regent, Princess Caroline, who was the subject of much gossip in the late-1810s. Also present are retainers in court dress. On the right a man in military uniform greatly resembles the hero of the battle of Waterloo, the Duke of Wellington. This identification is supported by the placement of some 'petararoes' or small cannon near the soldier. At the 1817 garden party such guns were fired in honour of the Prince Regent. A soldier is drumming up interest in joining the army, recruitment for which is taking place next to him, and a large flag billows from a tree above the army contingent.

This detail may have derived from a similar feature to be found in Claude's *Landscape with a Rural Dance*,[21] now on loan to the Dulwich Picture Gallery but in Turner's day owned by one of his patrons.[22] Artistic associations are respectively introduced on the extreme left and nearer the centre by a cello and a portfolio waiting to be used or perused.

Stylistically, Turner's landscape enjoys an obvious link with Claude, while the elongated necks of a great many women viewed from behind are reminiscent of similar forms encountered in the works of Watteau and Fuseli. The Claude and Watteau connections are particularly appropriate, for both of these French painters had often projected an earthly paradise, and that appears to have been Turner's intention here as well. His suggestion of the inner, organic life of the trees contributes greatly towards the attainment of that end, for as idealised arboreal forms they surely equal the perfected human forms of, say, Praxiteles or Michelangelo. In sum, then, and as the prefix of the title makes evident, in *England: Richmond Hill on the Prince Regent's birthday* Turner set out to survey the state of his native land, and he found it a very happy one in the process. Now Britain really was at peace, with its citizens very evidently contented. As 'radiant Summer opens all its pride', people of all ages, occupations and classes are at ease both with themselves and with the world.

In 1836 Turner made the last of his state-of-the-nation images, and again he returned to Richmond Hill, Surrey in order to do so (fig.120). Now, however, he employed watercolour as his medium, just as he had done in the 1793 *Britain at Peace*. The 1836 drawing was created for subsequent reproduction in the most ambitious engraving scheme with which Turner would ever be involved, the series of prints entitled 'Picturesque Views in England and Wales' for which he elaborated one hundred designs between 1824 and 1838.[23] In 1834 King William IV had ordered the construction of a terraced walk from the bottom of Richmond Hill to its summit near the Star and Garter Inn (which is visible on the left of Turner's watercolour), and that explains why the artist entitled his work 'Richmond Terrace, Surrey' rather than 'Richmond Hill'. The watercolour would prove to be his last depiction of the vista, and in it he not only celebrated the creation of the new walkway but also matched a splendid visual panorama with a complementary social one.

Fig. 120   J.M.W. Turner,
Richmond Terrace, Surrey,
summer 1836, watercolour on
paper, 28 x 43.5 cm,
Walker Art Gallery, Liverpool

On the left we see a man in court attire accompany two ladies towards the Star and
Garter Inn. Another man wearing a top hat and slightly less formal clothing talks to an
elegantly dressed lady who is surely the mother of the podgy little boy wearing
fashionable Scots garb. (As we are gazing out from a relatively low height in this
watercolour, Highland dress on the small boy seems rather witty: an inveterate
punster, Turner liked making such jokes.) On the extreme left a uniformed coachman
looks down upon the scene. Given the dress of everyone in this left-hand grouping of
people, the individuals who comprise it could easily stand for the monarchy, the
aristocracy and the servants upon whom they depended.

In the centre, to the right of a gap that contains playful children and equally
playful dogs, are figures that include a student wearing a mortar-board and two
young women carrying parasols; given their fairly well-dressed state, they could
well have been intended to exemplify the middle classes. And finally, on the right,
may be seen strolling figures in their 'Sunday best' and an apparently exhausted
hawker slumped beneath a tree, all of whom Turner surely intended to represent

the labouring classes. Nearby, a barrow of fruit and flowers perhaps alludes to the produce of their labours.

Affixed to the tree above the slumped hawker is the board containing the verses drawn from 'Summer' pertaining to the view from Richmond Hill. The light filtering through the trees is particularly lovely, as are those trees themselves, with their gracefulness of form and sense of inner growth and flowering. If anything they are even more beauteous than the trees painted in the 1819 view from Richmond Hill. Just as he had done in that earlier work, Turner here gives us a social survey of his native land, and a happy one at that, although it is perhaps tinged with a little sadness as though the passing show is transient, like the evening light and the dying day. By 1836 Turner was well aware of his own mortality. Although he would go on celebrating life with vigour during his remaining years – as everyone hopes the dedicatee of this book will do so just as fully – it is understandable that an occasional wistfulness breaks through, as it does here in the subtle distribution of light and the use of mellow colouring.

In his four state-of-the-nation works made between 1793 and 1836, Turner gave us a range of differing responses to landscape that demonstrates what the representation of wide panoramas can encompass in terms of related social meanings. In *Britain at Peace* the young artist had looked back at the state of the nation before war had threatened to change it, and perhaps to alter it for the worse. In the 1809 Windsor view entitled *Plowing up Turnips near Slough,* he had examined the effects of a later stage of that selfsame war and what it was doing to his native land, as well as suggesting that unless things changed there might be even more disastrous consequences, at least where the monarchy was concerned. By 1819, in *England: Richmond Hill on the Prince Regent's birthday,* war was just a memory and Turner was able to celebrate the return of peace while hinting at the role that a stable monarchy and an outstanding soldier had played in bringing about that admirable state. And in 1836, with *Richmond Terrace, Surrey,* he again examined the social order and its apparently harmonious condition, even if in one small detail he subtly alluded to the physical exhaustion that this might possibly entail.

It was clearly no coincidence that three of these four views were faithful depictions of the Thames valley, and even the exception – the early *Britain at*

Peace – includes within its idealised landscape a castle that stands on the banks of the Thames. Turner was a Londoner who had been born in Covent Garden, spent three years as a child in Brentford and then lived for a short time at the mouth of the Thames estuary at Margate. Subsequently he had lived in central London, as well as residing for part of the time in Isleworth, Hammersmith, Twickenham and back in Margate (and he would end his days in Chelsea). Clearly, the Thames valley embodied everything he found most stimulating about life in Britain. It is therefore entirely unsurprising that he should have chosen that river or sections of it to make some of his most serious statements about landscape and the role that both its past and present history played within the life of his nation, in all its diverse political, social, cultural and artistic ramifications.

1   For discussion of the foregoing biographical matters, see Eric Shanes, *J.M.W. Turner: A Life in Art*, to be published by Yale University Press on behalf of the Paul Mellon Centre for Studies in British Art (in preparation).

2   This was his *View on the river Avon, near St Vincent's rock, Bristol* which was hung as exhibit 263 below the line just over halfway along the south wall of the 'Anti-Room' (as the Royal Academy habitually termed the space). There were 63 works hanging in that room this year. Unfortunately, the watercolour is now untraced and we have no idea what it looked like.

3   Britain had been at war since 1 February 1793 when France had declared war on the United Kingdom and upon the Republic of the United Provinces, as Holland was then called. A coalition between Britain, the United Provinces, Prussia, Austria, Spain and Sardinia had quickly formed to meet that challenge. Although there would be two breaks in hostilities that would each last under a year, with some of the foregoing powers being subjugated by the French, the war would continue for almost a quarter of a century, until the final defeat of Napoleon in 1815.

4   The watercolour was simply called 'A View of Windsor Castle' by A.J. Finberg in his *Complete Inventory of the Drawings in the Turner Bequest*, London 1909, p.66, where it was listed as XXXIII-H.

5   Finberg (*Inventory*, p.66) dated the drawing to 1796–97, while Andrew Wilton (*Turner in the British Museum*, exh. cat. The British Museum 1975, p.34, cat.16) dated it to around 1797–98, mainly on the basis of an identification of the 'mountain scenery' in question as being Welsh, and because it supposedly resembles a steeply embanked river drawn in the 1798 *Cyfarthfa* sketchbook (T.B. XLI), as well as a depiction of Cilgerran Castle upon a high cliff as drawn in the *Hereford Court* sketchbook of that same year (T.B. XXXVIII). However, Wilton did concede that 'in terms of style this watercolour seems to belong to a slightly earlier date'. More recently, the Turner Worldwide database on the Tate Britain website has assigned the watercolour to 1798–99 on the basis that the landscape depicted resembles scenery on the river Teifi in south-west Wales. None of these Welsh identifications are convincing and in any case all the suggested later dates seem erroneous because of the immense stylistic discrepancy that exists between this watercolour and everything else Turner created between 1796 and 1800.

6   Reynolds took this phrase from *The Principles of Painting* of 1699 by the French writer on art, Roger de Piles (1635–1709), which had been translated into English in 1743.

7   See Eric Shanes, *Turner's Human Landscape*, London 1990, for an extensive exploration of this subject.

8   The author is very grateful to Pieter van der Merwe for first identifying this building as a mill, and for sharing his knowledge of the Avon Gorge in relation to the watercolour.

9   See R.S. Fitton, *The Arkwrights, Spinners of Fortune*, Manchester 1989, pp.30, 50, 146, 201–2.

10 Wilton, *Turner in the British Museum*, p.34, cat.16. As stated above, the connection of the topography of the river valley in *Britain at Peace* with Welsh scenery is extremely tenuous and subjective. In any event, exact identification of the valley depicted is entirely irrelevant to our understanding of the work, as it was clearly not created as a topographical image.

11 The spelling of the title appears here as it is given in Turner's 1809 exhibition catalogue. Unfortunately, in the entry for the work in Evelyn Joll and Martin Butlin, *The Paintings of J.M.W. Turner*, London and New Haven, revised edition 1984, cat.89, the spelling of 'Plowing' was corrected to its modern English form and a comma inserted after the word 'Turnips'. Some aspects of the present interpretation of the painting were stimulated by an (unpublished) lecture given by Jean Golt to the Turner Society at the Paul Mellon Centre for Studies in British Art, London, both on 24 February 2007 and in more hurried form on a prior occasion.

12 Christiana Payne, *Toil and Plenty: Images of the Agricultural Landscape in England, 1780–1890*, exh. cat. Nottingham University Art Gallery 1993, pp.88–89.

13 See Michele L. Miller, 'J.M.W. Turner's Ploughing Up Turnips, near Slough: The Cultivation of Cultural Dissent', *The Art Bulletin*, vol. 77:4, December 1995, p.579. Although the copy of *The Pilgrim's Progress* in Turner's library would date from 1834, he surely read the book long before then.

14 Miller quite rightly makes the point ('J.M.W. Turner's Ploughing Up Turnips', p.579) that we are looking at an area of land adjacent to the Thames that was frequently flooded. As a consequence, the soil was very marshy.

15 As well as the drills and arms supporting them, it is also possible to discern in the original painting the coulter or long metal knife-blade that cut open the soil, thereby permitting the apparatus to advance smoothly.

16 Miller, 'J.M.W. Turner's Ploughing Up Turnips', p.582.

17 These were the other types of crops most usually rotated with turnips, with barley being the first to follow on from them.

18 For example, see Miller, 'J.M.W. Turner's Ploughing Up Turnips', p.572.

19 For discussion of this issue, see Shanes, *J.M.W. Turner: A Life in Art* (forthcoming).

20 Jean Golt, 'Beauty and Meaning on Richmond Hill: New Light on Turner's Masterpiece of 1819', *Turner Studies*, vol.7:2, Winter 1987, pp.9–20.

21 *Liber Veritatis* 13.

22 This was the Hon. Charles Anderson-Pelham (1781–1846) who would become the second Baron Yarborough upon the death of his father in 1823 and the first Earl of Yarborough in 1837.

23 For discussion of this series in detail, see Eric Shanes, *Turner's England*, London 1990.

JOSEPH BURKE
An Historian of Eighteenth-century British Art in the Antipodes

Patrick McCaughey

Fig. 121 Fred Williams, *Professor Joseph Burke*, 1977, oil on canvas,
197.5 x 95.5 cm, The University of Melbourne Art Collection

JOSEPH BURKE
An Historian of Eighteenth-century British Art in the Antipodes

Patrick McCaughey

When Joseph Burke arrived in Port Melbourne in December 1946, to take up the post of *Herald* Professor of Fine Arts at the University of Melbourne at the age of thirty-three, he had already had a remarkable career. From 1942 to 1945, he had been Private Secretary to successive Lords President of the Council, a cabinet seat, from Sir John Anderson to Clement Attlee and Lord Woolton. Attlee recalled Burke to 10 Downing Street as his Private Secretary in 1945 and he served in that capacity for the first fifteen months of Attlee's premiership. What persuaded him to swap Whitehall for Carlton – the inner city suburb of Melbourne which housed the university – was the reality of a full-time chair in the Fine Arts at a time when such opportunities existed in the UK only at the Courtauld Institute and the University of Edinburgh.

The chair of Fine Arts in Melbourne was the brainchild of Daryl Lindsay, Director of the National Gallery of Victoria 1942–56, and made possible by the philanthropy of Sir Keith Murdoch – father of Rupert Murdoch and Chairman of the influential newspaper group, *The Herald and Weekly Times* – and the Council of Trustees of the Gallery. The terms of the chair were exceptional and envisaged responsibilities for the incumbent beyond the academy. The *Herald* Professor was expected to teach 'the understanding and appreciation of the fine arts and the application of their principles and practices to the life of the community.' Such a remit suited Joe Burke – for so he was universally called in Australia – both intellectually and temperamentally. Originally there was no plan to create a Department of Fine Arts offering instruction to undergraduates and supervision to graduates. Eventually Joe Burke set up a distinguished Department with Franz

Philipp, a refugee from Nazi Austria and a former student of Julius von Schlosser, and Dr Ursula Hoff, a graduate of the Warburg Institute in Hamburg, now settled in Melbourne as Curator of Prints and Drawings at the National Gallery of Victoria. Later Bernard Smith, the eminent Australian-born art historian, joined them. Joe Burke loved to roam beyond the confines and administrative tedium of a university department.

Art historically, Joe Burke was the coming man in British circles. He read English at King's College, London in the early 1930s and wrote his MA at the Courtauld on 'A Critical Edition of Hogarth's *Analysis of Beauty* with a study of its place in the growth of aesthetic criticism in the 18th century.' The thesis was approved in 1935. Twenty years later the Clarendon Press would publish his edition of *The Analysis of Beauty with the rejected passages from the manuscript drafts and autobiographical notes.* It remained the standard edition until Ronald Paulson's revised edition of 1997.

Joe Burke continued his art historical studies at Yale on a Henry Fellowship 1936–37 undertaking research into the early career of Benjamin West. During this time he formed some important friendships with Chauncey Brewster Tinker and, most notably, Wilmarth Sheldon Lewis, editor of Horace Walpole's correspondence and founder of the Lewis Walpole Library in Farmington, Conncticut. Years later Joe Burke was fond of remarking that the true gentleman today is a New England gentleman. On his return he became Assistant Keeper – Second Class, as he would proudly declare – in the textiles department at the V&A. He was seconded to the Home Office at the outbreak of the war. During that time he continued with his scholarly work, delivering the Charlton Memorial Lecture in Newcastle in 1941, published as *Hogarth and Reynolds: A Contrast in English Art Theory* (OUP 1943). Reynolds was portrayed as 'the greatest exponent' of a theory of ideal beauty and the creator of an aesthetic orthodoxy and Hogarth as 'its most bitter foe'. Although from the start Hogarth was Joe Burke's man, noting the paradox that the *Analysis* was warmly received by men of letters and savagely attacked by artists and connoisseurs, he admired the 'tolerance' and 'catholicism' of Reynolds' taste. 'To study them [the *Discourses*] is to study the 18th century.' Such balance and moderation in art historical judgment would characterize Joe Burke's later contributions to the field.

Joe Burke remained a quintessential Englishman all his life. Tall, bespectacled, customarily dressed in blue, pin-stripe, double-breasted suits or white linen ones

Fig. 122 Sidney Nolan, *Death of Constable Scanlon*, 1946, enamel on composition board, 90.4 x 121.2 cm, National Gallery of Australia, Canberra

in summer, with a quick wit and sharp intelligence, he reminded one of a Wilfred Hyde White character with brains and energy. Yet from the moment of his arrival, he embraced Australia warmly without a trace of condescension. He was surprised at the 'distinction' of the University of Melbourne and formed an immediate and lasting friendship with Daryl Lindsay. Professor Jaynie Anderson in her pioneering study of Joe Burke and his Australian background noted 'how he fell in love with Australia, with the landscape, the eternal eucalypt, with the climate, with the art and architecture.'[1]

The latter point cannot be stressed too much. Modern Australian art was producing its first important artists in the 1940s. In Melbourne Sidney Nolan emerged at the head of a pack of gifted, iconoclastic and ambitious young artists. In Sydney, Russell Drysdale was galvanizing a small but influential following with his bleak and unaccommodating view of outback Australia as a pitiless wasteland.

Joe Burke who would write the first monograph on Drysdale (1951) noted that 'in his art Australia Indomitus takes the place of Australia Felix. He is deeply concerned with the tragedy of the drought stricken farmer not as individual victims but as a whole class of society.' Joe Burke formed lasting friendships with both Nolan and Drysdale and many other Australian artists.

In March 1948 in Melbourne Nolan showed his Ned Kelly series of paintings of 1946–47. Regarded now as classics of the modern movement in Australia, permanently and prominently installed at the National Gallery of Australia, they are a strange, still disconcerting amalgam of intense narrative drive, brilliantly recalled landscape and hard-edged primitivism. 'Begotten out of sunlight and the Douanier Rousseau,' as their author remarked. They depict the rise and fall of the bushranger, Ned Kelly and his gang, moving from tranquil landscapes to the fiery *auto-da-fé* of his capture at the burning hotel in Glenrowan. Joe Burke saw and admired these pictures of murder and mayhem in the Australian bush.

The mordant comedy of Nolan's Kelly paintings with his square black helmet and the *opera buffo* policemen falling from trees was not to everyone's taste in the Melbourne of 1948 (fig.122). But to a sensibility steeped in Hogarth, Nolan's synthesis of the heroic and the comic embodied pictorial qualities readily understood and admired. For Joe Burke, Hogarth was the artist who 'elevated wit to the level of poetry by its intensity of feeling' and Nolan would achieve the same in his Ned Kelly paintings.[2] Joe Burke was fond of quoting Charles Lamb's famous remark about Hogarth: 'Other pictures we look at – his prints we read'.[3] Burke clearly had no difficulty in applying the same to his new-found Antipodean master.

Joe Burke's friendship with Drysdale and Nolan would have lasting benefits to both these artists' careers and to the course of modern Australian art in England. In January 1949 Sir Kenneth Clark paid his one and only visit to Australia. Joe Burke was asked to draw up his program. After he had advised Clark that 'it's a mistake to see people, not places' he identified 'the two things most worth seeing in Melbourne – the Blake Illustrations to Dante in the National Gallery of Victoria and the Botanical Gardens, laid out by an Australian genius [William] Guilfoyle.'[4] After recommending that Clark visit one of the grander sheep stations in the Western District and dine in the Melbourne Club with the Felton Bequest Trustees, whom Clark had advised briefly and brilliantly in 1947–48,[5] he ended with the emphatic suggestion:

Sydney [*sic*] Nolan is the most imaginative and original painter whose work I have seen in Australia. He is young and technically immature but shows great promise. [John] Reed, a rather eccentric young man, owns the cycle of paintings illustrating the life of Ned Kelly, the bush ranger anarchist and hero of local school boys and communists.

Clark took Joe Burke's advice and the outcome was startling. In Sydney he bought paintings by both Drysdale and Nolan for himself. With limited time, Clark still made his way out to the Sydney suburb, Wahroonga, to visit Nolan in his studio. Cynthia Nolan, the artist's wife, recorded the event in an amusing letter of thanks to Joe Burke. So lavish was Clark's enthusiasm for the work that 'at first he [Sidney Nolan] thought he was being strung along and wasn't very sure whether he should knock him down … the phrase "corking good" was almost Sir K's undoing.' Clark went the extra mile for both artists. He introduced Drysdale to the Leicester Gallery in London who gave him a one-man show in 1950, the first of many. Clark was equally encouraging to Nolan who held a successful show at the Redfern Gallery in 1951. Clark's friendship with both men was genuine and long lasting, writing to Joe Burke at the end of 1950:

Drysdale lunched here last week and I have seen Nolan once or twice. They are both genuine artists and charming men. As for their wives, they are worthy of one another. It is a nice question which is more horrible. In such cases one always inclines towards the one seen last. It is a disaster that they should both be stuck with such women as they are doing them a lot of harm over here.

Shortly after Joe Burke arrived in Australia, he received two important commissions from Oxford University Press. One was to prepare the modern edition of Hogarth's *Analysis of Beauty* for the Clarendon Press which, as already noted, duly appeared in 1955. The other was the honorific invitation in 1949 by T.S.R. Boase, the General Editor of the Oxford History of English Art, to write Volume IX, covering the period 1714–1800. It was, as Jaynie Anderson observed, the 'plum' volume. The Oxford history would absorb Joe Burke for the rest of his academic life. It took over twenty-five years to produce. Joe Burke wrote his preface in 1973 and the book was finally published in 1976. T.S.R. Boase died in 1974 well before it appeared. The longer the book dragged on, the greater the burden it became for Joe Burke. The correspondence between editor and author makes for grimly amusing reading.[6]

In January 1957 Boase wrote: 'I am getting fairly well ahead with it [Volume X of the Oxford History of English Art 1800–1870] but am hoping that yours will get in first.' Joe Burke responded somewhat evasively in March: 'I have been dropping almost everything to get on with the book during the summer vacation and as no news is good news, I shall be writing at greater length as soon as I come out of semi-seclusion.' But in November 1958, Burke was assuring Boase that he was 'going into complete purdah between the 20 November and the end of March next to work on the book.' And twelve years later, in March 1970, Burke was telling his editor that he will 'cut down my text to size by about October.'

There are the obvious reasons for the delays and difficulties Burke experienced in completing the work. The remoteness from his sources – 'the tyranny of distance' – was one. Between 1950 and 1970 Joe Burke had only five periods of study leave overseas of any length. In a pre-internet age without email or digital photography, the gathering of references and photographs was a painfully slow business and Burke ran through a brace of research assistants on the way to completion. But Burke's ambition for his text was another cause. He embraced architecture, landscape gardening and the decorative as well as the fine arts, paying attention to the evolving aesthetic theories of the period. The volume was to be thematically and conceptually organized and not just chronicle art history. When eventually it was submitted, Joe Burke was as surprised as he was gratified to learn that the copy editor at OUP described the finished MS as 'scrupulously prepared.'

The long gestation of his Oxford history meant that Joe Burke engaged in eighteenth-century studies for virtually his entire scholarly life. The preparation of the longer work gave rise to lively and interesting studies along the way. Among the best of these is the deft and enterprising 'Hogarth, Handel and Roubiliac: A Note on the Interrelationships of the Arts in England c. 1730–1760'.[7] It might be of interest to preface the discussion of this article, key to understanding the cast of Joe Burke's mind, by pointing out that one of his greatest enthusiasms, amounting to a hobby horse, was the Bauhaus. He once proudly remarked that his flat in London was furnished with tables and chairs by Alvar Aaalto and Marcel Breuer ' … and I hung a Henry Moore drawing on the wall and I thought I was the cat's whiskers!' (The Moore drawing would later hang in his office in Department of Fine Arts and he generously gave it to the University of Melbourne, fig.123.)

His excitement over the Bauhaus was partly fired by his generation's dislike of all things Victorian and partly because he was fascinated by the interplay between

Fig. 123   Henry Moore,
Family Group, 1944, pen and ink,
chalk and watercolour wash,
55.9 x 43cm, The University of
Melbourne Art Collection,
gift of Joseph Burke

the fine arts and the arts of design. The particular aspect of the Bauhaus which intrigued him the most was the effect of Paul Klee and Wassily Kandinsky on the other workshops. The interrelations between painting and sculpture with theatre and music, metalwork and textiles, glass and typography interested him keenly. He was delighted to find that one of the original Bauhaus students and masters, Ludwig Hirschfeld Mack, was now working as the art master at Geelong Grammar School, a leading Anglican public school forty-five miles south of Melbourne. A close relationship grew up between the two men.

This awareness of contemporary practice found its way back into his eighteenth-century scholarship, enlivening it and making him look for the common threads

GEORGE FREDERICK HANDEL Efqʳ
born February XXIII. MDCLXXXIV.
died April XIV. MDCCLIX. *L.F.Roubiliac invᵗ et sᵗ*

between artist, composer and sculptor. They were linked through their association with two poles of London's eighteenth-century institutions, Vauxhall Gardens and the Foundling Hospital. Roubiliac's two portraits of Handel provided Joe Burke with his starting point. The Vauxhall Gardens version 'with his knees crossed, in nightcap and *negligée*, with one of his stockinged feet resting a slipper that he has carelessly cast off' (fig.124) is contrasted with the Handel Monument for Westminster Abbey (fig.125). 'The distinction' for Joe Burke lay 'between the familiar and the grand styles.' These qualities persist equally, he believes, in Handel – the grand style of the oratorios and the familiar style of the occasional music

Fig. 124 (left) L.F. Roubiliac, *George Frideric Handel* commissioned for Vauxhall Gardens, 1738, marble statue, height 135.3 cm, Victoria and Albert Museum, London

Fig. 125 (right) L. F. Roubiliac, *George Frideric Handel*, commissioned 1759 and erected 1762, Life-size marble statue, Westminster Abbey

Fig. 126   Lyonel Feininger,
*Cover design for the 1919 Bauhaus
Manifesto by Walter Gropius,*
1919, letterpress, zinc engraving
after a woodcut on greenish
paper, 32.1 x 19.4 cm,
Bauhaus Archive, Berlin

and some of the operas – and in Hogarth. For Joe Burke those two modes were the key to the mid-eighteenth century.

Between these two polarities of the grand and the familiar lies the essence of the mid-century, when the Augustans tempered the heroic with the humane and wit and poetry were in alliance.

The two styles moreover 'are part of a whole. A knowledge of one is required for an understanding of the other and *vice versa*.' For Joe Burke the overriding point was that Hogarth, Handel and Roubiliac, in mastering these polarities, forged 'a new mode of aesthetic sensibility, appropriate to the party of humanity.' The last phrase is of course Peter Gay's, from his book *The Party of Humanity: Essays in the French Enlightenment* (1964). Both book and phrase resonated deeply with Joe Burke and influenced his Oxford history.

One of Joe Burke's cardinal virtues as a lecturer (and he was a virtuoso in this role) was his insistence that every good lecture must have an argument. He applied this maxim to his Oxford history. The broad argument of the book is that the century moves from the Rule of Taste, exemplified by Richard Boyle, 3rd Earl of Burlington, buttressed by the treatises of Alexander Pope, Jonathan Richardson and Colen Campbell, to the Liberty of Taste exemplified by Robert and James Adam, preparing the way for the Picturesque and Romanticism. Hogarth and his mid-century contemporaries form the fulcrum between the two domains. The architectural emphases reflect again Joe Burke's Bauhaus predilections. Surprisingly, he rather took Walter Gropius at his word and saw its ideals embodied in Lyonel Feininger's woodblock cover design for the 1919 Bauhaus manifesto (fig.126). That profoundly expressionist image of a soaring, star encrusted cathedral demonstrated Gropius' belief that architecture formed the great umbrella to shelter all the other arts. Architecture for Joe Burke told the abstract chronicles of the age. It gave a certain stiffening (and stiffness) to his account of the early eighteenth century.

Here is Joe Burke in the Assembly Rooms in York (fig.127):

As Burlington paced up and down the completed hall, he may well have felt that old Rome, if not old Greece, had at last been 'transplanted to England'. For the solitary visitor ... the Assembly Rooms constitute the central shrine of classicism in England.[8]

Fig. 127 (left) Lord Richard Boyle Burlington, York Assembly Rooms, the colonnaded main hall, York, 1730, RIBA Library Photographs Collection

Fig. 128 (right) Robert Adam, Long Gallery, Syon House, Brentford, Middlesex

The Adam brothers form the bookends. After noting that the Adam Revolution was 'a revolution of the interior', Joe Burke gave this spirited account of Syon House (fig.128), the masterpiece of the Liberty of Taste:

> The entry in the middle was well suited to its function as a sculpture gallery. When the hall and collection have been admired, the drive is to the splendid ante-room and then on through dining-room and drawing-room to the Long Gallery spanning the entire length of the river front. The revelation of his intricate surface style is postponed to this last room in the style of a columbarium. In the further of the two closets that flank the Gallery is a playful rococo surprise, a circular Chinese room in which appropriately hangs a musical birdcage. The spatial sequence of state rooms is without peer in the British Isles, holding its own 'with the greatest palaces of the Continent'.[9]

At the outset of his history, Joe Burke gives as one of his ambitions to construct 'a narrative which based primarily on the individual achievements of artists.' His history is at its happiest when he is looking and responding to particular works or examining the pattern of an artist's or architect's career. Along with Robert Adam, his discussions of James Gibbs, Wright of Derby, George Stubbs and Richard Wilson form the most vivid passages of the history.

The climax of his account of Gibbs, whose contradictions and paradoxes Joe Burke relished such as 'the steepled temple' or the man who 'Palladianized Wren', draws from him a response, tinged with an exile's momentary nostalgia: 'Gibbs'

Fig.129 James Gibbs, St Martin-
in-the-Fields, London, 1726

synthesis [steeple and temple front, fig.129] completely eclipsed the
uncompromisingly classical design published in *Vitruvius Britannicus* and for this
reason St Martin-in-the-Fields, standing at the heart of Empire and expressing
both the religious and the secular ideals of the age, is the supreme symbol of
Georgian architecture in its imperial phase.'[10]

Joe Burke stresses time and again in his writings on eighteenth-century British
art that 'the Enlightenment in England is essentially a provincial phenomenon.'[11]
Such a view did not begin with Burke but his emphasis on the Provincial
Enlightenment – it forms the final section of his history – sheds much light on his
entire *Weltanschauung*.

First, there was strong desire to shift the aesthetic assessment of the eighteenth
century: 'Its reputation for elegance and civilized recreation should take a lower
place than its claim to artistic excellence in the sphere of wit inspired by

humanitarian sympathy.'[12] It was amongst the Provincial *Aufklärer* that Burke found his party of humanity even if Hogarth, Burke's touchstone for the elevation of wit and comedy, remains a stubbornly metropolitan figure.

Second, Joe Burke shared with his generation an aversion to the idea that eighteenth-century painting can be studied largely through portraiture. Such a view would have sounded more radical in the late 40s than in the mid 70s of the last century. It led to a curiously stilted and unconvincing account of Reynolds in the Oxford history. Such an aversion led to the steep revaluation of the subject pictures of Stubbs and Wright.

Third, Joe Burke's attempt to write the history of English eighteenth-century art from Melbourne between 1949 and 1973 contributed to his sympathy with and enthusiasm for the masters of the Provincial Enlightenment. He too knew what it was like to form a circle of like-minded friends and associates who shared his liberal opinions and commitment to scholarship far from other major metropolitan centres. Neither Melbourne nor its principal university could be accurately described as intellectual backwaters in the post-war period but you had to extend and exert yourself to have a fulfilling life of the mind. At this Joe Burke excelled. The brief of the *Herald* Professor of Fine Arts, to encourage 'the application of the principles and practices to the life of the community', was in itself a statement of Enlightened ambition. Joe Burke played an active part in such diverse causes as the protection of the Melbourne Botanical Garden, the Industrial Design Council of Australia, the Felton Bequest and the establishment of the Australian Academy of the Humanities amongst many others.

Re-reading *English Art 1714–1800* thirty-five years after its publication is, however, a salutary experience. The difficulties in undertaking so ambitious a work far from the resources necessary to carry it out obviously slowed its production. The delay between conception and publication exposed its limitations and shortcomings. Published before the wave of new art historical writing swept across the field of British art, exemplified in the work of Marcia Pointon, David Bindman, John Barrell, David Solkin and Anne Bermingham amongst others, Joe Burke's historical, social and political awareness is almost nebulous in the course of his narrative. He prefaces his history with the sweeping and contestable assertion that 'the achievement [of British artists] mirrored the ideals of a society dominated by a landowning oligarchy deeply conscious of its territorial influence and the rivalry

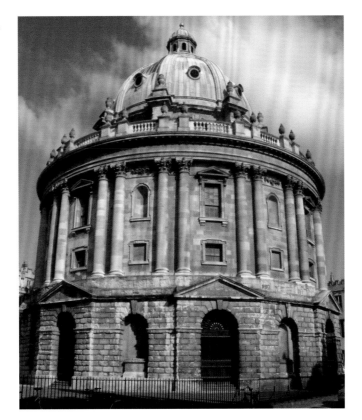

Fig.130 James Gibbs, The
Radcliffe Camera, Oxford, 1747

of its two main parties for political power and its rewards.' He swallows too easily
the paradox, crisply enough stated, in his preface:

> The ethos of this aristocratic society is singularly consistent, but much of the
> originality of English art in the period can be related to the confidence of the
> middle class of whose values Hogarth was so energetic a champion. …

The absence of a firm social context makes for an unanchored quality in Burke's
narrative as though works of art and architecture held a continuous dialogue
between themselves, uninfluenced by a patron's taste or interests or a changing
and changeable political scene. Joe Burke's comment on Gainsborough's *Cottage
Door,* that he 'brought to the observation of rustics the sensibilities of a Man of
Feeling', falls well short of a proper analysis, however well intended.[13]

Joseph Burke belonged to that generation of British art historians who were transformed intellectually by the arrival of the Warburg Institute in Britain in 1933 (incorporated into the University of London 1944) and the presence of such *émigré* art historians as Fritz Saxl, E.H. Gombrich, Edgar Wind and Rudolf Wittkower. Their famous 'tribute to Britain', the volume of essays collected in *England and the Mediterranean Tradition* (Oxford 1945), made a lasting impression on him, freely acknowledged at the outset of his Oxford history. When he turned to writing his own *magnum opus*, part of the challenge was to situate eighteenth-century English art within a European tradition, to show its Continental connections and contributions and move away from describing English art in insular terms. European categories and periodizations such as the Baroque, Rococo, Neoclassicism, Romanticism are deployed throughout his Oxford history despite a skepticism about their usefulness expressed in the Preface. 'The Radcliffe Camera is the last masterpiece of the classicizing English Baroque which concludes with an evocation of Roman grandeur as Augustan as anything built more strictly to rule by the Burlingtonians' (fig.130) is representative of Burke's analysis by category.[14] It clearly reflects a certain excitement at placing familiar monuments in a broader aesthetic and art historical context and not a defensive insecurity about the place and achievement of British art. But such an analysis belonged to the 1940s and 1950s when the impact of the original Warburgians was at its height. By 1976 these stylistic categories read like blunt instruments to interpret the great age of English art.

One other curious use of category analysis is Joe Burke's use of 'romantic' to characterize the more progressive elements in eighteenth-century British art. In *Omai*, for instance, 'the classical and romantic tendencies of the 18th century are fused in perfect reconciliation, so that the picture becomes a kind of summation.'[15] Stubbs' *Zebra* has 'a Blakeian intensity' and Richard Wilson's *The Daughters of Niobe* is hailed as 'one of the masterpieces of the century in which a classical scene is treated romantically.'[16] Indeed Wilson's progress as an artist is characterized in terms of his 'romanticism': 'Before nature he freed himself from dependence on his masters and comes closer to the threshold of true romanticism than either Reynolds or Gainsborough.'[17] The use of 'romanticism' in such a manner reflects the influence of Herbert Read whom Burke admired for his writings on industrial design and art education.

When, however, Joe Burke spoke of the creation of the landscape garden as 'a true spearhead of romanticism', he drew a riposte from Hugh Honour in an otherwise appreciative review of his Oxford history.[18] The landscape garden could 'alternatively be regarded,' Honour wrote, 'as the manifestation of an attitude to nature which was to be felled and cleared by the Romantics': 'the rouge of an antiquated coquette,' as Sir Walter Scott called them. Hugh Honour's admiration for the ambition and range of Joe Burke's history drew this measured estimation: 'a sound general account, a work of synthesis which … abounds in original and perceptive comments.' It was not shared by other prominent reviewers.

Both Ronald Paulson and Luke Herrmann jumped on the volume's shortcomings even while paying it some backhanded compliments.[19] In both cases the long delayed appearance of Joe Burke's history was the cause of remonstration. For Paulson 'the absence of new scholarly research and a remotely distant cut-off date of secondary sources' – nothing in the bibliography after 1970 and little scholarship after 1965 actually cited – were its crippling limitations. 'Nothing for a long while seems to have registered on Burke's assumptions.'

Herrmann was more caustic. He pointed out that the preceding volume of the Oxford History of English Art, Margaret Whinney and Oliver Millar's *English Art 1625–1714*, had appeared in 1957 and the succeeding volume, T.S.R. Boase's *English Art 1800–1870*, in 1959. Had Burke's volume appeared then or in the early 1960s it would have been welcome. Hermann found it 'difficult to ignore its shortcomings … the book as a whole is somewhat anachronistic as today the series is.' His final judgment was condescending: 'for the general reader and the average student … the book provides a far ranging and readable introduction.' Yet Paulson and Herrmann could not avoid admiring key elements and passages of the history. On every page,' noted Paulson, 'one feels an acute … intelligence seeking to understand and formulate with clarity the important aspects of 18th century English art.' Herrmann, more coolly, found the chapter on 'The Impact of the Rococo' 'conveys a sound impression of the variety of styles to be found in the decorative arts' and with 'Hogarth, Roubiliac and their Contemporaries' Burke 'summarizes the complexities of his material with admirable conviction.' The chapter on 'The Royal Academy and the Great Style' 'provides a particularly vivid account of the revival of History Painting.'

The overall impression given by these eminent reviewers in leading scholarly journals was that Burke's *English Art 1714–1800* had passed its 'sell-by date.' The tyranny of distance had claimed another victim. Joe Burke's disappointment which he kept to himself must have been intense given the length and laboriousness of his history. Paulson in his peroration did pay him a notable tribute: 'The best compliment I can give Burke's book … is that it can be read with care because the author has always looked for himself, read for himself and described what he has seen with elegance.'

But the Oxford history 'did him in' as regards further scholarly work and he published little more of substance in the field. Joe Burke, CBE from 1953, was knighted in 1980 shortly after his retirement from the University of Melbourne – an award which gave his friends and former students as much pleasure as it did him. He was a widely and genuinely loved man in Australia to which he had given much over the thirty years of his career, perhaps at the cost of his own scholarship. He was one of those able and educated Englishmen (Scots and Irish too) who came to Australia post-World War II and found a new country they could identify with quickly and completely. He never seriously contemplated returning to Britain. In 1961 T.S.R. Boase sounded him out about the position of Keeper of Western Art at the Ashmolean but when Edgar Wind informed him that a more experienced museum candidate had come forward, Joe Burke quickly withdrew. He wrote to Boase at the time (January 1961) 'an art historian makes certain sacrifices working in a remote and pioneering field but there are also very great rewards and something to be said for trying to see the job honourably through to the end.'

Joe Burke died in 1992 aged seventy-nine. Bernard Smith, his erstwhile colleague and longstanding friend, neatly characterized him in his obituary noting 'his kindness, generosity, sublime forgetfulness and proneness to the occasional tantrum.' Joe Burke certainly belonged to the party of humanity, that 'elite of civilized men and women, who knew the classics both of ancient and modern times, loved and practiced the arts, cared for conversation and participated in a kind of timeless assembly of the happy few.'[20]

I am most grateful for the assistance I have received in preparing this essay from Professor Jaynie Anderson, *Herald* Professor of Fine Arts at the University of Melbourne and to an unpublished paper by Sir Andrew Grimwade, 'The Legacy of Joseph Burke'. Jock Murphy, Director Collections, and Kathryn Wood, Reference Archivist, of the Baillieu Library were models of helpfulness. At the Yale Center for British Art, Lori Misura of the library staff helped me to track down various publications and I am most grateful to her. Emeritus Professor Jules Prown of Yale University kindly read and commented on the MS before publication.

1   Jaynie Anderson, 'Interrogating Joseph Burke and His Legacy', *Melbourne Journal of Art*, vol.8, 2005, pp.88–101; reprinted online *Journal of Art Historiography* May 2011 (arthistoriography.wordpress.com).

2   Joseph Burke and Colin Caldwell, *Hogarth: The Complete Engravings*, London 1968, p.6.

3   *Hogarth and Reynolds: A Contrast in English Art Theory*, Oxford 1943, pp.9–10.

4   Kenneth Clark–Joseph Burke Correspondence, reprinted as an appendix in Jaynie Anderson, 'Interrogating Joseph Burke'.

5   Kenneth Clark had successfully recommended the acquisition of Nicholas Poussin *The Crossing of the Red Sea*, Pierre Bonnard *Siesta* (formerly owned by Gertrude Stein) and Amedeo Modigliani *Manuel Humbert* amongst others.

6   T.S.R. Boase–Joseph Burke Correspondence. Joseph Burke Papers Box 42 1/90 University of Melbourne Archives.

7   *Eighteenth Century Studies*, vol. 3/2, winter 1969.

8   Oxford History of English Art Volume IX *English Art 1714–1800*, Oxford 1976, p.30 (hereafter OHEA IX).

9   OHEA IX p.336.

10 OHEA IX p.78.

11 *The Iconography of the Enlightenment*, Annual Lecture delivered to Australian Humanities Research Council [afterwards known as Australian Academy of the Humanities], spring 1969 (Sydney 1970), p.13.

12 OHEA IX p.ix.

13 OHEA IX p.219.

14 OHEA IX p.81.

15 OHEA IX p.205.

16 OHEA IX pp.226–27.

17 OHEA IX p.230

18 *Times Literary Supplement*, 21 January 1977.

19 Ronald Paulson in *Eighteenth Century Studies*, vol. 10, 1977; Luke Herrmann in *Burlington Magazine*, January 1978.

20 Peter Gay, *The Party of Humanity: Essays in the French Enlightenment*, New York 1964, p.289.

THE ARCHITECTURE OF ARSENAL

Steven Parissien

Fig.131 *Rainbow over Highbury Square, March 25, 2010*, photograph by David Price

THE ARCHITECTURE OF ARSENAL

Steven Parissien

*I*n 1913 Woolwich Arsenal Football Club's ebullient Chairman Henry Norris (created Sir Henry four years later) controversially moved the Arsenal from its current ground in Plumstead, deep in Southeast London, to a new location in Highbury – ten miles away, in the North London borough of Islington. Norris's reasons were purely financial: by the 1912–13 season Arsenal's attendances had fallen to below 3,000 a game, and were likely to fall even further: following the last game of the season on 26 April 1913, Arsenal were relegated from the Football League's First Division, having won only three matches all season. The club had already gone into liquidation once, in 1910 – which was when Norris had originally stepped in to take control – and could well do so again. In North London, Norris reasoned, the club could begin again and build a sustainable fan base; in Plumstead, it could only dwindle to nothing. Norris also had his sights on exploiting the club's audacious cross-London journey as a means of effecting the club's back-door readmittance into the First Division.

In the relatively short history of organised football in Britain to date, no other association football club had ever been moved so far, or so hurriedly. North London's existing Football League clubs were, predictably, far from pleased at Arsenal's impending arrival: Tottenham Hotspur and Clapton Orient (a club which, ironically, was itself forcibly moved – to Leyton – in 1937) both protested vociferously. And there was staunch opposition to the move from residents of both Woolwich and Highbury. The *Kentish Gazette* published a letter from an irate fan which confidently declared 'you cannot "franchise" a football club'[1] – not a claim many would dare to make today – while the *Woolwich Gazette* shrieked hysterically that 'Norris was kidnapping Kent's "only son".'[2] At the same time, residents in the quiet suburb of Highbury started a campaign to resist the building of a new football stadium in their midst. Norris, however, successfully persuaded Highbury's local businesses that football crowds would be good for business – as indeed they were – while he manipulated his newly made contacts in the North London press to muzzle Islington's protests. ('Mr Norris pulled some strings behind the scenes', was the laconic reminiscence of the new stadium's project architect, fifty years later.[3]) Norris's insistence that support for the club in West Kent remained feeble was undeniable. And, perhaps most importantly, Norris cultivated the President of the Football League's Management Committee, the fearsome former manager of Liverpool FC, John McKenna, and persuaded him to dismiss any League opposition to the move that was orchestrated by Tottenham and Orient.

Henry Norris was a tall, domineering bully with a long, horse-like face, piercing blue eyes and a forbiddingly large moustache. The archetypal entrepreneur, he could be a ruthless tyrant ('a tough nut: testy and a one-way man – his way', was one recollection of the former Chairman[4]). But he could also be ineffably charming when the occasion warranted, and used this combination of aggression and charm to great effect. He always, he believed, got what he wanted – and at Arsenal in 1913, his self-esteem appeared to be vindicated.

By the turn of the century, Norris had seen the development of football grounds as the best way to augment his fortunes. He had accordingly bought West London's Fulham FC (along with the Mayoralty of the Borough of Fulham) in order to convert Fulham's home of Craven Cottage into one of the country's finest football grounds – an aim which he had largely fulfilled by 1905. Now he sought to do the same for Arsenal, using the same architect–engineer, Archibald Leitch, who had built him the new stands at Fulham.

Leitch had, interestingly, recently designed a new stadium at Stamford Bridge, two miles east of Craven Cottage, for the builder–entrepreneur Gus Mears. Mears hoped to use the impressive new stadium to lure Norris's Fulham team away from Craven Cottage; but when Norris refused to budge, Mears decided to form his own team at Stamford Bridge, which subsequently became Chelsea FC. Norris now countered Mears' scheme with a highly ambitious plan to merge Fulham and Arsenal – a brazen proposal which, even with his numerous connections, Norris failed to steer past the Football League.

Prevented from moving Arsenal in with Fulham, Norris turned his attention to finding an appropriate new location for Arsenal's ground. In this he was able to deploy another choice contact he was keeping up his sleeve. A property developer who was also a leading Anglican churchman (at the same time as being a prominent and enthusiastic freemason), Norris had recently become a close friend of Randall Davidson, the Archbishop of Canterbury. Having failed to find a suitable site for Arsenal in West London, it occurred to Norris that the attractive, spacious playing fields at the theological college of St John the Divine in Highbury, North London, might be readily available from the Church of England at a knock-down price. (St John the Divine's own handsome neoclassical college buildings were, sadly, destroyed in a fire in April 1945.) When Norris managed to prise the land away from the Ecclesiastical Commissioners for a modest £20,000, the freeholders' signatory for the 1913 lease for the land was none other than Archbishop Davidson himself. Norris had cleverly used his familiarity with Davidson not only to obtain the land for a good price but also to win himself some excellent publicity into the bargain. The Church's only provisos for this deal were that no games were to be played there on a Sunday, and that there was to be no gambling or alcohol consumption on the site. The latter rule was soon ignored, while seventy years later games were being regularly played at Highbury on a Sunday.

Norris's ambitions for Highbury stadium were predictably grandiose. He envisaged that the new ground would be used to stage Cup Finals, which were then being played in Crystal Palace's inadequately sized and remote ground at Selhurst Park. (Wembley Stadium was not opened until 1924.) His brief for the project engineer, Leitch, was thus 'to provide a ground for the Cup Final to replace Crystal Palace'.[5]

Archibald Leitch (1865–1939) was a Glasgow blacksmith's son who from his earliest years was very familiar with engineering metal. He originally trained as a marine engineer, then joined the famous firm of Mirlees, Watson & Co as Head of Ordering in 1890. However, he made his name designing football stadia after landing the commission to design a new wooden stand at Glasgow Rangers' new home, Ibrox Park, in 1899. He worked with an unfashionable building type, and his designs were functional rather than inspired; yet his confidence and ambition earned him both a fortune and the social respectability he craved.

Leitch's career should have been cut brutally short when, on 5 April 1902, wooden terracing at the south-west corner of his new John Street stand at Ibrox collapsed during an England v Scotland international, killing 25 and wounding 517.[6] Leitch had designed the biggest timber terraces anywhere in the world; at the ground's opening, the *Glasgow Evening Times* lauded 'the very substantial, stable and artistic laying out of the grounds'[7] (a judgement it was to regret three years later). Yet Leitch, like Norris, was able to put his professional and society contacts to good use, and managed to wriggle out of any blame. The subsequent trial put the Ibrox timber merchant, McDougall, in the dock, and not Leitch. McDougall was cleared – to Leitch's irritation – but the engineer astonishingly managed to hold onto his lucrative post as Rangers' stadium architect, despite the fact that expert engineering witnesses had criticised his terrace design in the trial. It says much for Leitch's lack of remorse that, while the Scottish Football Association gave £5,000 to the fund for the families of the victims of 5 April, the evidently guilt-free engineer donated only ten guineas. He appeared far more worried about his future career than the deaths his negligence had caused, complaining to Rangers' Chairman that the McDougall trial was 'most disastrous to my future prospects here and elsewhere'.[8]

Despite his worries regarding the repercussions to the tragic disaster at Ibrox, in the ensuing years Leitch managed to build up a solid practice as the nation's self-appointed stadium expert, working at grounds ranging from Anfield in Liverpool and Ayresome Park in Middlesbrough to White Hart Lane and Selhurst Park in London. His stand and pavilion at Craven Cottage, the home of Fulham FC which he built for Henry Norris, rank as his best works and are now listed, though his acclaimed but unlisted Trinity Road Stand at Villa Park was demolished in 2000. He even experimented with the exciting new opportunities offered by the use of concrete, which he used as a base for his new stand for Huddersfield Town's London Road ground in 1906.[9]

Leitch's design for Highbury was typical of his work: functional but mundane. It comprised a new, single-tier east stand and banked terraces on the other three sides of the pitch, entered via the new 'Rush Preventive Turnstiles' of 1895. The roofs of his stands were not cantilevered, as those at the Emirates were to be, but constructed according to traditional, post-and-beam principles. The result was that, although Leitch professed to place great importance in preserving sightlines, not all spectators had an uninterrupted view of the pitch.

Leitch's original design was never built. London County Council (LCC) objected to his first plan, forcing him to lower the new east stand by one tier. (Leitch's initial scheme would have resulted in a high brick wall at the back of the stand facing the east side of Avenell Road.) The compromise was a far lower wall, and a reduction in the number of supporters the stand could accommodate, down from 11,000 to 9,000.

Leitch, much in demand for football stadia elsewhere in the UK and excessively ambitious, was rarely on site. He left most of the work – including the planning negotiations with the LCC – to his junior A.G. Kearney, who was later to run Leitch's lucrative Liverpool practice. Kearney later reminisced that 'Mr Leitch's time was taken up chasing likely financiers to support various works that might be influenced our way'.[10] It did not help Kearney that Leitch had weakly acceded to Henry Norris's impossibly tight deadlines; the inevitable result was that, although the new ground was able to be opened for the new season on 6 September 1913, despite Kearney's best efforts – and his frantic lobbying of the LCC's planners – the stadium was only half-finished, with the new East Stand covered not by a permanent roof but by tarpaulins. Kearney was left to face the music – and Norris's wrath – alone. As the site architect later recalled, Leitch, 'thinking that discretion was the better part of valour, had made himself scarce', and was nowhere to be seen on the opening day.

Finished or not, Norris was determined that Leitch's new ground should host to a First Division team. Accordingly, he lobbied his allies on the Football League to agree to promote Arsenal back to the top flight in 1919 – even though, in the last season played before football matches were suspended in 1915, Arsenal had only finished in fifth place in the Second Division. Norris built on this astonishing sleight of hand by ensuring that England's first postwar home international, against Wales in March 1920, was played at Leitch's Highbury – as, too, was the first true international, against Belgium, in March 1923.[11]

The Chairman's luck finally ran out in 1927. In that year the Football Association found Norris guilty of 'irregularities' relating to his paying for his new car and chauffeur out of club funds. In truth, these were minor charges; Norris had simply made too many enemies in the FA by his overbearing and aggressive manner. He sued the FA, but lost, and found himself banned for life from any involvement in football. He resigned from the Arsenal chairmanship in 1929, and died in 1934. And with Norris died any hopes Leitch may have nurtured of being recalled to Highbury to upgrade the stadium. When major new works were commissioned at Highbury in the 1930s, Leitch's firm was not even considered.[12]

Norris's replacement as Chairman was Sir Samuel Hill-Wood, a former Derbyshire cricketer and cotton magnate who had once owned Glossop North End FC (a team which enjoyed a brief sojourn in the First Division), and who had been made a baronet in Lloyd George's controversial New Year's Honours of 1921. Hill-Wood proceeded to build on Norris's impressive achievements – beginning with the ground.

In 1925 Norris had brought in a new manager for his ambitious club: Herbert Chapman, formerly the manager of Huddersfield Town FC. One of the most successful of all of Norris's initiatives, Chapman reinvigorated the club and led it to a spectacular series of cup and league victories during the subsequent nine years. And both Chapman and Hill-Wood soon agreed that, in order to create what they hoped would become Britain's most stylish as well as most successful club, they needed to rebuild Leitch's bleakly utilitarian stadium.

Chapman himself had a definite eye for design, and wanted the architecture of the new ground to reflect the newly fashionable Art Deco style, first seen at the 1925 Paris Exposition. Chapman himself redesigned the club badge in an Art Deco idiom. He also added the large clock to the North Bank[13] and, always with an eye to publicity, managed in 1932 to persuade the local tube line's owners, the Underground Electric Railways Company of London (soon to be absorbed into London Transport), to rename the adjacent Piccadilly Line station, Gillespie Road, simply as 'Arsenal' – a coup staged at no cost whatsoever to the club. And already, in 1930, he and Hill-Wood had hired a new architect to redevelop Highbury's West Stand.

Claude Waterlow Ferrier (1879–1935) was educated at Marlborough and brought up an ardent Francophile: he studied in France, and admitted that he had been hugely influenced by the groundbreaking Paris Exposition. (One of Ferrier's most lasting achievements was the publication of an English–French dictionary of technical terms.) A pupil of Aston Webb, he set up his own practice, initially on his own and later, from 1927, in conjunction with the Scottish architect William Binnie (*c*.1885–*c*.1963). Ferrier designed some impressive large buildings in London, using the rather ponderous classical style espoused by Aston Webb, though without Webb's lightness of touch and the Art Deco flair Ferrier himself was to exhibit at Highbury (fig.132). Ferrier's Royal National Institute of the Blind headquarters of 1909–14 still stands; yet his more imaginative rebuilding of the Army and Navy Club in St James's Square of 1925–26 (which adapted C.O. Purnell and Alfred

Fig.132 Claude Ferrier,
133–39 Highbury Hill, London N5,
1931–32

Smith's lively original of 1848–51) was inexplicably demolished after the Second
World War, and replaced with a tediously bland modernist block by T.P. Bennett
of 1962–63.

William Binnie studied architecture at Glasgow School of Art and in 1910 moved
to New York to work with Warren and Wetmore, helping the firm to detail the new
Grand Central railway terminus. Returning to Britain in 1913, he began to work for

the architect Leonard Martin in London. While the First World War – in which he rose to the rank of major – interrupted this career, it also provided him with a lucrative new role. From 1919 he began work as architect for the Imperial War Graves Commission, becoming the Commission's Deputy Director in 1920. His war graves work came to dominate his life: aside from his work for the Commission, his East Stand at Highbury and the Hotel Phoenicia on Valetta, Malta of 1939 (which was badly bombed in 1942–43), Binnie subsequently built little else.

Ferrier's new West Stand at Highbury of 1931–32, costing £45,000, was at the time the most advanced and the most expensive football stand ever built in Britain. It was opened in 1932 by the Prince of Wales (subsequently King Edward VIII and the Duke of Windsor). Built over the old Spion Kop terrace,[14] it incorporated three flats and an electric lift. And under its cantilevered concrete roof, it boasted luxurious 'Windsor' padded tip-up seats which were covered with 'Rexine' moquette in the more expensive rows. With some irony, the building contractor Ferrier used for this work was the firm of W.J. Cearns, whose eponymous managing director was also a director of West Ham United, and who became the Hammers' Chairman in 1935.[15]

To reach the new stand from the west, Ferrier had to demolish houses on Highbury Hill (numbers 133–139). However, he filled the gap with an eccentric new gatehouse for the ground, which he provided with a castellated parapet, a projecting central bay, large Crittall steel windows, and prominent Art Deco lettering. Although today the building stands sadly derelict, at the time of writing (January 2011) it is due to be refurbished and converted to provide eleven flats of affordable housing.

Chapman died unexpectedly on 6 January 1934, aged only fifty-five. By 1935 Ferrier, too, was dead, struck and killed by a passing motorcycle. However, the rebuilding programme Chapman and Ferrier had initiated was continued. Hill-Wood and Chapman's successor as manager, George Allison, brought in Ferrier's partner, William Binnie, to build a new East Stand to match Ferrier's West. In fact, Binnie's stand eclipsed his late partner's achievement (figs.133–135). The elevation (which looked the same height as Ferrier's stand, but was actually five feet lower) was more ostentatiously Art Deco in inspiration than Ferrier's, depending on a grid of red-painted steel windows for its regularity, and incorporating a projecting central bay decorated with Chapman's club badge and the cannon crest. At the foot of the central bay was Binnie's imposing, stripped-classical entrance, executed in black

Figs.133–135 William Binnie,
Highbury Stadium, East Stand,
principal elevation, 1936

Figs.136 and 137   William Binnie, Highbury Stadium, East Stand, central bay, 1936

marble (figs.136–137). Behind these doors lay the 'Marble Halls', an impressively scaled entrance hall (actually paved with terrazzo, not marble) which contained Jacob Epstein's splendid bust of Herbert Chapman. Unusually for the time, Binnie's advanced East Stand also boasted a players' gym (a facility that was later moved to the club's training ground at London Colney). Its luxuriance also ensured that it cost far more than Ferrier's predecessor: £130,000, as opposed to £45,000 for the West Stand.

Ferrier and Binnie's Highbury was soon the most admired football stadium in Britain. It became a favourite venue for film and television: in 1937 the first televised football match – between Arsenal's first and second teams – was staged here, while in 1939 the ground was used as the backdrop for the hit film *The Arsenal Stadium Mystery*, adapted from the novel by Leonard Gribble and starring Leslie Banks. After the war the ground was used for all of the international football matches at the 1948 London Olympics.

By the end of the 1980s, however, the two Art Deco stands were looking tired and delapidated, while the other two, utilitarian stands were in grave need of modernisation. In 1988–89 the Clock End, on the south side of the ground, was remodelled, and fifty-three executive boxes were added – all finished in dismal, corrugated grey metal cladding devised by designers A D Consultants, a treatment far removed from the stylish Art Deco tradition of Ferrier and Binnie. In 1992 the old North Bank was demolished to enable work to begin on an all-seater stadium in order to comply with the recommendations of the Taylor Report of 1990, which had been commissioned following the Hillsborough disaster of the previous year. At the same time A D Consultants were – somewhat surprisingly, in view of the widespread criticism of their refurbishment of the Clock End – asked back to rebuild the North Bank. The lacklustre design that they produced, however, was excoriated in the local press, and condemned as being mediocre at best. In the face of a well-informed protest group – the 'Group for an Alternative Arsenal Stand' – the club hired instead stadium experts the Lobb Partnership who, led by project architect Sean V. Jones (and in partnership with engineer Jan Brobrowski), designed the far more satisfactory North Bank that was completed in 1993.

With seating introduced, Highbury's capacity now stood at 38,419. (On 9 March 1935 the terraced stadium had entertained a crowd of 73,295.) This was clearly inadequate for major league games, to say nothing of international club matches. Accordingly, the decision was taken at the end of the 1990s to move the football club away from Highbury Stadium, yet still remain close enough so as not to disrupt nor antagonise the existing local fan base, and to continue to take advantage of the Arsenal tube station. Accordingly, after ideas of moving to the new Wembley Stadium had been dismissed as unrealistic (largely as Wembley was too far away from the core of Arsenal's fan base), it was proposed to move the club half a mile to the west and build a new stadium on former Midland Railway land, now used partly as a recycling centre and partly for a Royal Mail sorting office. The old Highbury site would be redeveloped as housing – taking care to incorporate as much of the historic structure as possible and avoid building on the old pitch. (By this time Binnie's East Stand was listed Grade II; yet, puzzlingly, Ferrier's admittedly more modest West Stand was not. In the event the former was sympathetically restored during the rebuilding, while the west wall of the latter was retained in the new development.) Crucially, the profits from this Highbury development were to be used to help pay for the vast cost of the new stadium.

Fig.138 Christopher Bradley-Hole,
Highbury Square Garden,
2009–10

In contrast to 1913, when Islington Borough Council was highly suspicious of the club's proposed arrival at Highbury, seventy years later the council was enthusiastically supportive of Arsenal's move. Outline planning permission was granted as early as 2001, and listed building consent from English Heritage to enable the conversion of the listed East Stand soon followed. English Heritage insisted, though, that the old Board Room and its trophy cabinet be relocated to the new site, and that the new north and south blocks at Highbury be reduced in height and stepped down to street level, so that so they would not dominate either the surrounding streets nor the converted East and West Stands. Islington Borough Council also initially stipulated that 25% of the new development should be allocated to affordable housing, although this proportion was gradually eroded as negotiations progressed.

In 2005 the big, experienced architectural practice of Allies and Morrison, founded in London in 1984, was appointed to devise a masterplan for the Highbury

Figs.139, 140 and 141 Allies and
Morrison, Highbury Square,
London N5, 2007–10.
Views from the south end of the
former pitch

site in collaboration with developers Vision Four. At the same time, landscape
designer Christopher Bradley-Hole – who had previously worked with Allies and
Morrison at the BBC's White City 'Media Village' in 2004 – was appointed to
landscape the old pitch (fig.138). Bradley-Hole was a cutting-edge, modernist
landscape designer; author of *The Minimalist Garden* of 1999, his work was
inevitably uncompromising and contemporary, and often based on grids and
rectangles. His brief was to retain the pitch area (under which car parking for the
site would be provided), and landscape it as a resource for the locals, including a
children's park of 75 square metres. Areas of old turf where supporters' ashes had
previously been scattered were to be carefully lifted and relaid at the new stadium.

Allies and Morrison completely demolished the North Bank and Clock End
stands, and replaced them with anonymous housing blocks. The new block on the
north side was of seven floors at pitchside, descending to four facing onto Gillespie
Road, with two large internal courtyards. From the former pitch, the glazed walls
and glazed stairwells of the new east and west blocks now dominated the new
elevations. Binnie's splendid facade on Avenell Road was retained, however, with
the 'Marble Halls' serving as an entrance to eighty-seven apartments on six floors.
Across the old pitch, far less survived of Ferrier's West Stand, which now comprised
ninety-four apartments and a ground-level nursery school for seventy children.

In 2010 the new development at the old stadium site, now loftily rebranded as
'Highbury Square', was completed. Seven hundred and eleven housing units had
been built on the site, those on the footprint of the old East and West Stands being
priced at the premium end of the scale (the prime apartments in both of these
ranges all boasting a 'pitch view'). At time of writing only ten units – half of them
premium penthouses, priced at between £775,000 and £950,000, atop Binnie's
former East Stand – still remain unsold.

Overall, the development of Highbury Square works well (figs.139–141). While
some of the new blocks at the north and south ends are reticent to the point of
banality – making the division between affordable and private housing all too
obvious – the east and west ranges artfully combine the Art Deco character of the
old stands with the rectilinear modernism so beloved of Allies and Morrison.
Perhaps the least successful element of the scheme is the landscaped pitch, whose
rigid grid of partitions and unnecessarily fussy punctuations seem to deter, rather
than encourage, access.

Figs.142 and 143
Rod Sheard/HOK Sport,
Emirates Stadium, London N5.
Exterior from the southwest

Barely a mile away from Highbury stands the new Emirates Stadium,[16] built by architects HOK Sport, the international architectural practice. HOK was founded in Kansas City in 2003 and has grown exponentially since; its one-time subsidiary, HOK Sport, has built countless sports complexes round the world, including Wembley Stadium, Stratford's 2012 Olympic Stadium, Wimbledon's rebuilt Centre Court, the new Ascot Racecourse and Chicago's Wrigley Field. Having completed the Emirates, in 2008 the management of HOK Sport bought themselves out of the parent company and changed their name (somewhat curiously) to 'Populous'.

HOK Sport's lead architect on the project was the Australian-born Rod Sheard (b.1951). Sheard had already worked on new football grounds on greenfield sites – most notably, Bolton Wanderers' Reebok Stadium and Huddersfield Town's

Figs.144 and 145
Rod Sheard/HOK Sport,
Emirates Stadium, London N5.
The West Stand

Galpharm Stadium – and had indeed been part of the Lobb team that had redesigned the old North Bank at Highbury in the early 1990s. (In 1999 Lobb had been absorbed into the growing maw of HOK.) In 1995 Sheard's Galpharm Stadium won both the Royal Institute of British Architects' 'Building of the Year' Award and the Stirling Prize for Architecture. It is unsurprising, then, that Sheard used his award-winning Huddersfield design to inform his work at Arsenal – particularly the vast banana trusses which, at Huddersfield, stretched in a low arc across the main stands to allow uninterrupted viewing of the pitch from all seats, while still providing these seats with shelter from the wind and rain. Sheard introduced long, low, arcing trusses on all four sides of the Emirates Stadium, ensuring that any spectator could see the whole of the pitch (if not always the whole of the crowd).

The design relationship between the Emirates and the Galpharm also served to help cement the longstanding links between Arsenal and Huddersfield Town – the team that Herbert Chapman had managed before he arrived at Arsenal in 1925.

The new stadium seats 60,355 – roughly 22,000 more than Highbury in its final, all-seater guise. It is the biggest football stadium in the country after Old Trafford, and cost £470 million to build. There is no overall roof. Instead, a cantilevered roof over the stands swoops over the seating to maximise airflow and (if there is any) sunlight. The seating in the Emirates is (with the exception of MK Dons' stadium at Milton Keynes) the only supporter seating in the UK to be padded. And the need for corporate support has been prioritised: the 'Club Level' middle tier of seats comprises 7,139 premium seats, together with the Directors' Box, while the slender tier above comprises 150 corporate boxes, seating a total of 2,222.

Indoors, the new dressing rooms were designed with the advice of the current club manager, Arsène Wenger, who for the home dressing room applied the principles of feng shui, ensuring that there were no right angles or sharp corners in the new complex. The dressing rooms also boast underfloor heating – as indeed did Ferrier's highly advanced dressing rooms at Highbury.

Soon after the Emirates opened in July 2006,[17] however, criticism arose from supporters that the new stadium was too commercially obsessed and did not take the fans' needs, nor Arsenal's impressive footballing heritage, sufficiently into account. As a result, a large clock (not the old Highbury clock, but a new version with a far larger face) was added to the south end of the stadium in August 2010, and work was begun on decorating HOK Sports's curved external elevations with giant murals featuring thirty-two great Arsenal players of the past. At the same time the four sides of the stadium were named after the old Highbury site: thus were the Clock End, the East and West Stands and the North Bank magically reborn.

As architect Rod Sheard has noted, the quality of, and public regard for, the architecture of football has improved enormously since Archibald Leitch's day, and today football stadia 'can be regarded as among the most important buildings a city possesses'.[18] His Emirates Stadium certainly supports that claim. A superb landmark building, it is an invaluable architectural asset not just for Arsenal FC and for the Borough of Islington, but for the whole of London. Henry Norris and Herbert Chapman would have been justifiably proud.

1 Quoted in Brian Glanville, *Arsenal Stadium History,* London 2006, p.31.

2 Quoted in Jon Spurling, *Highbury and the Story of Arsenal in N5,* London 2006, p.9.

3 Simon Inglis, *Engineering Archie,* English Heritage, London 2005, p.39.

4 A.G. Kearney in Arsenal Match-Day Programme, 21 December 1963, quoted in Inglis, *Engineering Archie,* p.39.

5 Simon Inglis, *Football Grounds of Britain,* London 1996, p.18.

6 Surprisingly, although the disaster occurred at 3.40pm and the scale of the fatalities was known by half-time, the game was played to its conclusion – even though it ended with some of the players in tears.

7 Quoted in Inglis, *Engineering Archie,* p.16.

8 Archibald Leitch to James Henderson, 19 June 1902, quoted in Inglis, *Engineering Archie,* p.25.

9 Leitch's employment by both Huddersfield and Arsenal constitutes the first of what were to become historic links between these two venerable clubs. Huddersfield's London Road ground was abandoned in 1994, and swiftly demolished.

10 Kearney, quoted in Inglis, *Engineering Archie,* p.39.

11 Norris's campaign to have England's Cup Finals staged at Highbury, however, did not succeed. Much to Norris's chagrin, the Cup Finals of 1919–21 were staged at Stamford Bridge, which had a bigger crowd capacity than Highbury.

12 Leitch died in 1939. His son carried on the practice, but with diminishing returns. The firm finally folded in 1955.

13 In 1935 Chapman's clock was moved to the opposite, 'Laundry' end, thereafter known as the Clock End.

14 Following the British army's ignominious defeat on the hillside of Spion Kop, near Ladysmith, in January 1900, a curious footballing tradition evolved by which steep, open-air terraces were named after this battle. The first recorded use of the term in relation to a stadium terrace was at Arsenal's old Manor Ground in Plumstead in 1904. In 1906 Liverpool built the celebrated 'Kop' at Anfield – designed by Archie Leitch.

15 In 1980 West Ham United, the club that the Cearns family did so much to foster, beat Denis Hill-Wood's Arsenal 1–0 in the FA Cup Final at Wembley.

16 In October 2004 Emirates Airlines signed a 15-year deal to name the new stadium. Owing to prohibition on such commercial ties, however, for UEFA the site is merely known as 'Arsenal Stadium'.

17 The official opening, by HRH The Duke of Edinburgh, was not until 26 October 2006.

18 Rod Sheard, Foreword to Inglis, *Engineering Archie,* p.7.

Photographic Credits